Constructing Global Enemies

Constructing Global Enemies asks how and why specific interpretations of international terrorism and drug abuse have become hegemonic at the global level. The book analyses the international discourses on terrorism and drug prohibition and compares efforts to counter both, not only from a contemporary but also from a historical perspective.

Utilizing poststructuralist theory of the relationship between hegemony and identity, Herschinger argues that hegemony is much more than just the dominance of a single country in international life; rather it is the emergence of a hegemonic order that can best be understood as the production of a new collective identity. Offering an in-depth discussion of the methodology of discourse analysis, the book explores how such hegemonies emerge and persist in the field of security. This serves to explain the widespread disagreement regarding the fight against international terrorism as well as the successful suppression of counter-hegemonic projects in the field of international drug prohibition.

Constructing Global Enemies will be of interest to students and scholars of international relations and security studies.

Eva Herschinger is a research associate and lecturer in the Department of Political Science at the Universität der Bundeswehr München, Germany.

The New International Relations
Edited by Richard Little
University of Bristol
Iver B. Neumann
Norwegian Institute of International Affairs (NUPI), Norway
Jutta Weldes
University of Bristol

The field of international relations has changed dramatically in recent years. This new series will cover the major issues that have emerged and reflect the latest academic thinking in this particular dynamic area.

International Law, Rights and Politics
Developments in Eastern Europe and the CIS
Rein Mullerson

The Logic of Internationalism
Coercion and accommodation
Kjell Goldmann

Russia and the Idea of Europe
A study in identity and international relations
Iver B. Neumann

The Future of International Relations
Masters in the making?
Edited by Iver B. Neumann and Ole Wæver

Constructing the World Polity
Essays on international institutionalization
John Gerard Ruggie

Realism in International Relations and International Political Economy
The continuing story of a death foretold
Stefano Guzzini

International Relations, Political Theory and the Problem of Order
Beyond international relations theory?
N.J. Rengger

War, Peace and World Orders in European History
Edited by Anja V. Hartmann and Beatrice Heuser

European Integration and National Identity
The challenge of the Nordic states
Edited by Lene Hansen and Ole Wæver

Shadow Globalization, Ethnic Conflicts and New Wars
A political economy of intra-state war
Dietrich Jung

Contemporary Security Analysis and Copenhagen Peace Research
Edited by Stefano Guzzini and Dietrich Jung

Observing International Relations
Niklas Luhmann and world politics
Edited by Mathias Albert and Lena Hilkermeier

Does China Matter? A Reassessment
Essays in memory of Gerald Segal
Edited by Barry Buzan and Rosemary Foot

European Approaches to International Relations Theory
A house with many mansions
Jörg Friedrichs

The Post-Cold War International System
Strategies, institutions and reflexivity
Ewan Harrison

States of Political Discourse
Words, regimes, seditions
Costas M. Constantinou

The Politics of Regional Identity
Meddling with the Mediterranean
Michelle Pace

The Power of International Theory
Reforging the link to foreign policy-making through scientific enquiry
Fred Chernoff

Africa and the North
Between globalization and marginalization
Edited by Ulf Engel and Gorm Rye Olsen

Communitarian International Relations
The epistemic foundations of international relations
Emanuel Adler

Human Rights and World Trade
Hunger in international society
Ana Gonzalez-Pelaez

Liberalism and War
The victors and the vanquished
Andrew Williams

Constructivism and International Relations
Alexander Wendt and his critics
Edited by Stefano Guzzini and Anna Leander

Security as Practice
Discourse analysis and the Bosnian War
Lene Hansen

The Politics of Insecurity
Fear, migration and asylum in the EU
Jef Huysmans

State Sovereignty and Intervention
A discourse analysis of interventionary and non-interventionary practices in Kosovo and Algeria
Helle Malmvig

Culture and Security
Symbolic power and the politics of international security
Michael Williams

Hegemony & History
Adam Watson

Constructing Global Enemies

Hegemony and identity in international discourses on terrorism and drug prohibition

Eva Herschinger

LONDON AND NEW YORK

First published 2011
by Routledge
2 Park Square, Milton Park, Abingdon, Oxfordshire OX14 4RN

Simultaneously published in the USA and Canada
by Routledge
711 Third Avenue, New York, NY 10017

First issued in paperback 2014

Routledge is an imprint of the Taylor & Francis Group, an informa business

Typeset in Times New Roman by Pindar NZ, Auckland, New Zealand

British Library Cataloguing in Publication Data
A catalogue record for this book is available from the British Library

Library of Congress Cataloging in Publication Data
Herschinger, Eva.

Constructing global enemies: hegemony and identity in international
discourses on terrorism and drug prohibition / Eva Herschinger.
    p. cm. — (The new international relations)
  Includes bibliographical references and index.
  1. Hegemony. 2. Terrorism—Prevention—International cooperation.
3. Drug control—International cooperation. I. Title.
  JZ1312.H47 2010
  327.101—dc22   2010022696

ISBN 978-0-415-59685-5 (hbk)
ISBN 978-1-138-81143-0 (pbk)
ISBN 978-0-203-83638-5 (ebk)

To Hannelore

Contents

Figures and tables

Figures

Tables

Preface

For some governments around the world, terrorism and illicit drugs began to be viewed at an early stage in the twentieth century as significant albeit separate threats to the stability and well-being of the state. By the start of the twenty first century, however, these threats have often been depicted as existential in form and are regarded not only as inextricably intertwined but also inherently global in scope, requiring a cooperative response from the international community. It is now regularly argued that there is a need for the international community to wage a collective war on both terror and drugs.

At first sight, it might seem that at least in the context of drugs the reference to war is metaphorical, but in practice this reference to war is increasingly becoming literal. After NATO began to wage war in Afghanistan in 2001, for example, the Office of Drug Control Policy, established by the United States in 1988 to eradicate drug abuse, admitted that Afghanistan represented a 'challenging security situation' that complicated the task of fighting a war against drugs and terror at the same time. By 2009 the situation had steadily deteriorated and a United Nations Report from the Office on Drugs and Crime stated that Afghanistan was responsible for ninety two percent of the world's opium production and that the opium market, worth $65 billion, was being used to fund global terrorism. This sudden and dramatic escalation in the scale of the mutual threat now apparently posed by illicit drugs and terrorism is all the more remarkable when it is noted that hallucinatory drugs and terrorism have both been important elements of the human condition for thousands of years.

Without doubt there is a very broad consensus that illicit drugs and terrorism do indeed pose the international community with a fundamental problem that must be addressed collectively and comprehensively if we are to stand any chance of eradicating either the abuse of illicit drugs or the indiscriminate use of violence by terrorists against innocent victims. By the same token, there is also wide agreement that the linkage of these two problems severely complicates the task of solving either of them. But this apparent consensus masks some fundamental disagreements about how to tackle the problems posed by both illicit drugs and terrorism. So, for example, there is a significant school of thought that argues that at least some of the most intractable problems associated with the existence of illicit drugs would be solved by decriminalizing the use of these drugs. At the international level, however, there is huge resistance to this kind of move. By contrast, when we focus on terrorism it is immediately apparent that there are deep-seated cleavages within the international community not about terrorism in the abstract but who in practice is engaging in terrorism. In other words, everyone can agree that terrorism is unacceptable but there is no agreement about who are the terrorists or what constitutes a terrorist act.

It follows that although the international response to illicit drugs and terrorism is superficially very similar, both requiring the international community to engage in a collective war against the perpetrators of these global problems, in practice there are some very important differences that deserve to be exposed and accounted for by means of a comparative investigation. What Eva Herschinger aims to do in this book is to develop an approach that will help us to understand how drugs abuse and terrorism have emerged as problems that must be addressed by the international community and why the consensus that cloaks and legitimises the response to illicit drugs has not been extended in the same way to terrorism.

Herschinger draws on the form of discourse analysis favoured by poststructural theorists to develop her approach. Poststructuralist theorists presuppose that there is a constant political struggle about how we define the world that we live in and, as a consequence, political actors inevitably strive to establish a hegemonic order where there is a general consensus about the definitions that they favour. Herschinger focuses on how the struggle to define drug abuse and terrorism has played out in the United Nations and she reveals that there are important differences in these two cases. Nevertheless, in both cases the struggle to establish and maintain a hegemonic order has led to an increasingly polarized view of the world that thereby justifies the international community engaging in a war against drug abuse and terrorism.

By drawing on poststructural discourse theory, however, Herschinger is able to unpack this line of argument in a very sophisticated fashion. But she is also able to develop her argument in much more detail by exposing the United Nations documents that her analysis is based on to the kind of very systematic investigation more usually associated with positivism. On this basis she is able to reveal very precisely how the attempts to establish hegemonic orders that define both illicit drugs and terrorism have evolved as well as diverged across time.

Although Herschinger concludes that her analysis is unable to provide specific policy solutions to the complex and multifaceted problems posed by illicit drugs and terrorism there is no doubt that she does successfully demonstrate that it is erroneous to presuppose that the use of violence is the only route to solving these problems. Her intriguing approach demonstrates the value of poststructural theory and the virtue of subjecting it to sustained empirical analysis because by doing so it enables her to show that the wars on terror and drug abuse are necessarily the product of the sustained struggle to define drug abuse and terrorism within a hegemonic order that determines their relationship with the international community. The growing polarization of this relationship, with the international community now being identified with all that is light and good and terrorism and drug abuse being associated with all that is dark and evil, has meant that alternative ways of defining the relationship between the international community and both illicit drugs and terrorism have been pushed aside. Since the prevailing policies generated by the international community have demonstrably failed and indeed have served to exacerbate the problems associated with drug abuse and terrorism there is an obvious and urgent need to rethink the identities of and relationship between the international community, on the one hand, and terrorism and drug abuse on the other. This is the essential first step to the task of reformulating the legitimate practices for managing drug abuse and terrorism.

Richard Little
University of Bristol

Acknowledgements

Writing a book is an enterprise that involves intellectual, financial and emotional support and whose ultimate outcome is never guaranteed. This may be a cliché but the grain of 'truth' to it is the deep satisfaction to thank those who have provided me with the support I needed to complete this project.

A number of institutions have granted me financial and technical support but have also served as the main arenas for many intellectual encounters required for such an undertaking. In particular, *Jacobs University Bremen* not only provided me with the financial means of a write-up grant to finish my PhD thesis on which this book draws but also proved fruitful ground in the context of my work. This book began within a research project on the internationalization on the state monopoly of force with the Bremen *Collaborative Research Center 597 'Transformations of the State'*, which served as a platform of flourishing academic interaction. The project and Center are funded by the *Deutsche Forschungsgemeinschaft* and I gratefully acknowledge its generous financial support. I would also like to thank the *Staatsbibliothek zu Berlin* for providing the space to exercise my creative thinking.

I have begged favours from many people during the course of my research. First, I wish to thank Markus Jachtenfuchs. During the past few years he helped me to shape my thoughts into a final, coherent product while urging me on in his gentle but demanding and critical manner. I would like to extend my gratitude to Margrit Schreier, who provided me with an enormous amount of intellectual support and thoughtful criticism and has always encouraged me to pursue my path in qualitative methodology. I am also highly indebted to Thomas Diez, whose sharp and pertinent but always friendly criticism has been an inspiration and motivation much needed and feared at the same time. Thank you!

Earlier drafts of this book enjoyed the discerning gaze of a number of friends and colleagues. These include Cornelia Brüll, Kristina Hahn, Christiane Kraft-Kasack, Martin Nonhoff, Frank Sauer, Jochen Walter and Silke Weinlich. Their comments and feedback provided me invaluable support for expressing my arguments in a clearer fashion. Furthermore, I would like to thank Werner Schneider for his advice on how to carry out discourse analysis in a practical manner. I am particularly happy that Markus Baierl allowed me to use his painting 'Kandahar' as book cover since its atmosphere aptly captures the impossibility of drawing clear-cut borders. Many thanks go to my colleagues on empirical research, Jörg Friedrichs and Dana Trif and to Dayna Sadow for her proofreading of the manuscript.

However, not only intellectual and critical engagement is required to write a book. I am deeply indebted to Dennis, who never complained about me becoming highly ignorant to the 'lowly spheres of daily matters' while working on this book. I am equally indebted to my parents who have given me constant and emphatic support throughout all my years of study. I know I am fortunate to have them.

Introduction

This book is about the discursive production and transformation of hegemonic orders in the discourses on international terrorism and drug prohibition, the identities constructed thereby and the practices legitimized by these orders and identities. It analyzes how both discourses have installed, justified and sustained dominant orders by asking how and why specific interpretations of international terrorism and drug abuse have become hegemonic at the global level. The study especially questions how these agreements have or have not been achieved, since enacting policies against both phenomena – to globally wage a 'war on terror' and a 'war on drugs' – necessitates a high degree of political and social consensus which is not possible without agreeing upon a particular meaning of terrorism and drugs.

Yet, for international cooperation against terrorism and drug abuse to function and potentially to succeed, the practices of 'war' must not only be institutionalized, regularized and accepted but also appear as the only option for worldwide peace. Those authorities who claim to be in charge of determining the parameters of anti-terrorism and anti-drug policies have to present themselves as disposing of authoritative knowledge about the nature of terrorism and drug abuse to provide both phenomena with a distinct meaning. Inducing consent on what terrorism and drug abuse are about, on why and how to fight them and normalizing the practices of 'war' requires the creation of a new universe, a new vision that is able to dominate the view on both phenomena in order to produce approval and suppress counter-hegemonic projects at the same time. Thus, to establish hegemonic orders, a new world must be in the making, creating a dominant and unquestioned understanding of terrorism and drugs in which violent counter-measures become normal, appropriate and legitimate.

The present book explains this process of hegemonic orders 'in the making'. It reconstructs different understandings of terrorism and drugs in their struggle to become dominant, to become the *one and only* interpretation – more precisely, how terrorism and drug abuse have turned into threats to state and society alike. Terrorism is constructed as an omnipresent menace to humankind and terrorists as evil, fanatic individuals who only strive for the establishment of a barbaric regime, tossing the values and achievements of civilization to the wind. And drugs are the parasites on the healthy body of the good citizen, aided and abetted by internationally operating drug dealers preparing for the 'drug holocaust' (United Nations 1991: 9) which will throw humankind into a hell of addiction. Meanwhile, some citizens do not only invest their mental power and creativity to fight terrorism and drugs but also a great number of them risk their lives in these wars to preserve the rest of humanity from the acts of the evildoers. In fact, these men and women have no other option than to fight, since neither the sinister ages of barbarism nor a holocaust may be permitted to happen again. Indeed, 'good battles evil and civilization itself stands against the dark forces of barbarism' (Jackson 2005: 2) and within these universes the 'wars' are rational, reasonable and the only option – they are the right thing at the right time to do. And, most importantly, constructing terrorism and drug as an evil, which has to be overcome, announces a new vision, the dawning of a new world free from both threats. It is this vision that looms at the end of a long fight against terrorism and drugs.

However, today's homogenous picture conveyed by the two 'wars' is only half of the story. Efforts to tackle international problems like terrorism or drugs are not without precedent. Instead, attempts to solve them are written into a discursive terrain that is already partially structured through previously articulated interpretations and identities. Both phenomena can be interpreted in radically different ways: terrorism, for instance, can be considered either as an act of resistance against economic exploitation, or as a manifestation of barbarism. Just as the well-known cliché states: your terrorist is my freedom fighter. The use of drugs, on the other hand, may be considered as illegal and therefore deviant behaviour, or can be tolerated as an alternative way of life. These meanings are equally possible and they can be (and are) advocated within the discourses on international terrorism and drug prohibition. Moreover, different perspectives prevail on who disposes of the authoritative knowledge on the nature of terrorism and drugs and who is in the position to respond to both phenomena.

In light of these heterogeneous pictures, this book has two objectives. First, it seeks to explore how hegemonic orders have been established in the discourses on terrorism and drug prohibition at the global level. It examines how and why specific meanings of international terrorism and drug abuse become dominant; it explains the identities constructed thereby (Who is/has become the enemy? Who are we? Who are the ones to – legitimately – fight them?) and elucidates why a consensus is necessary for a 'war on terror' and a 'war on drugs'. Second, the book aims at reconstructing the heterogeneity of both discourses by retracing the struggles of different hegemonic projects that promote competing understandings of terrorism and drugs and, thereby, different perspectives on what they consider as appropriate international anti-drug and anti-terrorism measures. The book's *central argument* is that the establishment of hegemonic orders at the international level in both fields is a dual process, which can be conceptualized on the one hand as the constant attempt to homogenize the image and the interpretation of the Other. On the other hand, I argue that focusing on the Other and on processes of othering does not suffice. Instead, one also needs to accord a central place to the construction of the Self. Thus, for hegemonic orders to emerge, the attempts to create a cohesive vision of the Self that is shared by the discursive agents jointly opposing the Other is of equal importance. To allow for the adoption of internationally accepted measures against the Other, this vision of the Self needs to be based upon a political consensus between the agents concerned. To reconstruct the heterogeneity of both discourses, the analysis compares the international efforts to counter terrorism from 1972 to 2010 with the developments against drugs from 1961 to 1988.

There are a number of reasons why the emergence of and struggle for hegemonic orders against international terrorism and drug abuse is a subject for inquiry. First, installing a hegemonic understanding of terrorism and drugs as a threat or attempting to do so has only lead to more violence so far, i.e. measures against drug dealers and terrorists have mostly not gone beyond the reflexive application of massive counter-violence. If one does not precisely know the nature of terrorism and drug abuse, the dangers of violent anti-drug and anti-terrorism policies – most importantly, the moral hazard of becoming like terrorist and drug dealers through the abuse of civil and human rights or by criminalizing drug use and destroying the livelihood of drug cultivators – one might end up worse off than when one started (Jackson 2005: 4). Despite good intentions things might not be that easy. Both phenomena are complex problems, which defy simple responses in the form of a hegemonized 'us vs. them'.

Therefore, and secondly, the language of war in both discourses needs to be thoroughly scrutinized. As chapter one will elaborate in more detail, in the context of the book language is treated not as a mere reflection of reality but as constructing reality. By saying it, something is done as, for instance, in betting, giving a promise or naming a ship (Austin 1976). With regard to security this implies that naming a certain development a security problem – to call it an 'existential threat' – specific agents move this development into a specific area, and thereby claim a special right to use whatever 'extraordinary measures' are necessary to block the threat (Buzan, Wæver and de Wilde 1998: 12). And what more of an extraordinary measure than declaring a 'war on drugs' and a 'war on terror'? Still, speaking of a 'war' does not only allow extraordinary measures on one side but also on the other. Comparing the actions of drug dealers with the doings of the Nazi-regime and calling terrorists barbarians does not only put them outside the realm of civilization but also enables dealers and terrorists to continue pursuing their sinister objectives. Thus, there is more than a genuine risk that the current policies will rather reify the global cycle of violence and counter-violence than eliminate it. Yet, my purpose is by no means to justify violent actions of terrorists or drug abusers! Rather, by systematically analyzing the discourses, the study lays open the current foundations of thinking on both phenomena and thereby allows seeing how much the ones countering terrorism and drugs are themselves involved in the cycle of violence and where there is the possibility to elaborate a different language – 'one that illuminates rather than obfuscates' (Jackson 2005: 4) – and which might lead to the peaceful and safer world people are aspiring ever since.

In a related sense, thirdly, the exercise of power by hegemonic orders needs to be questioned. A general politicization of the public is necessary in order to control authorities dealing with perceived security menaces. Public interrogation can avoid the abuse of power and articulate different responses to these threats, which do not exclusively rely on antagonizing the Other and counter-violence. Critical examination of the enemy constructions and the respective measures can resist their institutionalization within which abuses of civil liberties tend to become routine. Yet, so far, international cooperation against terrorism and drugs has not yielded strong resistance from the public; the normative consensus that security can only come by the price of freedom seems to be already very much part of current thinking (Herschinger, Jachtenfuchs and Kraft-Kasack forthcoming). Accordingly, by carefully analyzing the foundations of the judgements on terrorism and drugs the critical impetus of the overall public can be strengthened. This book aims to fuel the debate on whether and how current constructions of and reactions to drugs and terrorism can be and need to be altered.

The approach of the book

Discourse and hegemony, identity and language – these key terms indicate that this book is based on various literatures and is located at disciplinary intersections. The focus on discourse, hegemony and security issues situates the study within the discipline of International Relations (IR).[1] Here it shares company with the so-called poststructuralist[2] approaches. In addition, it exhibits intimate ties with poststructuralist discourse theoretical reflections by, most importantly, Ernesto Laclau and Chantal Mouffe, Jacques Derrida and Michel Foucault.

As such the book makes two crucial contributions. First, it fills an important gap in the empirical literature on international terrorism and drug prohibition. At present, relevant writings focus on national policies and tend to consider either those directed against terrorism, or those directed against drugs in isolation. On a theoretical level, current writings concentrate on national policies and their respective counter-measures in only one of the two policy-fields, or offer a largely policy-oriented analysis of both phenomena at the international level while lacking conceptual rigor. The large number of books on international terrorism is indicative of the high level of academic interest, and of the importance of the issue for academics, politicians, practitioners and journalists alike (to name just a few: Wilkinson 1974; Lacqueur 1987; Hoffmann 1998; 1999; 2003; Waldmann 2004; Guelke 2006; Richardson 2006). However, a much smaller number of books approach the topic from an IR perspective (Osman 2003; Boulden and Weiss 2004; Gioia 2006), but most of those focus on questions of international law or deal with counter-terrorism measures in the context of the European Union (Gal-Or 1985; Schmid 1993; Chalk 1996; van Krieken 2002; Archick and Gallis 2003). If the literature is theory-guided it follows the classic state-centred and interest-focused positivist approaches, such as the various incarnations of realism, liberalism, institutionalism and, in part, conventional constructivism.[3] In general, this implies that authors explain the shape and effectiveness of anti-terrorism policies with reference to national interests, states' preferences, institutional constraints and/or external factors. However, such explanatory attempts have not brought about a satisfying answer regarding the question of why efforts to find globally acceptable anti-terrorist measures have failed since the Munich attacks in 1972.

With regard to drug prohibition, a handful of monographs, edited volumes and articles applying a political science perspective on the issue exist (see among others Bruun, Lynn and Rexed 1975; Bewley-Taylor 1999; van der Veen 2000; Busch 2001; Gerber and Jensen 2001; Bewley-Taylor 2003). Nonetheless, few writers explicitly adopt an IR perspective (exceptions are Nadelmann 1990; 1993; Friesendorf 2007, although they focus exclusively on the United States drug policy). If studies engage with the international sphere, they predominantly analyze the effect of drugs from a European perspective (Albrecht and van Kalmthout 1989; Estievenart 1995; Elvins 2003; Boekhaut van Solinge 2004)[4] or from a historical perspective (McAllister 2000; Briesen 2005). This literature convincingly explains the emergence of a global regime on international drug prohibition by referring to the spread of particular norms and the influence of epistemic communities. However, there is a lack of critical engagement with the question of how the consensus in this field was able to overcome considerable national and cultural differences in the interpretation of what should be classified as a drug, and which measures are deemed appropriate to fight the spread and use of drugs. In contrast, a burgeoning body of literature analyzes terrorism and drug prohibition from a discursive, critical perspective (see among others Connolly 1997; Booth and Dunne 2002; Silke 2004; Bigo 2005; Booth 2005; Jackson 2005; MacCoun and Reuter 2005; European Political Science 2007; Ranstorp 2007; Neal 2010), and the present analysis ties in with the assumption of the constructed nature of the two phenomena and the need for critical investigation of the politicization of both issues for legitimizing far-reaching security measures. Still, comparative, critical IR-studies on terrorism and drug prohibition, analyzing the role of hegemony and identity are scarce (for few exceptions from non-discursive, non-critical perspectives see Friedrichs 2007; Jachtenfuchs *et al.* 2008; Herschinger, Jachtenfuchs and Kraft-Kasack 2010). The present book aims to fill this gap. Indeed, choosing and comparing international terrorism and drug prohibition allows explaining not only why two issues that have been widely perceived as major threats to nation-states and international peace and security witness such different fates and international measures countering them have mostly involved massive violence instead of consequently asking for different ways to deal with both phenomena. The comparison also brings about central insights into the formation of hegemonic orders otherwise difficult to obtain.

Therefore, the book's second contribution is of a theoretical-conceptual and methodological nature. Starting with the latter, so far, poststructuralist studies in IR systematically carrying out stringent and methodologically coherent research in general and on the politics of hegemony in the security field in particular are few and far between. This has added to the strength of 'one of the few axioms shared within the discipline of IR, namely that poststructuralism and methodology don't mix' (Hansen 2006: xviii). When Stephen Walt feared the seduction of IR by poststructuralism (Walt 1991: 223) and Peter Katzenstein, Stephen Krasner, and Robert Keohane stated that poststructuralism denies the necessity and use of evidence, rationalists agreed that poststructuralism is incapable of epistemological and methodological rigor (Keohane 1989; Katzenstein, Keohane and Krasner 1999).

However, I fully agree with Lene Hansen that the 'culprits' must be sought in the lines of poststructuralism as well: 'a search through the canon of poststructuralist IR reveals that the explicit concern with methodology has not been given prominent a place' (Hansen 2006: xviii). The critical aim of poststructuralism in the beginning years may partly explain this tendency to abstract theory and, above all, deconstructive readings of the history and discipline of IR. Of course, to confront the positivist mainstream theories, methodology was surely not the first and obvious choice; this called for a critical examination of the ontological and epistemological grounds upon which the main theories of IR rest. Methodology has been somewhat forgotten in this debate but it would be hazardous not to improve the standing of poststructuralism in this respect since scarce attention to methodological issues tends to put one at disadvantage within the research community (Milliken 1999: 226). Yet, not to be misunderstood: I am not arguing in favour of an all-pervasive methodology that every poststructuralist has to apply. Rather, it is about making methodological choices and decisions explicit and, hereby, increasing the plausibility of one's results, taking the idea of transparency serious and daring to question the credibility of one's enterprise. To address issues of credibility and plausibility within this study by no means surrenders to the positivist view of a method founded on the belief that the mere observation of specific methodological rules guarantees the truth of the results (Torfing 2005: 25).

With regard to the two central concepts of the present study – hegemony and identity – one observes that some junctions have been more frequently taken than others. First, the current usage of the term 'hegemony' refers to the relatively trivial idea of the primacy of the United States in vital security issues and is conceptually, empirically and normatively unsatisfying. Yet hegemonies are far more than power relations based upon coercion alone and/or embodied by a dominant country (Charbonneau and Cox 2008: 305–6; Walker 2010: 76). Considering it essentially a question of power which interpretation or meaning of an issue becomes dominant and, thereby, taking struggle and resistance as starting point, I argue that a poststructuralist approach opens up space for an alternative, critical conceptualization of hegemonies in the international field. However, only a small number of IR poststructuralist writings have dealt with identifying the efforts made to stabilize and fix dominant orders (see for instance Shapiro 2004), while the greater part has investigated alternative, previously excluded discourses, i.e. how dissent was made and unmade (see for example Manzo 1992; Sylvester 1994; Fierke 1998; Saco 1999). Still, there has been a relative neglect of engaging appropriate methods and criteria in the analysis of the production, persistence and transformation of hegemonic forms of international order. To address this desideratum, the book develops a poststructuralist framework of hegemony based on a model of discursive strategies, revealing how it is possible that a concrete meaning of international terrorism and drugs has spread throughout the respective fields. This allows for the examination of how different forces have been forged into a common hegemonic endeavour, as well as of the ways in which these processes construct particular identities. Overall, the book addresses the neglect of appropriate methods for the analysis of the production and persistence of hegemonic forms of international order. It heeds the ever louder call for a genuine poststructuralist methodology in IR specifically and in the social sciences in general, and therefore constitutes an important contribution to current research in these fields (Milliken 1999: 254; Glynos and Howarth 2007: 6).

With respect to the second central concept of the study, identity, poststructuralist scholars have advanced an understanding of identity as relational entities. The meaning of an entity depends on a different entity against which it can be differentiated, i.e. a Self is distinguished from an Other. This comprehension has led IR poststructuralists to investigate at large the discursive practices of the state as it is considered the locus of the most fundamental division between a Self – the inside – and it(s) Other(s) – the outside. In this context, national security policies have received considerable attention, since security has been considered as a boundary-drawing practice that helps a community to define 'who it is' and where the enemy can be found. Security discourses constitute identities in terms of a national, benevolent Self that needs to be protected from a foreign, menacing Other (Ashley 1987: 416–7; Walker 1993: 159–61; Campbell 1998b). Such concentration on the exclusionary practices of the Self produced a rather uni-dimensional understanding of the Other as threatening, as a radical Other (Weber 1995; Campbell 1998a; 1998b; see among others Wæver 2000; Milliken 2001; Doty 2003. Notable exceptions are Inayatullah and Blaney 2004; Shapiro 2004). In comparison, collective identity construction 'among states' and 'beyond states' to paraphrase Alexander Wendt (1994: 106), i.e. at the international level has received less attention – not only quantitatively (with regard to the number of studies) but also qualitatively (with regard to theorizing collective identity construction). In these analyses, national identity construction serves as role model for collective identity construction in general, which makes it difficult to conceptualize how other types of collective identities are made and unmade in the first place. Most importantly, how a *common* Other is construed and how a *collective* Self is established needs to be analyzed. This study will shed light on these modes of construction by developing a concept of collective identity constitution without taking national identities as a role model. By joining Hansen's call for acknowledging that an 'Other is situated within a web of identities rather than in a simple Self-Other duality', the book will make a case for a concept of identity whose ontological flexibility allows for the empirical study of different and varying degrees of otherness (Hansen 2006: 40–1). In sum, focusing on the reproduction and transformation of hegemonic orders, the book investigates the conditions upon which the emergence of a stable consensus in international discourses on terrorism and drugs rests. This serves to explain the widespread disagreement regarding the fight against international terrorism as well as the successful suppression of counter-hegemonic projects in the field of international drug prohibition. Such procedure allows engaging directly with the question of why particular interpretations of security phenomena guided and animated the shape of accordant policies while others did not.

Perhaps those well versed with IR poststructuralism have already missed delineation of its 'history' in IR. However, as the goal of this study is to speak to the subject matter, I refer to the various accounts on the ways IR poststructuralism has travelled since the mid 1980s (see among others Wæver 2004; Diez 2006; Hansen 2006). The study's contribution to the discipline resides in embarking on the 'next step in IR poststructuralism', which implies facing the challenge of substantive research and what is commonly subsumed under the term 'operationalization', or as Foucault has circumscribed it, a systematic and methodologically plausible, convincing problematization of various issues (Foucault 2006).

The content of the book

By outlining the study's understanding of language and discourse, practice and strategy as well as hegemony and identity, chapters one and two present the theoretical and methodological backbone of the study. The first chapter 'On hegemony and identity in international security discourses' sets the scene of the book by establishing a close link between discourse and language, hegemonies and identities in the field of security. Its underlying assumption postulates that the spread of a hegemonic pattern throughout a political field is justified by constructing particular identities and by means of using a specific type of language. Construing international terrorism and drug abuse as threats does not only employ a language that assumes radical differences, but also confers a specific meaning on both phenomena, which allows drawing boundaries within the discourse. Thereby, two diametrically opposed entities emerge: an Other (the 'evil terrorists/drug abusers') confronts a Self (the 'good citizens/the civilized international community'). Still, a Self is not only forged via the differentiation from an Other but equally through the creation of a vision of itself, of what the world would look like without being endangered by the respective Other, terrorism and drugs.

In this process, discursive agents present themselves as having the power to draw boundaries in a field criss-crossed by numerous contradictory meanings, and the authority to decide how to respond internationally to both phenomena. However, efforts to deal with both problems by establishing hegemonic orders are confronted with a discursive terrain already inhabited by and structured through previously articulated understandings of terrorism and drugs. If one acknowledges that different understandings of the Other are possible, one also admits that constructions of identities can produce varying degrees of otherness. This in turn implies that identity construction does not necessarily depend upon juxtaposition to a radically threatening Other. The book develops a concept of identity, which is ontologically flexible to account for different degree of otherness; thus, a concept sensitive to the differences drawn between, for instance, a drug addict as a criminal or sick individual. Despite an acknowledgement of these degrees, and of the necessity of examining them to get a thorough conception of Other and Self, the book argues that hegemonic orders rely essentially on the construction of an unequivocal, radically different, and menacing Other. In light of these considerations, the book's *central argument* is that the establishment of a hegemonic order at the international level in both fields under investigation depends on the constant attempt to homogenize the image of the Other, that is, to create a homogeneous, clear-cut interpretation of the Other. Furthermore, since the establishment of a hegemonic order is a twofold process, attempts to create a cohesive vision of the Self shared by the discursive agents jointly opposing the Other are of equal importance. And in order to allow for the adoption of internationally accepted measures against the Other, this vision of the Self needs to be based upon a political consensus between the agents concerned.

Chapter two 'Opening the "black box": the construction of international hegemonies' establishes the analytical framework of the book. It develops methodological tools necessary to analyze the practices of hegemonic orders, giving insights on how a concrete meaning of terrorism and drugs has spread throughout the respective fields and marginalized alternative understandings. In doing so, the chapter explains the way in which specific identities are constructed as authoritative. To this end, the book develops a discursive model of hegemonic operations, which is based on the vocabulary of poststructuralist discourse theory. It takes into account a number of its central concepts (e.g. 'antagonism', 'identification', 'tendentially empty signifiers' etc.) and refers back to the general logics of critical explanation. Most prominent in this context is the logic of equivalence, which establishes chains of equivalence linking different political forces into a common hegemonic project, and the logic of difference, which counters this type of linkage. At the heart of the book's discursive model lies a classification of the multitude of hegemonic strategies into productive and counter-hegemonic strategies, depending on their impact on the construction of hegemonic orders at the international level. The model allows for an analysis of the extent to which hegemonic orders are justified with reference to specific identities. Furthermore, it is sufficiently flexible to analyze how homogenous or heterogeneous an Other is constructed, what visions of the Self are articulated, whether they are shared unambiguously by the discursive agents, whether or not a political consensus is formed and, ultimately, when one can speak of the establishment of a hegemonic order in the respective field. As such, the book's framework offers a format for systematic comparison of the two discourses under scrutiny.

Chapter two also lays open the methodological aspects of the study. It explains the reasons underlying the choice of international terrorism and drug prohibition as case studies: for more than five decades, both have been perceived as threat not only to a single nation-state but also to international peace and security. The two issues have been present at the contemporary international agenda for roughly fifty (drugs) and forty (terrorism) years respectively, which represents a sufficiently long period to carry out a meaningful discourse analysis. The different time periods chosen for the two case studies are justified with reference to the decisive periods of framing of both discourses: whereas the international drug prohibition discourse was framed from 1961 to 1988, the framing of the international terrorism discourse is still underway. While the main material for the analysis stems from the United Nations (UN) debates on international terrorism and drug prohibition, the database encompasses a significant number of documents from other institutions like the European Union (EU), Europol, the International Narcotics Control Board (INCB) or international non-governmental organizations (NGOs) as well as from various national sources such as newspapers, reports and documents from government officials. In the present context, including a large number of UN-documents is warranted as the UN represents not only the central source of legitimacy for both discourses but also the forum within which key discursive agents struggle for a global vision of what the world should look like if terrorism and drugs no longer existed. Therefore, the UN is an ideal place for analyzing the attempts of constructing not only an Other but also a Self, i.e. for investigating the validity of my central argument. Overall, the book's database covers 485 documents from these different types of sources.

Chapter three 'International drug prohibition: constructing the "drug-free world"' argues that drugs were gradually construed as presenting an international threat. Today's perspective on narcotics is the outcome of a conflict between defining drugs as requiring concerted international action or preventing a definition of that sort. The chapter traces the historical roots of today's dominant interpretation of drugs as illicit and their use as deviant. As it was only under the aegis of the UN that global drug prohibition turned into a worldwide system structured by a series of international drug treaties, chapter three concentrates on the official debates of the three major conventions in the area: the UN *Single Convention on Narcotic Drugs* (1961) and the UN *Conference to Consider Amendments to the Single Convention on Narcotic Drugs* (1972), the UN *Convention on Psychotropic Substances* (1971) and the UN *Convention Against Illicit Traffic in Narcotic Drugs and Psychotropic Substances* (1988). Chapter three identifies the hegemonic strategies constructing drugs as the antagonistic Other and traces those, which aim at constructing the identity of a 'drug-free world', of the Self confronting the drugs Other through inducing a consensus. The latter is also meant to justify a range of international measures to fight the 'war on drugs' as the analysis of documents from sources like the EU, INCB and various international NGOs as well as from national governments will indicate.

In order to allow for comparison between the two case studies, chapter four 'Writing the "war on terror": the struggle of hegemonic projects' is structured analogously to chapter three. Emphasizing the historical contingency of the current interpretation of terrorism, chapter four outlines the development of the term from its first known appearance during the French Revolution to the attempts to find a universal definition of terrorism at the level of the UN starting in 1972. Data examined in chapter four encompass the debates on a comprehensive convention against international terrorism at the level of the United Nations (which started in 1972 and are still underway), the Europol-US agreements on the exchange of data and the EU-US agreements on judicial cooperation in criminal matters. Though identifying different hegemonic strategies in the discourse that share the common aim of constructing terrorism as antagonistic Other, the book's analysis stresses the enormous difficulties of contemporary efforts to forge a global consensus on a definition of international terrorism. Chapter four also maps out the hegemonic strategies aimed at the establishment of the Self, i.e. the entity opposed to the terrorist Other. While there is a certain level of agreement that a world safe from terrorism should be achieved, there is also a far-ranging conflict regarding the question of *how* this vision can be achieved. Consequently, chapter four puts forward the controversial and possibly surprising finding that no hegemonic order at the international level has emerged in the terrorism discourse since 1972 – and this remains the case even after the events of 11 September 2001. The flip side of this finding is that without significant political consensus a tenable justification of a 'war on terror' appears largely impossible at the international level.

The aim of chapter five 'Comparing the "war on drugs" and the "war on terror"' lies in pulling together the findings from the two case studies. Comparing both discourses brings about the central insight that the international drug discourse has resulted in the establishment of a hegemonic order at the international level, whereas the international discourse on terrorism has failed to do so. To explain why this difference has occurred, the chapter carries out a fine-grained comparison of both discourses by focusing on the language of war, the constructions of Self and Other and the justification of counter-measures in presence and absence of hegemonic orders. Since the book was originally meant to address the current lack of systematic and methodologically coherent research of the politics of hegemony in the security field, the chapter closes with some general methodological reflections on broader evaluation criteria from qualitative methodology in the social sciences.

The conclusion reviews the book's critical perspective and extends its boundaries. It highlights the function of the war-like language on international drug prohibition and terrorism and explores the dangers of hegemonic orders that are based on such radically different but inevitably intermingled constructions of Self and Other. It highlights the way in which these constructions normalize the pattern of inclusion/exclusion and examines how such orders endanger the stability of a presumed moral community. The conclusion critically reflects upon the extent to which such representations allow negating a Self's responsibility towards an Other, and questions whether different types of hegemonic orders in the field of security can be imagined which could pave the way for policies searching for long-lasting solutions to the phenomena international drug abuse and terrorism.

1 On hegemony and identity in international security discourses

In one of his children's short stories, *Ein Tisch ist ein Tisch*[1], Swiss author Peter Bichsel writes about an old man who wanted to change his life by giving new names to familiar, ordinary things like tables, chairs and beds but also to specific activities. Henceforward, a table was no longer a table but a rug. A bed he called a painting, a cupboard turned into a newspaper and the old man himself was no longer a man but a foot, while the foot was a morn and the latter was called a man. 'To skim through' he called 'to lie something down' and 'to lie' was signified by 'to ring'. This 'new language' changed the old man's life completely because after a while, he was unable to understand the others. Worse, he began to fear speaking to other people, since it was not only he who could not understand them – they also could not understand what he was saying. Ultimately, the man ceased to speak. 'He kept still, spoke only to himself and did not even greet others' (Bichsel 1969: 25).

The failure of the old man to change his life for the better, to wreak havoc on the world of communicated ideas, aptly demonstrates what is at stake when dealing with language. Language is ontologically significant and productive since it is through language that subjects or material factors come into being, dispose of meaning and are given a particular identity. This is precisely the study's point of departure. It is driven by the underlying assumption that the spread of a hegemonic pattern throughout a political field like terrorism and drug prohibition is justified by constructing specific identities and using a specific type of language, because the concepts introduced in the course of this chapter – hegemonic orders, identities and legitimating practices – need to be articulated to have a political and analytical presence. Therefore, chapter one will establish a close link between the book's central concepts, discourse and language, hegemonic orders and identity. By explaining how language is deployed in the construction processes of hegemonic orders and identities, the chapter conceptualizes the two concepts within an integrative poststructuralist framework, which provides the book with a solid theoretical grounding. Theorizing on the intimate connection between discourse, hegemonies and identities serves further to develop the book's central argument on the dual process of establishing hegemonic orders: an unequivocal, radically different, and menacing Other is as much needed as the creation of an accordant unambiguous vision of the Self which is based upon a political consensus among the discursive agents jointly opposing the Other and, thereby, allowing the enactment of internationally accepted measures countering the Other.

Language and articulation, discourse and practice

For positivism, language works as a transparent medium for the indexing of data giving us a clear view *on* reality while the interpretation of reality can rely on correlations and facts. In contrast, poststructuralism conceives of language as ontologically significant and productive. Such an understanding situates the study within theories that comply with the 'linguistic turn' in the social sciences: they refuse to conceptualize language as a means of representation, as a transparent medium or key for the researcher to investigate an objective perception of reality. 'Reality' cannot be objectively perceived; hence, there is no objective or 'true' meaning behind or beyond linguistic representations. The discourse functions as the theoretical horizon on which objects are constituted: all objects are objects of discourse, as their meaning depends on a socially constructed system of rules and significant differences (Howarth and Stavrakakis 2000: 3). This is the tragedy of the old man: the productivity of language allowed him to turn the table in a rug and the bed into a painting; it allowed him to construct a world of his own full of things and objects with new meanings. But language is also a socially constructed and collectively shared system of rules, codes and conventions to which individuals have to comply in order to be understood and to participate in societal life, language can never be a private property – there is no private language exclusively for the old man (Wittgenstein 2001: 75/243).

To further understand language as political not only makes it a site of social interaction but also a space for producing and denouncing specific subjectivities within the political realm – language is a site of exclusion and inclusion. For instance, the understanding of drug use in the nineteenth century was radically different from today: drug use was a tolerated behaviour, people in various societal strata consumed drugs for pleasure, recreation or for medical reasons, and states even promoted the drug trade by claiming the monopoly on, for example, the trade with opium. Such a stance is inconceivable today, since the political nature of these formerly accepted practices became subject of contestations and, eventually, exclusions: states would not act as trader of drugs anymore and consuming drugs is considered as deviant, sick and illegal behaviour. Thus, drug prohibition (and equally terrorism) are not a mere liguistic reflection of processes or patterns of behaviour one can discover in the world 'out there' and described 'as they are'. They are as much in need of interpretation as they open up space for interpretation. How they are interpreted and why some interpretations dominate and others do not is – as this book argues – a question of hegemonic orders.

By claiming that it is only through language that things acquire meaning, the imagination of an extra-discursive realm able to determine the meaning of an object is excluded. However, such a stance does not imply that objects of knowledge might not exist independently of language, that there is no materiality of say a body or a table outside of discourse.

The fact that every object is constituted as an object of discourse has nothing to do with whether there is a world external to thought, or with the realism/idealism opposition. An earthquake or the falling of a brick is an event that certainly exists, in the sense that it occurs here and now, independently of my will. But whether their specificity as objects is constructed in terms of 'natural phenomena' or 'expression of the wrath of God' depends upon the structuring of a discursive field. What is denied is not that such objects exist externally to thought, but the rather different assertion that they could constitute themselves as objects outside any discursive conditions of emergence.

(Laclau and Mouffe 2001: 108)[2]

Hence, poststructuralism conceptualizes language in a twofold manner. First, language is highly structured, since – as Derrida once argued – it is a system of differential signs, and meaning can only emerge through a series of juxtapositions, where one element is valued over its opposite and not via the essence of the thing itself (Derrida 1980). In principle, signs are composed of the *signifier* (the letters on the page or the sound that bounces off our eardrum) and the *signified* (the concept that appears in our brain when we read or hear the signifier). Hence, a drug addict can only be identified as such through a differentiation from the non-user, a terrorist needs to be delineated from the legitimate freedom fighter and a state's national identity acquires meaning via juxtaposition with a different national identity.

While signifier and signified capture the structured nature of language, meaning within linguistic structures is organized by articulation. Against the background of the ontological significance of language, poststructuralists valorize the role of articulatory practices in the structuring of social relations by claiming that every social process of putting elements together is to some degree articulatory. In this respect, and secondly, poststructuralists conceive of language not only as highly structured but also as instable at the same time. Due to this instable nature of language, the practice of articulation is 'the construction of nodal points which partially fix meaning' (Laclau and Mouffe 2001: 113). By speaking of the *partial* ability to fix meaning only, Laclau and Mouffe highlight the instable nature of language. Signifiers are always referring to other signifiers without ever coming to an irrevocable meaning. Derrida circumscribed this process with his neologism *différance*: words and signs can never fully summon forth what they mean, but can only be defined or explained by using more words; thus, the 'fuller' meaning is always postponed in language, there is never a moment when one can say the meaning is complete (Derrida 1972).

Such diverse writers as Derrida, Julia Kristeva, Foucault, Roland Barthes, Jacques Lacan or Laclau and Mouffe acknowledge that the articulatory practice always alters the identity of each articulated element. '[C]ontingency now inhabits not only the different elements that are linked together to form a discourse, but also the hegemonic projects or subjects that strive to fix meanings' (Glynos and Howarth 2007: 179). This brings about a conceptualization of *discourse* as 'the structured totality resulting from the articulatory practice' (Laclau and Mouffe 2001: 105). Hence, discourses refer to systems of meaningful practices that form the identities of subjects and objects; they relate elements to establish meaning, since elements need to be set in relation to other elements to acquire meaning. This is implied when the meaning of a terrorist can only be established by juxtaposing it to a non-terrorist. Discursive structures are not cognitive entities, they are articulatory practices, which constitute and organize social relations.

Although being defined as a structured totality the process of constantly relating elements and organize meaning rules out the impression of discourse as a static, fixed structure. On the contrary, discourse is a structure penetrated by contingency and temporality, marked by fissures, ruptures and breaches. Attempts to halt the inherent dynamic that haunts discourses and to fix meaning around closed structures are in vain: 'neither absolute fixity nor absolute non-fixity is possible' (Laclau and Mouffe 2001: 111). Thus, what counts for the articulatory practice also counts for discourses: meaning can be partially fixed because without partial fixations the very flow of differences would not be possible and no identity or social formation would ever be constructed. Partial fixations are achieved as any discourse situates itself as 'an attempt to dominate the field of discursivity [. . .] to construct a centre' (Laclau and Mouffe 2001: 111–2) and subjects search for a constitutive decision articulating social meaning in one particular way rather than another – to paraphrase Derrida's 'undecidability' of any text.

One central implication of denying the existence of an extra-discursive realm within which things and objects can be constructed consists of acknowledging that policies like the 'war on terror' and the 'war on drugs' are based on specific discursive representations of the security problem they want to address and on specific constructions of identities, of Self and Other. But how are linguistic representations and policies like the two 'wars' linked exactly? In this respect, the notion of practice is crucial. Practices are the ongoing, routinized forms of human and societal reproduction. As largely repetitive activities (not entailing a strong notion of self-conscious reflexivity), they contribute to the reproduction of wider systems of social relations. However, every practice is also articulatory 'as human beings constantly engage in the process of linking together different elements of their social lives in these continuous and projective sequences of human action' (Glynos and Howarth 2007: 104).

While such social practices and the identities they maintain tend to dissimulate the inherent contingency that inhabits social systems, the ghost of this contingency leaves its traces within the structure: discursive structures are precarious, they are full of breaches and gaps, i.e. any social edifice suffers from an inbuilt defect which may become visible in moments of dislocation (Lacan 2006: 693). Dislocation destabilizes a discourse due to events that cannot be symbolized by this very discourse – it refers to the 'decentring' of the structure through social processes which disrupt the structure (like a severe crisis), as they cannot be mastered by it. In such a moment, new opportunities arise, allowing (but also forcing) a subject to situate itself anew as its former points of identification have vanished in the process of dislocation. We will see later in how far the terrorist attacks at the Olympic Games in 1972 represent such a moment of dislocation as they could not be represented in the discourse on terrorism at that time.

Yet, dislocation is problematic and productive at the same time, since the dislocated social practices give rise to political practices, as in the moment of dislocation, of a crisis, grievances or dissatisfactions are publicly articulated as demands. Thus, political practices are about struggles challenging and transforming current norms, institutions and practices – or an entire regime of practices – in the name of a different, particular idea, ideal or principle (Howarth 2000: 108–9). If political practices are successful in challenging existing norms and institutions in the name of something new, they bring about a transformative effect, since they can modify or reorder an entire regime. Indeed, to the extent to which political practices are not only able to challenge an existing regime of practices but also link various forces and demands into a new regime of practices, they exercise an enormous transformative effect in the political landscape. Even more: political practices can be characterized as 'more or less hegemonic depending on the degree to which the political demands articulating a grievance are formulated in terms that succeed in having more or less universal appeal' (Glynos and Howarth 2007: 123). In this sense, a regime of political practices has a structuring function by ordering a system of practices against something else: the institution of a particular regime is always dependent on frontiers relating to what cannot be incorporated in the differential system of the regime. The establishment of these limits serves to exclude antagonistic otherness, represented by those elements that have nothing in common with the regime from which they are excluded. Quite obviously, defining a regime of practices in contrast to an antagonized regime shapes both of them. Labelling a drug addict as a criminal or defining her as a sick person leads to different practices on how to deal with her addiction – either by repressive and punitive measures or by prevention and clinical cure.

Furthermore, considering something as a threat, i.e. to 'securitize' an issue by designating it as an existential threat and request for extraordinary measures, is all but interest-free (Buzan, Wæver and de Wilde 1998: 23–6). It legitimizes the subject that securitizes to go beyond the limits of routine political behaviour and demand extraordinary measures and instruments. In most of these cases (since these types of demands are most frequently voiced by powerful stakeholders within a state), the measures serve to discipline the rest of society and reaffirm the rule of particular subjects over society. By invoking the extraordinary measures and practices to defend against the alleged threat, resistance to these practices becomes increasingly difficult. Moreover, resistance can easily be described as being subversive and playing into the hands of the threat.

To characterize practices and regimes, to account for their relationship, to explain how and why they change or resist transformations, we need to elaborate on the logics or modes of construction on which they are based. Most importantly, in order to address how and why specific regimes become hegemonic it is especially necessary to clarify what is understood by hegemony. This is the task of the next section.

Hegemony in International Relations

In its most general, encyclopaedic meaning, hegemony is defined as the dominance or supremacy of an individual or collective actor relying on different types of resources (military, economic, political or cultural) and their combination. Despite its central role in IR hegemony 'has remained a relatively imprecise and under-analyzed concept' (Lentner 2006: 107–8); its 'key attributes remain diverse and notoriously slippery' (Clark 2009: 205).[3] To date, mainly two approaches offer an explicit conceptualization of hegemony in IR: the *theory of hegemonic stability* and the neo-Gramscian school of thought. Both constitute materialist accounts in that they share the idea that hegemony is reducible to coercive resources (i.e. military and/or economic capabilities). The theory of hegemonic stability (Kindleberger 1973; Gilpin 1975; Keohane 1980; 1984) employs the term 'hegemony' to explain the origins and functions of the post-1945 international economic order, con-ceptualizing it as a structure organized around a single dominant country – the hegemon – with leadership responsibilities and privileges (Lake 1993).

The alternative account uses Antonio Gramsci's understanding of hegemony to question the prevailing world order. Among those scholars critical theorists in International Political Economy (or 'neo-Gramscians') have been most prominent.[4] Especially Robert Cox attempted in the early 1980s with a Gramscian reading a revision of current international theory by conceptualizing hegemony as more than the dominance of a state in the international system and opening new avenues for innovative thinking on the notion of hegemony. Dissatisfied with common explana-tions of social transformation and change, Cox used Gramsci's understanding on hegemony to question the prevailing world order.[5] His theory of hegemony 'does not take institutions and social and power relations for granted but calls them into question by concerning itself with their origins and whether they might be in the process of changing' (Cox 1981: 129). Referring to Gramsci, he defined hegemony as a structure of values and meanings about the nature of the order that pervades the system of states and non-state entities. Values, norms and meanings are not really questioned, because in a hegemonic order they appear to most actors as 'naturally' given, i.e. they are expressed as universally valid. Although hegemony is a form of dominance, it is interpreted as the expression of a broadly based consensus that becomes manifest in the acceptance of ideas and is supported by material resources and institutions (Cox 1981: 139).

Inasmuch as neo-Gramscians think of hegemony as an 'opinion-moulding activ-ity' (Cox 1996: 151) instead of the application of brute force or dominance, the process of its emergence comes into focus. Starting point of the analysis of hege-monic mechanisms for neo-Gramscians are patterns of production (this includes all kinds of production – knowledge, morals etc.) which are referred to as 'modes of social relations of production'. These relations encompass specific configurations of social forces, which become the power bases across states and within a specific world order. Hegemony, then, is constructed (and/or contested) by social forces through national political frameworks, which occupy a leading role within a state

(Cox 1987: 4). Once hegemony has consolidated itself at the national level, it may expand and move outwards on a world scale.

> A world hegemony is thus in its beginnings an outward expansion of the internal (national) hegemony established by a [. . .] social class' [and] 'to become hegemonic, a state would have to found and protect a world order which was universal in conception, i.e. not an order in which one state directly exploits others but an order which most other states (or at least those within reach of the hegemony) could find compatible with their interests.
>
> (Cox 1983: 171)

The merit of the neo-Gramscian approach lies in broadening the concept of hegemony beyond the description of a single country as hegemon as argued by the theory of hegemonic stability. However, reviewing recent neo-Gramscian inspired literature, one finds numerous examples discussing *why* hegemonies emerge but not *how* they come into being, *how* hegemonies vanish and *how* different socio-political forces struggle to establish hegemonies (see among others Bieler and Morton 2001). Yet, it is an imminent necessity to address this process of 'becoming hegemonic' systematically to advance a coherent analysis of the politics of hegemony from a poststructuralist perspective. With respect to these mechanisms, the neo-Gramscian approach remains vague and unsystematic. To consider that hegemony implies to 'find' a universal 'world order', i.e. an order which most other states could 'find compatible' with their interests, proves to be very difficult to pinpoint not only once it comes down to empirical analysis. With regard to an assessment of the emergence, the inner workings of hegemony and the establishment of the consensus, the neo-Gramscians themselves consider precisely these questions as important research desiderata (Cox and Schecter 2002: 33; Halliday 2002: 87).

While the merit of Cox and the neo-Gramscians clearly resides in contesting the mainstream understanding of hegemony, their concept does not go far enough for the present purpose. Applying a poststructuralist approach allows developing an independent perspective on the production of hegemonies in international politics. More precisely, I argue that the integration of poststructuralist discourse theory in its variant of the *Essex School of Discourse Theory* proves highly beneficial (on the uses of discourse theory in IR see Wæver 2005: 59). First, while the integration allows retaining the neo-Gramscian conceptualization of hegemony as being based on a consensus (see below), the material understanding of hegemony advocated by the neo-Gramscians cannot be sustained. This contradicts the study's claim that a discourse functions as the theoretical horizon of the constitution of objects and that their meaning depends on a socially constructed system of rules and significant differences.

Second, bringing in the Essex School of Discourse Theory allows advancing current poststructuralist conceptualizations of hegemony. So far, IR poststructuralists put forward the idea of hegemonies as discursive frameworks or regimes of practices. While researchers have been concerned with identifying efforts to stabilize and fix dominant orders as well as to investigate alternative discourses that had previously been excluded (see for instance Shapiro 1989; Manzo 1992; Sylvester

1994; Fierke 1998; Saco 1999), there has been little engagement with appropriate methods and criteria to analyze the production, persistence and transformation of hegemonic forms of international order. However, a number of noteworthy exceptions have reflected on hegemonies (see Inayatullah and Blaney 2004; Shapiro 2004; Lash 2007). One path to conceptualize hegemonies as discursive phenomenon has been pursued by drawing on Foucault, especially his works on discourse, resistance, and the power/knowledge nexus and applying them to international regimes. Here, regimes are interpreted as a hegemonic discourse/discipline set: if a set is accepted, it can produce desired behaviour on the part of the actors concerned by the regime (i.e. desired behaviour as in accordance with the objectives of the regime). But such acceptance comes at the price of contestation and struggle: '[b]esides a hegemonic discourse we may find a range of other formulations that either have never gained formal recognitions as regimes of truth or have lost that status. These are "subjugated knowledges"' (Keeley 1990: 91). In consequence, subjugated knowledges and resistance to the regime might surface if the regime's definition of order to a public space and realm of action is not accepted by the actors concerned. On their part, they would seek to transform the present order and the hegemonic regime incorporating the order (Keeley 1990: 91–9).

In a similar vein, hegemonies are conceptualized as a set of political practices establishing a framework that determines the general conditions of a specific way of life, thereby constructing identities of nation-states (Klein 1990, 1994; Agnew 2007). Here, again, resistance and contestation are endangering this way of life and need to be suppressed in order to ensure its persistence and stability. While these accounts to capture the politics of hegemony highlight the discursive production of and the power inherent in hegemonic structures to exclude alternative knowledge and identities and constitute a small but valuable basis for a poststructuralist framework, a coherent account of how discourses or specific regimes become hegemonic is still lacking. Since this study seeks to fill this gap through a systematic and critical analysis of how specific regimes become hegemonic, what 'happens' within them and what this implies for the subjects targeted or embraced by these discourses, it argues that the Essex School of Discourse Theory offers the most up-to-date approach to the politics of hegemony, provides for the means to analyze the inner mechanisms of hegemonies and, moreover, allows integrating a concise understanding of the creation of the Self.

A discourse theoretical reading of hegemony

Aiming to develop a theory of hegemony that can serve as a framework for political analysis, the founding figures of the Essex School of Discourse Theory, Ernesto Laclau and Chantal Mouffe, used Gramsci's thoughts as a point of departure but radicalized them further (Stäheli 1999). I will briefly elaborate on Gramsci's conception of hegemony to fully appreciate its later adaption to modern political processes by the Essex School. Gramsci's reflections on hegemony derived from the simultaneous experience of the Bolshevik Revolution and the failure of a communist regime in Western and Central Europe. He located their different fates in the presence or absence of a (bourgeois) civil society. While in tsarist Russia no such group hampered the revolutionary process, the European countries were marked by a strong and resilient civil society that impeded the success of the communist revolutions. Here, the fight for civil society demanded alternative means, which slowly built up the social foundations of a new state and did not consist of coercion solely but were based on consent.[6]

In the present context, three elements of Gramsci's thinking are of importance: first, his conceptualization of hegemony, second, his idea of hegemonic subjects, and, third, how hegemonies emerge. Gramsci perceives hegemony as the moment 'in which one becomes aware that one's own corporate interests, in their present and future development, transcend the corporate limits of the purely economic class, and can and must become the interests of other subordinate groups too'. This is the genuine political moment marked by an ideological struggle, which tries to unify economic, political and intellectual objectives 'placing all the questions around which the struggle ranges on a "universal", not a corporate level, thereby creating the hegemony of a fundamental social group over a series of subordinate ones' (Gramsci 1971: 180–3). As such, hegemonies are defined as a process – the production of a new collective *identity* (Torfing 1999: 108).

Second, if hegemony suggests that one group dominates others, the question arises what kind of 'fundamental social group' Gramsci speaks about. Obviously, this group has to take into account the interests of other groups to become hegemonic in the first place; furthermore, 'it also presupposes a certain equilibrium, that is to say that the hegemonic groups will make some sacrifices of a corporate nature' (Gramsci 1971: 180–3). While it seems clear that Gramsci speaks of collective subjects (groups) involved in the hegemonic process, the interesting feature lies in the fundamental. On the one hand, a fundamental group is a group that occupies one of the two poles in the present relation of production (for Gramsci these are the proletariat and the bourgeoisie). On the other hand, with the fundamental group economism sneaks in, since only a fundamental class can become hegemonic: '[t]hough hegemony is ethico-political, it must also be economic, must necessarily be based on the decisive function exercised by the leading group in the decisive nucleus of economic activity' (Gramsci 1971: 161).

Third, it remains to answer how this hegemonic process of fusion comes about, i.e. how hegemonies emerge – and this is arguably the most interesting aspect of Gramsci's work for the present context. As hegemony is no longer the attempt to forge a political alliance but the total fusion of different objectives (which are animated by a fundamental group), there needs to be something that allows for this fusion and keeps the different groups under a hegemonic 'heading' together. Thus, for Gramsci, hegemony involves the 'creation of a *higher synthesis*, so that all its elements fuse in a "collective will" which becomes the new protagonist of political action during that hegemony's entire duration' (Mouffe 1979: 184, original emphasis). How is this collective will established? In the process of unifying, Gramsci conceives of ideology as the lubricant between the fundamental class and the subordinated groups. They are allied by ideology when the latter is able to 'spread throughout the whole of society determining not only united economic and political objectives but also intellectual and moral unity' (Gramsci 1971: 245–6; Mouffe 1979: 185–6).

The collective will is formed through ideology but its very existence depends on the creation of an ideological unity, which serves as the foundation of the will. What is decisive here is Gramsci's conceptualization of ideology as a battlefield, as a terrain of permanent struggle in which political subjects are created. Consequently, a collective will is not based on something exterior, but is forged via the confrontation of different ideological elements for the most part already present in the ideological universe. It is the task of the fundamental class to ensure the unity of this will and to re-order, re-assign these elements in their new context. In fact,

> [i]deological struggle [. . .] consists of a process of *disarticulation-rearticulation* of given ideological elements in a struggle between two hegemonic principles to appropriate these elements; it does not consist of the confrontation of two already elaborated, closed world-views. Ideological ensembles existing at a given moment are, therefore, the result of relations of forces between the rival hegemonic principles and they undergo a perpetual process of transformation.
>
> (Mouffe 1979: 193–4, original emphasis)

Hence, with Mouffe we can consider Gramsci's concept of hegemony as an ideological struggle for meaning in which one group is able to make another group share its specific goals, beliefs or world views to create a collective will. Most importantly, this allows us to conceptualize hegemony as a discursive phenomenon. Building on this insight as much as on Gramsci's claim that the articulation of collective wills takes place in the midst of political struggles within the state, economy and civil society, which, in turn, determine the fate of competing hegemonic projects, Laclau and Mouffe, however, removed the economistic residue of Gramsci, who insisted that the social classes, due to their structural position, have a privileged role in the struggle for hegemony. Insofar as they part from Gramsci's determination in the last instance by the economy (and, thereby, equally from the neo-Gramscian approaches), both theorists pave the way for a broader application of the concept (Torfing 1999: 109; Laclau and Mouffe 2001: 69).

Yet, how do they conceptualize hegemony and the processes of its emergence, persistence and transformation? Essential in this regard is Laclau and Mouffe's perspective on how discursive elements are related or, more precisely, on the kinds of relations articulated in hegemonic practices. While many agree that the relation between discursive elements is by no means arbitrary, accidental or indefinite and that there are only a limited number of relations, the question of what type these relations are has been answered differently. Despite the potentially endless number of combination, Foucault, for instance, speaks of a limited amount of specific rules that regulate the formation of statements (Dreyfus and Rabinow 1994: 79–83), whereas Laclau and Mouffe further condense the number of regularly emerging relations in political discourses to only two: substitution and combination. Whereas substitution denotes the ability of each element to substitute every other element in a specific context of meaning, combination describes the relation and constitution of elements via differentiation (Laclau 1997a: 59).[7] Combination and substitution can be translated into relations of difference and equivalence respectively. Let us start with *difference*, since it is the most basic type of relation between discursive elements (Howarth and Stavrakakis 2000: 20). Discursive elements have to be different because without difference they would be identical and the question of their relation senseless, as there would be only one element and not two. Indeed, the difference makes them conceivable as elements: *a* is different from *b*, *b* from *c* and so forth. Given that difference alone is enough to relate elements of a discourse, it is necessary to stress that difference is not sufficient to modulate and model the discursive topography on its own. To shape the discursive terrain (which is always an uneven space) difference is subverted by equivalence. An example from Laclau and Mouffe's *Hegemony and Socialist Strategy* illustrates the functioning of equivalence:

> In a colonized country, the presence of the dominant power is every day made evident through a variety of contents: difference of dress, of language, of skin colour, of customs. Since each of these contents is equivalent to the others in term of their common differentiation from the colonized peoples, [. . .] equiva-lence creates a second meaning which, though parasitic on the first, subverts it: the differences [of dress, language etc.] cancel one other out insofar as they are used to express something identical underlying them all.
>
> (Laclau and Mouffe 2001: 127)

Hence, equivalence makes differences equivalential: *a*, *b*, *c* are equivalent, but – and this is important to stress – *with regard to something identical underlying them all*. Accordingly, *a*, *b*, *c* are equivalent (but not identical!) with respect to *z*. Contrary to relations of difference, equivalence reduces the complexity of the discursive space, since differences are concentrated under a common reference point, the 'general equivalent'.

Now, referring to a *logic of equivalence* and *logic of difference* implies that relations of equivalence and difference enable us to understand the way a practice or regime of practices was instituted or is being contested or instituted. Thereby, logic should be understood as 'the type of relations between entities that make possible the actual operation of that system of rules' (Laclau 2000a: 284). Thus, analyzing how the logic of equivalence and logic of difference operate is at the heart of the construction of hegemonics and identities. Insofar as political practices entail the constitution of new frontiers challenging old structures in the name of an ideal or principle – i.e. imply-ing a new set of inclusions and exclusions – the logic of equivalence is dominating. That is to say, the logic of equivalence captures the substitutive aspect of discursive relations 'by making reference to an "us-them" axis: two or more elements can be substituted for each other with reference to a common negation or threat' (Glynos and Howarth 2007: 144). The elements are not equivalent as they share a positive property – though, empirically they may have something in common! – but insofar as they have a *common enemy*. Briefly said, the logic of equivalence entails the construction and privileging of antagonistic relations as it weakens the dimension of difference on each side of the frontier. By contrast, when there is a breaking down of the frontiers to maintain existing structures – thus, preserving the old or current distribution of inclusions and exclusions – the logic of difference predominates. Difference captures the combinatory aspect of the relations between discursive elements, which accounts not only for the differences in identity among these elements but also for keeping the elements distinct, separate and autonomous. For instance, the age-old-practice of 'divide and rule' 'in which an occupying power seeks to separate ethnic or national groups into particular communities [. . .] is invariably designed to prevent the articulation of demands and identities into a generalized challenge to the dominant regime' (Glynos and Howarth 2007: 145).

Overall, both logics 'cannot do with or without each other': both are always present in the sense that each presupposes the other. While the logic of difference distinguishes the elements of a discourse, the logic of equivalence equates differences by establishing an antagonistic frontier. They always interact in a complex manner, but none of the logics dominates a discourse completely as only partial fixations are possible. The realization of a pure logic of difference would lead to a differential system set in stone. Every subject would have only one single, unchangeable meaning. An untainted dominance of the logic of equivalence is also impossible, as every subject would stand for nothing more but belonging to the same discourse. Both logics are in their way, because one is diluted by what the other is trying to fixate. Both logics need each other, as a certain degree of difference is conditional to establish equivalential chains (Stäheli 1999: 149). However, since discursive structures are contingent and not fixed, we have a means of specifying the dynamics as both logics highlight the dynamic process by which political frontiers are constructed, stabilized, strengthened or weakened (Laclau 2005: 79).

Essential in our context is the insight that the logic of equivalence institutes practices or regimes of practices by drawing frontiers, by separating a discursive space into two antagonistic camps – the good vs. the bad, the Self vs. the Other: the evil, barbaric terrorist/drug abusers vs. the good citizens/the civilized international community. This relates to what has been outlined on political practices and the structuring function of regimes of practices. Since the logic of equivalence dichotomizes discursive space by constructing frontiers and privileging antagonistic relations, it addresses explicitly *how* hegemonic practices and regimes are produced.

To summarize so far, the Essex School understands hegemony as the dichotomization of a discursive space by conferring a particular meaning upon antagonistic poles. This refers to the book's underlying assumption, namely that there is a close interrelation between hegemonic orders and the construction of identities. To explain how this relationship is forged, it is necessary to develop the study's notion of identity.

Identity – failed identity

In IR, preoccupation with identity originated mainly from the observation that some phenomena could not be explained with the help of the classical factors like power or interests and for the traditional school of thoughts in IR identity seemed to be an answer (Mercer 1995; Weller 1999: 252). However, it turned out to be rather difficult to incorporate an enriching notion of identity into the existing analytical frameworks. For rationalists, actors deploy identity strategically like any other resource to spur their interests; for realists identity is 'at best, derivative of the distribution of capabilities' (Katzenstein 1996: 17) without any independent explanatory power. In consequence, most of the identity-based approaches in IR attempt to enlarge the explanatory power of interest-based accounts by considering identity as a variable that explains state behaviour contradicting structurally determined interest (Katzenstein 1996: 22).

IR constructivist and poststructuralist approaches have ventured far beyond an instrumentalist notion of identity. In IR constructivist studies – and here the 'conventional', 'thin' or 'moderate' constructivists are meant[8] – identity is considered as a feature of which states dispose, as an 'attribute' (Wendt 1999: 224), and this renders identity 'a variable that can be inserted into already existing theoretical commitments' (Campbell 1998b: 218). This led conventional IR constructivists to reject the conceptualization of identity as a relational identity. For instance, Alexander Wendt argues that states have pre-social (what he terms corporate) as well as social identities. As the former is self-organizing there is no need 'for a particular Other to which the Self is related' (Wendt 1999: 225) because 'the self-organizing hypothesis' does not deny an 'ongoing process of boundary-drawing' but only implies that this is an internally driven process which does not involve 'the agency and discourse of outsiders' (Wendt 1999: 74). Furthermore, identity as a relational difference has to be repudiated because one can distinguish between role identities and type identities, which are intrinsic to the individual actor. Collective identities, in turn, are a distinct combination of role and type identities, 'one with the causal power to induce actors to define the welfare of the Other as part of that of the Self [. . .]' (Wendt 1999: 229). The relationship between a Self and its Other(s) is understood as an uni-dimensional continuum that ranges from negative to positive identification, offering the Self the possibility to perceive of the Other as an extension of the Self or as an anathema to it. Such a comprehension based on interaction between Self and Other allows the Self to act according to the issue and Other at hand: a state may positively identify with the defence ideas of another state, but in human rights issues align itself with the ideals promoted by the UN, i.e. with the globe. Thus, the nature of the identification determines the boundaries of the Self (Wendt 1994: 386).

However, pre-social identities treated as a 'property of intentional actors that generates motivational and behavioural dispositions' imply ultimately 'exogenously given' identities (Wendt 1999: 225, 328). Yet, '[i]f identity is assumed to be ontologically intrinsic, then it cannot be identified through a discursive epistemology but has to be attributed externally by an analyst' (Hansen 2006: 24). But can one really imagine a collective pre-social identity? As Hansen has convincingly argued, even if one thinks of the example of an isolated community without knowledge of other human beings, a group is still composed of distinct individuals and this ultimately involves the construction of each individual in relation to the group. Furthermore, at the level of the collective identity, why only think of the unrelated Other as a human being? Temporal or spatial Others (or even animals) are also imaginable as non-related Others (Wæver 1998a: 90; Diez 2004: 325; Hansen 2006: 24).[9]

This premise of exogenously given identities is even more problematic for the aims and questions of the study, since with this assumption the question of *how* identities are constituted by hegemonic operations is abruptly settled. IR constructivism in its conventional version focuses less on how collective identities are constructed but much more on the question how these identities *matter* for the determination of particular policies. The treatment of identity as something that is attached to and negotiated between pre-existing anthropomorphic actors requires conceptualizing identity as a unitary, circumscribable concept and this is problematic not only from a poststructuralist perspective but also for its subsequent treatment by constructivism itself.[10]

IR poststructuralists have conceptualized identity neither as pre-social, exogenously given nor as unified. Rather, with poststructuralism identity took centre stage in the analysis of international politics. Precisely herein lies 'one of the main contributions of poststructuralism to international relations theory', according to Thomas Diez, namely in 'the theorisation of identity, and in particular its relationship to difference' (Diez 2004: 321). Poststructuralism in IR conceives of identities as discursively constructed and contingent products of social or political action. To invoke, for instance, the international community in a UN-debate on terrorism or drugs is not simply understood as the inclusion of a new term but as a political act inscribing the notion of an international community in the discussions. Such acts construct an identity (in this case the international community) across diverse and often intersecting, antagonistic discourses and discursive practices (Diez 2004: 321). This discursive constitution implies that identity can only be present if it is constantly rearticulated by various discourses and rules out the location of an objective identity in any kind of extra- or non-discursive realm, functioning as a variable against which behaviour and material factors can be juxtaposed and measured. Hence, identity is non-essentialist, as it does not engage with an essence that has to be protected – it is less about 'who we are' or 'where we came from'. A performative character of identity is much more about 'what we might become', 'how we have been presented' and what this means on 'how we might present ourselves'. Non-essentialist identities emerge within the modalities of specific plays of power; consequently, they are more the product of marking difference and equivalence 'than the sign of an identical, naturally-constituted unity' (Hall 1996: 4).

At the same time identities are increasingly fragmented and can be only partially fixed. For poststructuralism, identity

> does not signal that stable core of the self, unfolding from the beginning to end through all the vicissitudes of history without change; the bit of the self which remains always-already 'the same', identical to itself across time.
>
> (Hall 1996: 3)

On the contrary, to conceptualize identities as fragmented and fluid is to argue that their discursively constructed nature always allows for alternative constructions against which other, dominant – or, to be more precise, hegemonic – identity notions have to be protected and defended. The contours of this hegemonic identity are the subject of constant (re)writing/(re)reading: not rewriting in the sense of changing the meaning, but rewriting in the sense of inscribing something as to render more permanent that which is originally contingent (Campbell 1998b: 31). Accordingly, discourses construing an identity of, say, an international community as an uninterrupted, linear 'identity history' are conveying the impression of an essence that is always visible and tangible, regardless of how different the times are. But there is neither any kind of core nor are hegemonic constructions stable, rather, they vary synchronically and diachronically (Laclau and Mouffe 2001: 112–3).

However, the most important element resides in the concept of identity as constructed through difference – identity is relational. Identity is constituted against an Other and discourses articulating identity articulate a *Self* against a series of *Others*. Identity is unimaginable without a difference. 'There is no way that a particular group living in a wider community can live a monadic existence – on the contrary, part of the definition of its own identity is the construction of a complex and elaborated system of relations with other groups' (Laclau 1995: 147). Thus, 'I cannot be myself if there is not you from which I am different'; Germany cannot be Germany without France or the United States from which it is different and 'a community of liberal democracies' cannot be democratic if there are not non-democratic communities: our identities are radically interdependent (Campbell 1993: 95).

Conceptualizing identities as relational paves the way to consider the details of the actual process of identity construction in light of hegemonic operations. Crucial to relational identity construction is the moment of identification. Identification captures that someone is identifying with something, i.e. one identifies with a signifier in a discursive field, for instance, with the notion of 'ecology' in order to acquire an identity as 'ecologist', to become an 'ecologist'. Becoming something is more than just calling oneself an 'ecologist' – identifying with a signifier in a discourse turns one into a subject in this very discourse. '[I]dentification is the moment of the radical subject, which discloses the subject as an agent in its world' (Glynos and Howarth 2007: 129). Yet, things are not that easy. The 'problem' with identification is that one cannot deny identifying. An act of identification is marked by an urgent necessity, as 'one needs to identify with something because there is an originary and insurmountable lack of identity' at the root of each subject (Laclau 1994: 3).

What is this lack of identity about? How does it come into being? Let me illustrate this with an example by Slavoj Žižek (1996: 128–31). Imagine a subject that is involved in ecology action, say a feminist ecologist. For her, the threat of ecological catastrophe results from the male attitude of domination and exploitation. Feminism provides her with the specific content of her ecological identity. Accordingly, for her, someone that considers herself an ecologist but not a feminist cannot be a 'true ecologist'. The same counts for someone considering himself as socialist ecologist (the cause of ecological crisis is rooted in profit-orientated capitalism) or a conservative ecologist (the crisis is to be found in man's false will to dominate the universe) and so forth. In either case, one that considers herself a non-socialist or non-conservative at the same time cannot be a 'true ecologist', as the content of socialism and conservatism provides for their specific interpretation of ecology.

Of course, subjects are not restricted to identify with only *one* specific signifier but identify with various numbers of signifiers. However, any attempt to capture or define a 'substantial core of ecology, the minimal content to which every ecologist has to agree is necessarily doomed to fail'. What is at stake is how to fill the (empty) signifier 'ecology' (what does it mean to be an 'ecologist'), because one only becomes a subject when the 'universal signifier to which I refer ('ecology' in our case) is no longer connected by an umbilical cord to some particular content, but is experienced as an empty space to be filled out by the particular (feminist, conservative, [. . .] socialist . . .) content' (Žižek 1996: 131).

Žižek's example shows that the act of identification involves the articulation of a universal signifier, which acts as a 'stand-in' for the lack of the subject and, thereby, fills it. Moreover, his example clearly brings to mind that this movement is a deceptive one as there exists no minimal core of ecology that every ecologist would agree to. The deception explains, 'why there is a permanent and alternating movement whereby the lack is rejected and invoked, articulated and annulled, included and excluded' (Laclau and Zac 1994: 33). Thus, the moment of failure in the constitution of every identity gives rise to the lack of the subject, because every signifier in a discourse fails to represent a subject in its entirety. There is always a residue of the Self that cannot be represented.

Precisely this remainder allows considering each identity as constitutively split between universality and particularity: universality works as a horizon for identity, while each identity equally constructs itself as a particularity, as different from other identities to come into being. Thus, each identity is divided in a particular content and a universal function. For the feminist ecologist, the particular content consists in feminism that provides her with a specific interpretation of 'ecology'. The latter is the universal horizon for her identity. With regard to the case studies of the present book, one could argue that the international community – constructed as the place, which should be liberated from terrorism, promoting universal values of liberty, freedom and equality – brings in a universal horizon with which subjects identify. How such a vision of a terrorism-free world, of the international community would look like depends on each subject's particular interpretation of what terrorism is about.

In this sense, identities are always failed identities. They are never fully closed which renders them vulnerable to further dislocation. As Jason Glynos and David Howarth rightly emphasize, this allows to flesh out an avenue away from thinking about the subject as a mere discursive position towards reflecting about it as constitutively incomplete and split (Glynos and Howarth 2007: 129). Such a conceptualization is even more important in the context of a study working with the notion of 'strategy', which will be outlined in chapter two.

Identity construction in the context of hegemony

So far, identification has been a constantly occurring process: subjects need to identify with a signifier, but these acts fail due to the impossibility of any signifier to represent the subject in its entirety and the failure leads to new acts of identification. However, there are situations within which the experience of lack and failure turns into an experience of blockage. Subjects consider their identities as blocked and negated by a force that – and this is very important to underline – is *deemed* responsible for this blocking and, therefore, for the failure of the identity. This is what can be called an antagonistic relation. Antagonism occurs when the presence of an Other prevents me from being totally myself:

> Insofar as there is antagonism, I cannot be a full presence for myself. But nor is the force that antagonizes me such a presence: its objective being is a symbol of my non-being and, in this way, it is overflowed by a plurality of meanings which prevent it being fixed as full positivity.
>
> (Laclau and Mouffe 2001: 125)

Accordingly, the point is not that 'we' are nothing because we cannot be a full presence of ourselves, but it is the drive to destroy the antagonistic force that impedes us from acquiring our full identity. Precisely this drive towards annihilation – and this is especially the case in security discourses – allows externalizing the constitutive lack to the Other, i.e. 'our' lack is placed on an Other which embodies 'our' self-blockage. Therefore, our political actions will be conducted by the illusion that overcoming the antagonistic force will permit us to become the fully constituted 'we' that we have always sought to be and which the Other is blocking (Laclau 1990: 253; Žižek 1990: 221–5; Torfing 1999: 128–9). Of course, antagonism necessarily involves establishing limits between a Self and its antagonistic Other by 'relating to that of the other which cannot be incorporated in the differential system of the discursive formation in question' (Torfing 1998: 92). This establishment serves to exclude the constitutive outside, i.e. those elements that have nothing in common with the differential system from which it is excluded. Since the constitutive outside is coterminous with antagonism, we can conclude that the latter is the condition of possibility and impossibility of a subject at the same time (Laclau 1995: 151; Torfing 1999: 124).

Let me illustrate this dense passage with an example from the study's empirical cases. When terrorism is represented as the absolute opposite of the international community and defined as barbaric and a threat to the international community, terrorism prevents the community permanently from being what it originally is or should become – a peaceful, civilized place for every man, promoting universal values of liberty, freedom and equality. Accordingly, the international community cannot attain a full-fledged identity as long as international terrorism endangers it: its identity is blocked. A typical assertion in this regard would be, for instance, 'if we only eliminate terrorism, the world would be a civilized and safe place'. Yet, this specific interpretation of the international community as civilized is only possible *because* of its antagonistic Other, the barbaric terrorist. As the international community excludes with terrorism everything the community is not, and terrorism is defined as barbaric, the community is necessarily non-barbaric, i.e. civilized.

Without doubt, the implications of experiences of blockage and the ensuing antagonistic relations are particularly far-reaching in security discourses. Considering an Other as one's enemy responsible for the missing fullness of one's identity may result in legitimizing violent measures against this very Other. In this sense, discursive agents present themselves not only as having knowledge about the nature of the Other – terrorism and drug abuse – and the power to draw rigid boundaries in a field criss-crossed by numerous contradictory meanings. But also consider themselves in the possession of the authority to decide how to respond to both phenomena, i.e. promoting policies that privilege military measures (the 'wars on terror and drugs') instead of relying on instruments of law enforcement. The authority to respond also implies a responsibility to respond; the international community cannot remain inert in the face of terrorism or the drug problem, it must act.

It is precisely these problematic implications that have led IR poststructuralists to focus on the constitution of antagonistic Others in security discourses in the first place. Although representing the Other as threatening is an essential component of security policies, it is only half of the story, since the antagonist Other is 'often situated within a more complicated set of identities' (Hansen 2006: 37). Indeed, this insight has evolved only recently in IR poststructuralism. Maybe William Connolly's 'paradox of difference' is still too often related to the potential of perceiving the Other as threatening to the Self's identity and led IR poststructuralists to associate difference with conflict all too quickly.[11] Perhaps the paradox was too frequently read through the lenses of the classical discourse of national security with its radical difference between the national community 'in here', and international anarchy 'out there' having left its imprints on the conceptualization of identity. This result comes as no surprise, as there is a considerable drive in the ontology of national identity to set up rigid boundaries to separate a Self from an antagonistic Other. The political leaders of the modern state have always engaged in 'boundary-producing performances' of constructing other identities as inferior, barbaric, and hostile to legitimize their security policies (Campbell 1998b: 71). This paints, as David Campbell once admitted, 'a particularly negative picture of processes implicated in a state's identity', but he justified this position by outlining that 'the potential for the transformation of difference into otherness always exists' (Campbell 1998b: 70).

To equalize difference with antagonistic otherness seems to be highly contingent and mostly led by 'a tendency within poststructuralism to conclude too quickly that the only possible relationship between state and Other is the latter one [the one of antagonistic otherness]' (Hansen 1997: 390).[12] Still, I fully agree with Hansen that not only Connolly but also Campbell leave open the possibility of an identity not necessarily constructed against an antagonistic Other. Since the former has always conceded that 'the definition of difference is a requirement built into the logic of identity', he considered the construction of otherness only as 'a *temptation* that readily insinuates itself into that logic' (Connolly 1991: 64–5, emphasis added) and not as a necessity. To some this might appear casuistic, yet, Connolly further claims that a Self is not only constituted against an antagonistic Other but also against a variety of 'non-selves', like complementary identities or contending identities (Connolly 1991: 8–9; Hansen 2006: 39). The same is true for Campbell. Although Campbell has often been cited as arguing in favour of a simple Self-Other duality (as his first quotations above imply), he stresses that foreign policy as national security discourse 'implicated in all confrontations between a self and other, embraces *both positive and* negative valences' and that the 'representation of difference does *not* functionally necessitate a negative figuration [. . .]' (Campbell 1998b: 73, 88 emphasis added). Of course, Campbell's focus on foreign policy implies the dominance of antagonistic Others because especially in this domain 'the *temptation* of otherness has been uncommonly compelling' (Campbell 1998b: 88, emphasis added).[13] A more nuanced judgement is possible, instead of drawing hasty conclusions that, first, 'one of the most influential studies of IR poststructuralism' is deficient in this respect, and, second, that IR poststructuralism in general

> is ill-equipped to look for, and find, polarities containing more than two poles, overlapping identities, partial compatibilities though all these are theoretical possibilities and can be found in practice and are indeed the foundation on which security cooperation is built.
>
> (Müller 2002: 384)

While one should pay justice to Campbell's study (it aims at the representation of a state's identity in foreign policy discourse), it severely misses the point to read *Writing Security* as a general theory of foreign policy discourse.

Despite these insights, studies dealing with more ambiguous constructions of difference are still few and far between, i.e. explanations are missing how variations in the relationship between Self and Other are possible within the overall logic of identity/difference. Tying in with a burgeoning body of works[14], I argue that the idea of identity being based on difference does by no means imply that the construction of antagonistic Others is the sole product of identity construction. To define in advance that antagonistic forms of difference are the only form of identity constitution would entail an unnecessary theoretical limitation that – as critics have pointed out – makes it difficult to satisfy the demands of an analysis of concrete discourses. Such a limitation would deprive a poststructuralist conception of identity formation of a lot of its potential and, indeed, would produce a static view of security discourse and identity (Neumann 1996: 167; Rumelili 2004: 36). If one concedes that difference in itself cannot be considered as the cause of conflict, of antagonistic otherness, variations in the way the Self deals with its Other(s) come into view. Thus, one needs to draw a distinction between *antagonistic* and *differential* relations since antagonism is a subcategory of difference, a specific structuration of it: '[d]ifference is an overarching category that refers to the relational construction of identity' (Dyrberg 2004: 249).

Thus, identity construction produces varying degrees of otherness and does not necessarily depend upon a juxtaposition to a radically threatening Other: international terrorism and drug abuse can both be interpreted in entirely different ways – terrorism can either be considered as a legitimate act of resistance against economic exploitation, or as a manifestation of barbarism. The use of drugs, on the other hand, may be considered as illegal and therefore deviant behaviour, or it can be tolerated as an alternative way of life. While being a double-edged sword, however, the most important aspect of antagonism evolves from the specification that antagonism is one mastery of the single space of representation but *not the only one*. This equally implies that antagonism is one possible outcome among others; it is not a teleological aim of identity construction. Instead of presupposing any kind of antagonism as pre-existing to be studied, one rather needs to lay open the discursive *strategies* constructing a particular antagonism (Torfing 1999: 131; Stäheli 2004: 239; Thomassen 2005: 17). In light of this, the study considers it as an empirical task to exhibit these strategies and to retain whether non-antagonistic Others are, for instance, cooperation-partners or subjects that are disassociated from the antagonistic Other.

Now, to fully develop my central argument, identity construction needs to be considered in the context of hegemonic practices. The argument reads that the establishment of a hegemonic order is a dual process, which can be conceptualized, first, as the constant attempt to homogenize the image and interpretation of the Other. I argue further that focusing on the Other and on processes of othering does not suffice. Instead, one also needs to accord a central place to the construction of the Self. Thus, and second, for hegemonic orders to emerge, the attempts to create a cohesive vision of the Self that is shared by the discursive agents jointly opposing the Other is of equal importance. In order to allow for the adoption of internationally accepted measures against the Other, this vision of the Self needs to be based upon a political consensus between the agents concerned.

Having said that constructing the Other as antagonistic is one possibility among others implies that the construction of an Other as antagonistic or not necessarily involves some element of force, repression and authority. By establishing discursive limits and separating the social space into two opposed camps, antagonism is a strong moment of force – synonymous with radical exclusion – and permits to conceptualize the relation between a Self and its Others as relations of power. In this respect, antagonism is integral to the logic of equivalence since the latter dichotomizes the social space into two antagonistic camps, entailing the constitution of (new) frontiers. As I have outlined, the logic of equivalence privileges antagonistic relations as it weakens differences on both sides of the frontier. Hence, the dichotomization of the discursive space established by hegemonic practices creates specific identities that are blocked by a force negating them. This force is respectively constructed as a 'common enemy'.

Yet, such conceptualization should not imply that hegemonies are dependent on antagonism: on the contrary, it is important to stress that a prerequisite for antagonism is the power inherent in hegemonic operation. It is the way in which the Other is constituted as a negated entity that can be seen as an act of power. Therefore, antagonism evolves from hegemonic articulations as they implicate the negation of an Other – i.e. antagonism is a product of hegemonic articulations. And in general, the force behind these articulations will tend to construct the Other as a threat to the Self (Torfing 1999: 120) and attempt to construct a highly homogeneous interpretation of the Other. Hence, identities constituted by equivalential practices, i.e. hegemonic practices tend to share a common enemy, a commonly antagonized Other.

Let us now turn to the Self. I have argued that hegemonic orders rely on the attempts to create an unambiguously shared vision among the discursive agents which consider a specific Other as their enemy and that this vision is constructed via a political consensus between the agents. While the Self is forged in opposition to the common enemy – terrorism, drugs – this is only one half of the dual nature of hegemonic operation. In addition, the logic of equivalence links identities into a joint project: fighting the common enemy in order to overcome the lack at the root of each identity, to achieve the vision, which is blocked by the presence of the Other. Hence, at the international level a Self (which is of course a collective Self) is forged through the promise of a different world – a world free of terrorism, free of drugs. This vision attempts to link different political forces to the common project, since they share a consensus on the threatening character and evil quality of the Other. To determine whether the often cited international community is able to act as a 'stand in' for the common vision is the task of the empirical analysis, while the question of how the Self is forged and how an antagonistic Other is shaped exactly will be developed in chapter two. To summarize, the present study conceptualizes hegemony in close context to identity. Hegemony is the production of a particular type of identity: as hegemonic practices dichotomize the discursive space by conferring a particular meaning upon antagonistic poles, they are creating a Self and its Other(s).

2   Opening the 'black box'

The construction of international hegemonies

So far I have explored the concepts of hegemony and identity and discussed their intimate relationship as hegemonic orders construct specific identities, i.e. a Self is created by opposing it to an antagonistic Other. However, to systematically address these processes of exclusion and inclusion – to open the 'black box' of international hegemonies – a number of further steps needs to be taken. The present chapter develops the methodological tools to analyze the practices of hegemonic orders, which offer insights on how a particular meaning of terrorism and drugs has dominated the interpretation of both phenomena and marginalized alternative understandings. Essential to hegemonic operations is the ordering of the discursive space allowing for the orientation of meaning. Accordingly, equivalential relations with their ability to dichotomize this space are of crucial importance. How these relations are forged needs to be explored in detail to explain the construction of hegemonies. The same applies to differential relations, since their functioning can obstruct the establishment of hegemonies.

In this context, the notion of strategy is central to analyze the rise and fall of hegemonies. Most importantly, chapter two introduces the cornerstone of the book's poststructuralist framework by establishing a discursive model distinguishing the multitude of hegemonic strategies into productive and counter-hegemonic strategies, depending on their positive or negative impact on the construction of hegemonic orders at the international level. Thereby, the model analyzes the interplay of hegemonic regimes and identities, and, most importantly, reveals the extent to which hegemonic orders are justified with reference to specific identities. It is also flexible enough to analyze the homogeneity or heterogeneity (i.e. the various degrees of otherness) of the Other construction, the nature of the Self's vision (and whether the vision is shared unambiguously by the discursive agents present in the discourse), and the kind of political consensus required to speak of the establishment of a hegemonic order in the respective field. Chapter two concludes with important methodological remarks on the practical procedure of the present study.

I have explained that the logic of equivalence is about erecting an antagonistic frontier, as subjects are rendered equivalent with regard to a common enemy, which confronts a collective Self. As these processes are central to hegemonic relations, we need to grasp the exact operations of this process. The same applies to the logic of difference, which keeps elements separate and autonomous and thereby pluralizes the discursive space countering the establishment of hegemonic orders. To keep the movements within hegemonic operations analytically separate, I will split the logics into their constituents. This separation is for analytical purposes only because none of the parts is able to trigger hegemonic effects of its own. For this reason, each constituent accounts for one hegemonic strategy. Together, six strategies form the *basic dimension* of hegemonic operations that will later be supplemented by a further dimension.[1] I will start with the three strategies of the logic of equivalence and then move on to the logic of difference.

The logic of equivalence: the basic dimension of productive hegemonic strategies

To begin with, productive hegemonic strategy *Universalization* encompasses the universalization of differential subjects. While subjects identify with a signifier in the discursive space, they express themselves as particular, as different from other subjects at the same time. The content of their particularity provides them with a specific interpretation of what the signifier means in their context (as in the example of the feminist ecologist within which feminism determined her interpretation of ecology). In equivalential relations, each subject experiences an incomplete surrender of its particularity, of its particular meaning. Emphasizing what a number of subjects share bespeaks of a second meaning that is parasitic on the particular meaning of each subject. However, the new meaning does not fully cancel out the particular meaning of a subject and universalizes subjects only with regard to 'something identical underlying them all'. Hence, via the universalization of subjects, an equivalential bond is forged stressing what they all have in common and a chain of equivalence is established.

How is it possible to universalize such obviously differential subjects striving for preserving 'the originality of a nations approach to terrorism' or 'reject to consider national liberation movements as terrorism' and characterize terrorism as 'evil and despicable'? To argue that the cancellation of a subject's difference functions by the reference to 'what underlies them all' points in the right direction; yet this cannot be something positive. First, a common positive determination would not need a relation of equivalence (this would be an internal positivity) and, second, a common positive external is inconceivable, since the reference to such an external would also function without an equivalential chain and could be constructed in a direct way (Laclau and Mouffe 2001: 127). Hence, what remains is the reference to a common negative internal or external. The common internal is ruled out because at the root of every subject is a lack that cannot be represented in a direct manner. Only the common external remains, i.e. the impediment of fulfilment of the subject by external oppositions. And here we are back at the concept of antagonism and its ability to dichotomize the discursive space.

I have explained that subjects suffer from an insurmountable lack that can only be eliminated if projected onto something represented as external. Further, I asserted that the construction of the external as threatening, as antagonistic Other is but *one possibility* to master the single space of representation. Thus, the common negative external cannot be represented in positive terms, i.e. as one more difference. As a consequence, the universalization of differential subjects goes in tandem with the dichotomization of the discursive space in two opposed camps or poles. It is productive hegemonic strategy *Establishing an antagonistic frontier* which builds such an exclusionary border. The frontier separates the equivalential chain from the negativity that threatens the subjects linked together by this very chain. As a result, two equivalential chains confront each other and the antagonistic frontier disassociates an *antagonizing* chain of equivalences (henceforth equally called *chain A*) from an *antagonized* chain of equivalences (hereafter equally called *chain Z*).[2]

While the 'something underlying them all' was formerly only the mediator between the universalized subjects, now, one signifier takes up the task to represent not only the links between the demands but the chain in its entirety. This qualitative change is the core of a hegemonic operation: by acquiring the function of representation the former mediator link serves as a base of the equivalential identities. At the end of this process we find a differential, particular signifier representing an entire chain. This particular signifier cannot represent something that is already present, something that is present in the subjects of the chain; for instance, the signifier does not incarnate 'the something underlying all subjects' – the general equivalent. Rather, the signifier acts as a 'stand in' for the lack at the root of each subject, for the unachieved but aspired full-fledged identity. Indeed, it represents not the lack of one particular subject but of a whole chain of equivalential subjects – while being part of the chain, it signifies the absent fullness of the chain, the desired identity of the chain.

Still, this particular signifier cannot 'be one more difference and not the result of the equivalential collapse of all differential identities' (Laclau 1994b: 174). It is from this impossibility of signification that the particular signifier has to be emptied of its particular content – it is an *emptied signifier*. Being split and representing a chain of equivalential subjects, it has to be deprived of the differential contents the subjects bring into the chain. Only in that way is the particular signifier able to encompass a chain and, thereby becomes empty. However, we will never meet 'purely' or 'completely emptied' signifiers, although they are emptied to the extent that their meaning is indefinite and disputed, i.e. *deutungsoffen* (Nonhoff 2001). For example, in political discourses, the particular signifier 'security' is the point of culmination of a large number of different and contradictory meanings and represents an equivalential chain of discourses of which western democracies are part. The relation between the particular and universal part of the signifier 'security' manifests itself as a dividing line because 'security' may still dispose of a specific remainder (the security of the individual) but needs to be emptied and universalized to represent the totality and the identity of the discourse (for instance, to represent the security of a regime). This remaining particularity makes the empty signifier only a *tendentially empty signifier*. Ultimately, the lesser the particularity of the signifier, the emptier it is, the better it is able to represent the chain of equivalence and to organize the discourse by aiming at establishing a horizon of closure of the discursive system (Stäheli 1999: 149–50; Laclau 2000a: 304).

Which particular signifier takes up the task of representing the whole chain, is contingent but neither accidental nor arbitrary. The unevenness of the social determines which signifier incorporates at specific moments in time the function of a tendentially empty signifier. Two theoretical conditions need to be satisfied: first, availability of potential signifiers in the discourse, and, second, their credibility as means of signification. While the first condition states that the signifier needs be already part of the respective chain of equivalence, the second refers to the competition between different signifiers. They are not equally able to take up the task, as it takes place in an already sedimented terrain permeated by relations of power, and different subjects struggle to construct and deploy potentially empty signifiers to advance their projects. However, these theoretical conditions cannot be exempt from thorough empirical analysis, as only such an investigation is able to determine how and why any particular difference performs the role of the empty signifier (Howarth 2004: 262; Thomassen 2005: 10–1). With the development of the third productive hegemonic strategy *Representation*, the logic of equivalence is outlined. Consequently, a hegemonic operation can be called the process when different subjects are articulated in a homogenous space of representation. Figure 2.1.[3] illustrates this operation in the discursive space.

A1[4], *A2*, *A3*, *A4* and so forth represent the subjects which are articulated in a chain of equivalence. Each *A* is split between a bottom semi-circle representing the particularity of the subject and a top semi-circle representing the (universal) meaning that makes the equivalential relation to the other subjects of the chain possible. *A1* is the tendentially empty signifier, as it has been able to empty itself of its particular content and represents the chain as a whole (while being part of the chain). *F* designates the antagonistic frontier, which has been created by

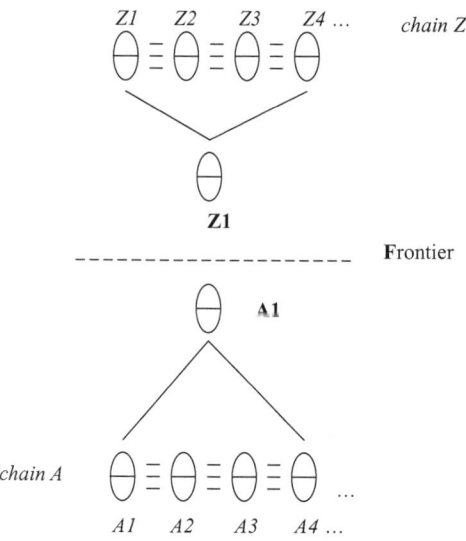

Figure 2.1 Basic model of a hegemonic articulation

establishing the antagonizing chain of equivalence (*chain A*) and projecting its lack onto something external – the antagonistic force *Z*, *Z1*, *Z2*, *Z3*, *Z4* and so forth represent the different subjects or discursive elements of the antagonized force and form the antagonized chain of equivalence (*chain Z*). Theoretically, *Z1* might take over the same task as *A1*.

The logic of difference: the basic dimension of counter-hegemonic strategies

Since relations of difference underlie any equivalential relation to a certain degree, the logic of difference explains how a dominant pattern and meaning is hampered in its spread and extension in a political field. Thus, subjects that have been universalized can again be particularized. The logic of difference does so by a differential absorption of the subjects. Counter-hegemonic strategy *Particularization* separates the subjects from their equivalential chain (Laclau 2000c: 193; Laclau and Mouffe 2001: 130). The more a chain of equivalence becomes extended, the more the logic of difference is strengthened. Subjects are increasingly able to withdraw from the chain by carrying out acts of differentiation, i.e. by referring to their particular part, which separates a subject from the rest of the chain. In result, the subject is (re)particularized.

As the particularization of formerly equivalential subjects leads to their stepping out of the chain of equivalence, ultimately, the chain breaks off: no bonds persist between the subjects any longer, no particularity is able to represent the equivalential chain any longer and the external Other vanishes. The subjects become (again) dispersed in the discursive space and disarticulated from the former equivalential chain. Thus, counter-hegemonic strategy *Breaking off the chain* implies not only the disassociation of some subjects from the chain but denotes the break off of an entire chain of equivalence.

Embracing the deterioration of the divide between Self and Other, counter-hegemonic strategy *Weakening the antagonistic frontier* displaces the latter 'to the periphery of the social' (Laclau and Mouffe 2001: 130); hence, the frontier still exists but 'somewhere else'. In a discourse dominated by the logic of difference, the sharp division of society is weakened and the frontiers are at the margins. Take the example of David Howarth's study on the transformation of the 'Black Consciousness' discourse in South Africa. Here, the National Party was faced with a growing opposition to its apartheid policies at the end of the 1970s and during the 1980s. It sought to expand its bases of consent by incorporating 'Indians', so-called 'Coloured's' and certain categories of 'urban blacks' into the discourse of the ruling party (which formerly only included 'Whites'). By bringing in 'Indians', 'Coloured's' and parts of the 'urban blacks', the 'rest' of the blacks was (still) excluded – but the frontier moved from the midst of society (white versus black people without any intermediate categories) to the periphery of South African society (Howarth 1997). Pacifying antagonistic frontiers, however, does by no means imply eliminating them.

Breaking equivalential bonds does not only apply to an antagonizing (*chain A*) but also to an antagonized chain (*chain Z*). The weakening of antagonistic frontiers means that the ties between both chains are targeted. In order to relegate the divisions to the margins of society, the differential absorption of equivalential subjects aims at 'both sides of the frontier'. Figure 2.2. illustrates the operation of the logic of difference in contrast to the logic of equivalence; accordingly, it completes the situation in the discursive space.

The arrow from *A4* to *A4a* and from *Z4* to *Z4a* designates the movements of counter-hegemonic strategy *Particularization*, which re-differentiates the subjects tied by the two equivalential chains. The arrow from *A4* to *F* stands for counter-hegemonic strategy *Weakening of the antagonistic frontier*. *Z4a* and *A4a* represent the particularized subjects. Their particularization becomes possible by the movement indicated by the arrow from *A4* to the sign of equivalence (between *Z3* and *Z4*) – representing counter-hegemonic strategy *Breaking off the chain*, which separates the members of the chain of equivalence. In the form of *A4a*, the subject *A4* is particularized and disarticulated from its former equivalential position in the chain.

To conclude, it is worth stressing that we now dispose of two sets of elements (the three strategies of each basic dimension) exposing the way a hegemonic pattern and meaning is constructed (via the logic of equivalence) but also how it is obstructed or disturbed (via the logic of difference). The three strategies of the basic dimension of productive hegemonic strategies are the following:

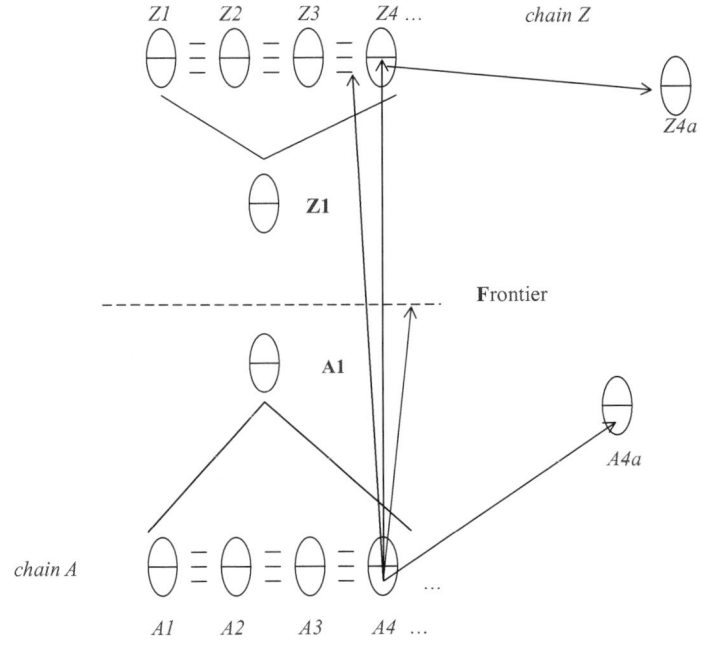

Figure 2.2 Basic model of hegemonic articulations confronting logic of equivalence and difference

- Universalization
- Establishing an antagonistic frontier
- Representation

Below are the three strategies of the basic dimension of counter-hegemonic strategies:

- Particularization
- Breaking off the chain
- Weakening of the antagonistic frontier

Having made a case for a concept of hegemony incarnated by the operations of the logic of equivalence and, most importantly, by the moment of representation, the question arises *when* exactly has a hegemonic order been established at the international level. I argue that this is essentially a question of success. In the present context, success is judged as a relative and not as an absolute value. To consider success as a fixed measurement would be unwary, since the success of a hegemonic project depends upon the context of the discursive field within which it is constructed (Nonhoff 2006: 204). The very moment to indicate success has already been described: at the moment one particularity assumes the representation of a chain of equivalence, i.e. functions as a tendentially empty signifier, a hegemonic operation has been successfully accomplished. Besides, this central moment bespeaking of a 'full-fledged' hegemony (as full-fledged as an impossible totality can be), the increase of the number of subjects a hegemonic project includes can contribute to the project's success. In principle, it indicates success if a wide range of different subjects identify with the signifier of a hegemonic project and the chain of equivalence is extended. Their acts of identification confirm, support and stabilize the general equivalent, i.e. what all subjects have in common. Yet, the increase is a double-edged sword, since an extended chain risks a break-off, as the general equivalent becomes thinner and thinner in order to embrace the growing number of subjects. Consequently, the increase needs to be seen in accordance with its performative dimension, i.e. the subjects stabilize the general equivalent by relating to the common enterprise. An increase extends range and depth of a hegemonic project and is conducive to its transformation into a hegemony but endangers it at the same time.

The ambiguity of an increase is not the only element able to impede the successful construction of a hegemonic order at the international level. As has been outlined, identities do not emanate from any kind of foundational or supreme instance; they are constructed via an articulatory practice. Each identity is construed through differentiation from other identities and thereby acquires meaning. The negative reference on what the identity is not leads to a homogenization of its inner differences. Internal differences are one type of difference, emanating from the constitutive split of each subject in a particular and universal part (the other type is the constitutive difference that separates the discourse from its constitutive outside). More precisely, the largest part of the process of homogenization of a discourse evolves by universalization, when a subject experiences an incomplete surrender of its particularity, underlining what it has in common with all other subjects of the chain.

The concept of *heterogeneity* encompasses those internal differences, which have neither been mitigated by universalization or by the construction of a common frontier nor by the moment of representation. Heterogeneity disposes of a threefold presence in discourses: first, it is the condition for the possibility of a homogenous construction of the Other as without heterogeneity, homogeneity would not be conceivable. It represents the particularity, which cannot be eliminated. Therefore, and secondly, heterogeneity is the very ground of equivalential relations. Finally, it 'is also what prevents some of the demands from incorporating themselves in the equivalential chain' (Laclau 2005: 152). Thus, heterogeneity represents the remaining particularity, the differential remainder of each subject as much as the unmitigated particularity of the antagonistic Other. As we will see, the presence of heterogeneity within chains of equivalence is of special importance to the analysis. While not presupposing any 'content' of heterogeneity and in particular of the differential remainder beforehand (as to determine its specificity is an empirical task); however, I assume that heterogeneity refers to a particular type of remainder. Remember the example of the feminist ecologist: her identity as a feminist procures her with a distinct interpretation of ecology, different from the one of a socialist or conservative ecologist, as feminism represents the differential remainder of the feminist ecologist. It is therefore very likely that in both discourses elements of national identity, national culture or religion are frequently referred to as they provide subjects with a yardstick to interpret terrorism or drugs at the international level. Thereby, these elements do not need to be referred to explicitly in the texts, since it is not about verifying whether and how often, for instance, the term 'national identity' occurs. Rather, elements of national identity are traced by self-descriptions or characterizations, by references to a specific tradition or a particular cultural feature, to specific values or norms. For instance, invoking cultural habits like coca leave chewing or khat smoking in the discourse on drugs are a case in point. They are equally present as political, cultural narratives that define, however implicitly, the meaning and nature of the respective national identity.

What are the effects of heterogeneity? On the one hand, it impedes the homogenization of a discourse and can thus restrict the transformation of a project into a hegemony. Thereby, heterogeneity's main effect 'is to put limits to those links which can become part of the equivalential chain' (Laclau 1997b: 261). As a number of fixed 'members' is established, however, the extension is restricted by their particularities. In a relation of equivalence between 'chastity', 'daily prayer' and 'charity' their remaining particularity would resist the incorporation of 'free love' in the chain: although love underlies 'chastity', 'daily prayer' and 'charity' as much as 'free love' the latter is contradictory to, for instance, the differential remainder of 'chastity' (Laclau 1997a: 73). On the other hand, heterogeneity can be conducive if internal differences are raised in a beneficial manner to the hegemonic project: by outlining a difference and simultaneously relating this difference to the respective general equivalent. For instance, in a relation of equivalence between states that subscribe to the global goal of fighting terrorism, pointing out that one has already introduced a counter-terrorist legislation would account for raising a subject's differential remainder in a positive manner to the respective hegemonic project. Hence, 'differential meanings are a limitation but, at the same time, a condition of possibility of the equivalence' (Laclau 1997b: 261). Indeed, heterogeneity appears inside of hegemonic operations when the moment of representation as much as attempts to universalize and to construct an antagonistic frontier are still underway.

Hegemonic strategies

However, how does a hegemonic project become successful? I argue that the notion of *hegemonic strategy* provides for a highly suitable means to address this question. Yet, to introduce the notion of strategy in a poststructuralist study seems to open up Pandora's box, since it is about the intricate relationship between discourse and subject, or to put it in IR terms, between agent and structure.[5] Indeed, how can one speak of the discursive structuring of the social and at the same time identify hegemonic strategies? Does not a self-conscious subject, does not intentionality sneak in here?

In IR, this question has been a bone of contention mainly between 'systemic theories', explaining international politics by reference to the structure (the international system) and 'reductionist' theories, explaining international politics by reference to the behaviour and properties of agents (states). In one of the last 'rounds' in the agent-structure debate, (mainly IR constructivist) scholars struggle to acquit the question of its either/or charge to avoid giving ontological or explanatory priority to either agents or structures. Rather, they intend to find a third way out of the dilemma by proposing a 'synthesis that can account for the powers of both' (Doty 1997: 367), and to consider structures and agents as mutually involved in the production of each other (Giddens 1984; Torfing 1999). However, for the present context, crucial is not whether a synthesis or third, fourth etc. way is possible, but to question the conceptualization of agents and structures put forward by IR constructivists vs. the ones by poststructuralists as much as scrutinizing the effects of their conceptions on the notion of strategy. While the former stick to an essentialist understanding of agents and structure, poststructuralism denies that structures, agents or subjects dispose of essential qualities (Doty 1997). Hence, what separates the two theoretical strands is the dominance of the performative character of structure *and* agency postulated by IR poststructuralism.

Still, IR poststructuralism is far from conveying a coherent understanding of the matter. While studies refuse to focus on the rational (or irrational) actions of agents and to explain and predict these by reference to individual calculations of self-interest, the degree of autonomy of the agent/subject remains disputed. However, to overestimate the structure leads, in the eyes of some, to a problematic distinction between cause (discourse) and result (policy) (Diez 2001: 13). Favouring the structure at the expense of the actors would understate the 'effort of the part of authorized speakers in order to produce and reproduce discourse' (Milliken 1999: 242). In a recent poststructuralist piece on the agency-structure problem, Roxanne

Doty (1997: 205) proposes to locate agency in the indeterminacy and undecidability of practice. First, practices are inescapably entangled with the social and discursive context within which they are embedded; second, practice is understood as being inseparably linked with the production of meaning; and, third and most importantly, indeterminacy and undecidability entail a de-centring of practice, since practice is of an ambiguous and open-ended character. Agency is still possible, as it is understood as a positioning of a subject via practice. Doty conceives of subject positions as being created by discursive practices and a subject is defined as a position within a particular discourse. Overall, 'agency results from a complex weaving together of the subject-positions and meanings that are available within multiple and overlapping discourses' (Doty 1997: 384–5).

Due to her concentration on subject positions and rather vague conceptualization of agency as the product of interwoven subject positions in multiple discourses, I argue that Doty's account is not far-reaching enough for the present purpose. If the discourse is offering various positions to the subject, then, in consequence, the subject constitutes itself predominantly with respect to discourse. Inasmuch as the actions of subjects emerge due to the contingency of discursive structures – a precariousness, which becomes apparent by the process of dislocation I have described above – the subject always needs to situate itself anew. It is the dislocatory effect that makes subjects reconstitute their failed identities and social meanings by articulating and locating themselves in alternative discourses, as it is in the 'nature' of the discursive constitution of the social that articulations never cease, that subjects always struggle to identify with a signifier (due to the need to identify with something) (Laclau 1996). It is political subjectivity, which is created in this process of constant identification. 'In this sense, the subject is not simply *determined* by the structure; nor, however, does it *constitute* the structure' (Howarth 2000: 109, original emphasis).

Precisely such conceptualization of subject and structure introduces a notion of *strategy* appropriate for a poststructuralist endeavour. This implies, however, not only a different understanding of strategy than advocated in rationalism but also in contrast to a strand of non-rationalist works. First, in most of the social sciences strategy commonly describes courses of action carried out by individuals aimed at overcoming an obstacle or an opponent. Strategy implies having and knowing a goal, careful and rational planning for attaining it, an anticipation of the likely behaviour of one's antagonists, and a set of alternative actions and reactions to prevail in spite of an attempt at foiling goal achievement. In contrast to tactics, strategy is generally understood to be followed for a longer period of time. Usually, strategy is associated with rationalism and often with rationalism's close relative, game theory. Here, individual actors make use of strategies, since a strategy is a plan for dealing with every possible move by the other player or players at every stage in the game (Torfing 1999: 145; McLean and McMillan 2003: 519). This, however, presupposes an objectivity and transparency of the social and of the strategic subject within the social of which we know that it can never be realized. From the point of view of poststructuralist discourse theory, the social is always already dislocated and permeated by antagonism. Or, as Laclau puts it:

[There is a] limitation of all efforts to interpret social antagonisms in terms of game theory. The latter entails a system of rules which sets down the possible moves of the players and consequently establishes their identity. But with antagonism, rules and identities are violated: the antagonist is not a player, but a cheat.

(Laclau 1990: 11)

And as it is a cheat, neither the subject's identity nor her interests nor her strategies can be objectively determined.

Second, in non-rationalist works, strategies have been approached from two angles: from the linguistic side and from a Foucaultian, Bourdieuan and/or Lacanian point of view. Forms of discourse studies that draw more directly on operational ideas from linguistics, conversational or speech-act theory show how people go about saying something concretely, how they make use of the language system in order to achieve their conversational goals. Such analysis is typically less a picture of the whole and discursive strategies are primarily understood in the sense of people's success to achieve a certain goal (see for an example Chilton 1996). A different, but influential way to conceptualize strategies is taken by the proponents of Critical Discourse Analysis. In the context of their works on the discursive construction of national identity, Ruth Wodak and co-authors are inspired by Pierre Bourdieu's definition of strategy and conceive of the notion as more or less conscious, elaborated plans of action that are situated at different levels of our mental organization. Such an understanding brings their notion of strategy (semantically) closer to linguistic concepts like frames (Wodak *et al.* 1998: 73–5; Fairclough 2003). However, to follow Bourdieu means equally to subscribe to a certain weak determinism opening up a room of manoeuvre for the individual – an understanding at odds with the concept of failed subjects as will be explained below.

Most analyses targeting the broader discursive landscape attempt to come to grips with the notion of strategy by considering Foucault as their point of departure (Klein 1989; Campbell 1998; Milliken 1999; Shapiro 1999). Foucault's use of strategies has to be seen in the context of his analyses of power. By power, he understands 'the name one attributes to a complex strategical situation in society' (Foucault 1990: 93), which provides for a terrain of crisscrossing power strategies. Power strategies may be called the totality of means put into operation to implement power effectively or to maintain it, and they constitute modes of action upon possible action of others. Since the power strategies insert themselves into the strategical situation (while the situation conditions the ways in which the various strategies transform, strengthen and subvert each other), they are conceptualized at a lower level than the strategical situation. Hence, the mechanisms introduced in power relations can be termed power strategies through which one can constantly direct the conduct of others: power strategies are 'strategic plays' by which individuals attempt to influence and determine the behaviour of other actors (Foucault 1982: 224–6). Yet, it would be rash to conclude that an intentional subject comes into sight, as for Foucault it is not the subject, but power that is intentional and non-subjective.

Power strategies are guided by a series of aims and objectives but they cannot be mastered by an individual subject since subjects are themselves constructed by discursive strategies (Torfing 1991: 80). This ties in with the formula of 'strategies without a strategist' and Foucault's notion of 'intentional non-subjectivity', allowing for the conceptualization of strategies as structured around intentions, objectives and aims without inevitably relating them to self-conscious subjects (Torfing 1991: 80; Dreyfus and Rabinow 1994: 187).

The study's own conceptualization of *hegemonic strategies* should be read as a merging of Foucault's power strategies and the relations between decision, structure and subject in poststructuralist discourse theory inspired by Lacan and Laclau. To begin with, three important aspects of the concept of the subject in poststructuralist discourse theory – the subject as dislocation, the subject as myth, and the failing subject – allow theorizing strategy within the book's framework. First, the subject 'equals the pure form of the structure's dislocation' (Laclau 1990: 60); it appears as an interruption of a spatialized structure of discourse, since the presence of a subject introduces gaps and cracks into the structure. At the same time, the structure is only articulated at the very moment in which it is dislocated; it can therefore only exist as dislocated structure. Thus, structure, dislocation and the appearance of the subject are insolubly intertwined, and none precedes the other. In a way, the same holds true for strategy: strategies are modes of dislocation. But they do not exist outside of a spatialized structure in which they are then employed. In politics, unlike in board games or in game theory, there is no given 'theoretical set' of strategies to which one can resort. In their specific constitution, strategies – as well as the specific structure or situation in which they are applied – materialize only when they are employed. And they will always be overdetermined and thus contingent on power relations. Hence, while an individual has intentions in mind whenever a strategic intervention is made, the properties and effects of a strategy an individual employs will depend on much more than the individual's intentions. Strategy is never simply a function of intention.

Second, 'any subject is a mythical subject' (Laclau 1990: 61). It is mythical in the sense that its appearance is not only tantamount to dislocation but at the same time is also connected to a vision of the full society – which, of course, can never be realized. Whenever I refer to a subject's influence, I therefore allude to both the introduction of a rift into a given structured order and a proposal to close that rift (in a different manner than before the gap appeared). Strategies also mediate between rift and suture: they seek to break up a structure of discursive elements in order to rearrange it or fix it differently. And the rearrangements aimed at always bear resemblance to 'better' or 'best' solutions. In that way, they are understood as facilitating or at least as approaching the general fullness of society. Strategies are thus modes of dislocation and closure at the same time.

Third, the subject is always a failing subject (Laclau 1990: 44). The subject comes into being through identifying with some image of fullness that it opposes to a structure, thereby arranging as well as dislocating the latter. This means nothing else but the fact that in hegemonic relations the condition of possibility of the subject is antagonism. Antagonism, in other words, is constitutive for the subject:

the subject can only appear because it articulates an entity that blocks this very subject's identity, and because this subject identifies with some project of fullness that it opposes to the blocking entity. Thus, the subject undergoes a process of identification in the face of its blocked identity. Hence, we could say that antagonism on the one hand shows the contingency of identity. It is blocked and endangered by a structure, but this structure is not a necessary one; it rests on power relations and is thus contingent. But on the other hand, it makes acts of identification possible (Laclau 1990: 20–1). The crucial point to be made, however, is this: as it is constitutive, no project of fullness, no act of identification will ever be able to prevail over antagonism. And therefore, the full identity of the subject can never be attained. The subject identifies, but it will never do so in a completely successful way. It is a continuously failing subject in the sense that it will always have a failed structural identity. The same can be said about strategy. Strategy is made possible by antagonism, and at the same time, it aims at overcoming it but can never achieve this goal. Strategies are ultimately always failing strategies, as they are never successful in bringing about the full society they target. We may conclude, therefore, that strategies are modes of dislocation and failing suture at the same time (Herschinger and Nonhoff 2008: 4–5).

Thus, one needs not resort to the phantasma of the self-conscious and self-transparent subject to work with the notion of strategy. In the struggle for hegemony, a subject, which is marked by incompleteness, contingency, and failure, will still make plans and follow strategies. More precisely, whenever the subject appears it will do so while resorting to a strategy, i.e. a mode of simultaneous dislocation and suture. But as the study's understanding of the subject is different from the rationalistic mainstream, so must be its understanding of strategy: first, there can never be a given and complete set of strategies to which the subject can intentionally resort. Second, the concrete form of strategies will always be contingent upon the moment of their actual employment (and the prevailing power relations). And third, the strategies will always be ultimately failing strategies (Herschinger and Nonhoff 2008: 6).

At a more practical level hegemonic strategies are a specific arrangement of discursive elements and subjects in time and space based on power calculations (Dyrberg 1998: 25). These elements and subjects are structured around specific objectives, intentions and aims. Eventually, this allows distinguishing between strategy and logic. While logics refer to the operational modus of the whole system and are always present, the development of the different strategies is based on these logics – accordingly, they need not to be always present in a discourse (Laclau 2000a: 284). In particular, this specification allows the practical identification of strategies in a specific document.

Strategies are further distinguished into strategies that strengthen vs. those hampering the spread of a hegemonic order. The distinction between *productive hegemonic strategies* and *counter-hegemonic strategies* designates these different types. While the former encompass strategies conducive to the emergence of hegemonies, the latter are concerned with their circumvention. The main difference between them resides in the arrangement of discursive elements and subjects in a discourse: either to promote the goal, aims and objective of a hegemonic project or to obstruct these aims. In consequence, whereas productive hegemonic strategies exhibit clear ties with the logic of equivalence, counter-hegemonic strategies experience an intimate link with the logic of difference and the concept of heterogeneity. They defeat the subversion of the differential remainder of each subject, which identifies with a tendentially empty signifier representing a particular hegemonic project. As heterogeneity emanates from this particular remainder of the subjects, these strategies impede the subversion of the remainder and, thereby, are detrimental to the success of a hegemonic project.

Identifying hegemonic strategies

It should be noted that the book's strategies are in one part developed deductively by drawing upon concepts from discourse theory, in the other part inductively derived from the material itself (and thus supplement the discourse theoretical range of conceptual tools). As both types of strategies are simultaneously rooted in the material through specific codes and anchored in discourse theory by localizing the strategies within the logic of equivalence and of difference, they are products of a deductive-inductive or deconstructive-reconstructive procedure. Theoretical concepts launch the development of the two types of strategies, whereas the insights of the empirical analysis extend, modify and substantiate the theoretical concepts – refined by the theoretical concepts and in their turn, re-articulated in the empirical context. Hence, the strategies stem as much from my specific reading of post-structuralist discourse theory as from the reconstruction of the particularities of both discourses and, therefore, are as much theoretically inspired as empirically grounded. This is not a circular process but a process of 'jumping back and forth between theory and analysis' – not to gain the best interpretation of the meaning of texts but to come up with the most plausible *reconstruction* of specific discursive practices. At the end of this process we will dispose of a discursive model arranging the multitude of hegemonic strategies into productive and counter-hegemonic strategies, depending on their impact on the construction of hegemonic orders at the international level.

However, when proposing to develop a discursive model of strategies, I may give the impression of constructing and, thus, supposing a given set of strategies apart from the discursive praxis. This is, of course, a valid charge. But I would like to counter it with two precautionary measures: on the one hand, the model of strategies is not thought to encompass 'real' strategies. On the other hand, it is considered to be open and non-exhaustive. As the analysis will show, different strategies can be discerned in different discursive contexts. My set is a set of what I have encountered, not an encompassing set.

In methodological terms, I identified the strategies via inductive coding in the empirical material. In the broadest sense, coding consists of assigning labels – 'codes' – to 'different segments or instances in the data' (Coffey and Atkinson 1996: 27) which either emerge out of the data or are attached to it by the researcher and are the product of her theoretical or contextual knowledge. Coding helps to organize and retrieve data, generates concepts from and with the data, brings those fragments together that have something in common or that are defined as having something in common and links all those data fragments to a particular idea or concept. Accordingly, codes are 'tags or labels for assigning units of meaning to the descriptive or inferential information compiled during a study' (Miles and Huberman 1994: 56). In the present study, the concept of a code is treated flexibly, i.e. a code could be anything that is plausible from the study's discursive point of view and the text line or passage under scrutiny. Therefore, codes serve as heuristic devices, as they reflect my analytical ideas and provide ways to interact with and think about the data. Inductive coding seems to be the ideal candidate to complement a poststructuralist discursive approach, as it is nothing more – and nothing less! – than a very promising way to systematize the empirical material for the ensuing discourse analysis.

In exchange with the theoretical concepts of hegemony and identity, strategy and subject I created five types of code families before I started to code the data: 'concept codes', 'strategy codes', 'Self codes', 'Other codes' and 'substantial codes'. Thereby, 'concept codes' relate to different concepts in discourse theory (such as the description of a lack) and to particular aspects of the research interest of the present study. 'Strategy codes' apply to any articulation that consists of a demand, includes or excludes subjects or refers to goals/aims/means (that can be supported or rejected). 'Self codes' are the description of any subject or collective identity in the discourse. They include articulations pointing out the distinctiveness of a subject with respect to other subjects or of a collective Self at the international level. 'Other codes' relate to any depiction of the antagonistic Others, terrorism and drugs regardless of whether articulations aim at differentiating the picture of the Other or underlining the antagonistic relation. Finally, 'substantial codes' apply to any content related or substantial issue raised in the debate, for instance, whether the text of the *Single Convention on Narcotic Drugs* should allow for reservations or not.

During the coding process, it became obvious that the basic dimensions of the logics of equivalence and difference would profit from a more detailed account of the dynamics encountered in the empirical material. Hence, in close examination with the strategies of the basic dimension, I introduced the *supplementary dimension* of hegemonic strategies.[6] It is particularly important to note that, first, strategies of the supplementary dimension also establish relations between elements of a discourse by substitution or combination; and, second, they do *supplement* the strategies of the basic dimensions but do *not replace* them. Whereas the threefold basic dimensions of productive and counter-hegemonic strategies are always sufficient to signal the emergence of hegemonic orders, the new dimension complements them and is not able to indicate hegemonic operations 'on its own'. Depending on whether they are productive hegemonic or counter-hegemonic, the newly introduced strategies either hamper or foster the construction of hegemonies; without the simultaneous presence of the basic strategies, however, no hegemony can be discerned. The strategies of the supplementary dimension increase or decrease the scope and range of a hegemonic regime or project and thereby influence its success. Overall, they are necessary to fully grasp the breadth of a hegemonic regime and its inner operations.

Productive hegemonic strategies and equivalential articulations

In chapter one, I have outlined that the political aspect of a practice evolves from the public articulation of grievances or dissatisfaction as *demands*. This implies not all demands pertain to hegemonic analysis. Of sole interest is a demand articulated out of a sense of disappointment and frustration with a given situation. Fulfilled demands are irrelevant because 'a fulfilled demand ceases to be a demand. It is only the lack of fulfilment [. . .] that gives a demand materiality and discursive presence' (Laclau 2005: 127–8).

Demands can appear in two different contexts – and with regard to the productive hegemonic strategies, the first type is of prominent interest (for the second one see below). Demands can be articulated out of dissatisfaction and if they are fulfilled, the problem is settled. However, if they are not satisfied and the problematic situation remains unchanged over a definite period, it depends on whether a certain accumulation of unfulfilled demands emerges and whether the institutional system in which they have been articulated is able to absorb them in a differential way, i.e. treats and satisfies each demand on its own (Laclau 2005: 73). If not, these accumulated demands tend to enter an equivalential relation. In this sense, political practices can be considered as hegemonic practices by the degree to which the respective political demands are formulated in more or less universal terms. They either link various forces and demands into a new regime of practices or stabilize the existing regime. Such gathering of various subjects under the banner of a common goal, ideal etc. by equivalential articulations implies that subjects are treated as similar with regard to this common reference point. Among these articulations are references to *common goals* like 'it was more urgent than ever that the international community should adopt concerted measures to combat terrorism and establish an effective global legal framework' (UN Sixth Committee 2000b: 2). The general equivalent can also be inferred from the allusion to an *interest* that is considered above all individual interests and formulations implying a *consensus* like '(s)ince all countries were aware of the evils of that traffic' (United Nations 1991: 13) represent an 'ideal type' of equivalential articulations. Here, equivalence is invoked by attempts to even out any difference between subjects.

The above-cited examples all pertain to equivalential articulations of the antagonizing chain of equivalence (*chain A*) confronting its Other, terrorism or drugs. However, the subjects of *chain A* also voice equivalential articulations pertaining to the antagonized force. For instance, when intimate ties are established between drugs and illness '[s]ince the links between drug abuse and aids were obvious and growing' (United Nations 1991: 12) or between drugs and terrorism by claiming that 'the illicit traffic [in drugs] was also the root cause of problems such as terrorism, subversion and illegal arms trafficking' (United Nations 1991: 15).

With their potential to universalize the particularity of various demands and gather them under the heading of the 'something' underlying all demands, equivalential articulations are the backbone of productive hegemonic strategies, like of the already outlined strategies of the basic dimension *Universalization, Establishing an antagonistic frontier* and *Representation*. Let us now turn to the productive hegemonic strategies of the supplementary dimension. In the context of clarifying what is meant by success, I have indicated that an extension of a chain of equivalence is beneficial to the construction of hegemonic orders at the international level. Speaking about adding discursive elements or subjects to *chain A* means that this process sets in *after* the chain has come into being. Hence, the productive hegemonic strategy *Extending the antagonizing chain of equivalence* refers to the enlargement of a chain that has already been constructed and is now strengthened by being extended.

When subjects bound by an equivalential chain stress their agreement with the general equivalent, productive hegemonic strategy *Referring to a subject's agreement with the general equivalent* is at play. This is the case when doubts of one's commitment to the fight against drugs or terrorism are invoked and subjects renew their full cooperation or consent with the ultimate or common goals. The reference may mask the most contradictory, particular contents assembled in a chain, as long as their agreement with the general equivalent remains intact. The call for a consensus or the need for a majority to counter terrorism and drugs illustrates this reference: the appeal to consensus only arises if disagreements between the subjects persist and appear insurmountable due to the clashing definitions of drugs and terrorism and the contradictory opinions on what can be considered as an effective fight.

When subjects of a chain refer to their particularity, which is presented to hamper their agreement with the general equivalent but *simultaneously* underscore their subordination to it, the productive hegemonic strategy *Simultaneously emphasizing and downgrading the particularity of a subject of chain A* applies. In the fight against drugs, some states demanded that the use of drugs in indigenous medicine or the use by indigenous peoples be dissociated from criminal offenses. This demand was raised together with an emphasis on the country's engagement in the international fight against drugs. Hence, pointing out a subject's particularity (indigenous medicine/use) is constructed as not impeding its subordination to the general equivalent. It is important that the particularity is emphasized and downgraded *simultaneously* because without this characterization, the strategy would not qualify as a productive hegemonic strategy. Emphasizing the particularity without immediate reference to the subject's agreement with the general equivalent counts as a counter-hegemonic strategy (see below).

It has been stressed on various occasions that the antagonistic frontier is only temporarily fixed, despite being articulated as a strict and unchangeable divide. The frontier separating terrorism and drugs from the civilized world is articulated with all possible sharpness as fixed and stable; however, the inherent dynamics of the discourses subverts the partial fixation of the antagonistic frontier and impedes a permanent dichotomization of the discursive space. Still, it can be rewarding to cross the antagonistic frontier (Nonhoff 2006: 234), a movement incarnated by the productive hegemonic strategy *Crossing the antagonistic frontier in order to strengthen chain A*. The overall aim of such movements (moving in the sense of 'disassociating' and 'associating') is not to destabilize the frontier but to strengthen the antagonizing chain by extending it and increasing the number of subjects bound by the chain.

The last productive hegemonic strategy called *Enlarging the antagonized chain of equivalence* encompasses movements to extend the chain of the antagonistic Other. On the one hand, the extension is attempted by adding discursive elements that have formerly not been associated with the antagonistic Other. This is, for instance, the case when in the discourse on drugs the French representative calls for an inclusion of the 'new danger' synthetic drugs into the remit of the *Single Convention on Narcotic Drugs* (which has happened ten years later with the 1971 *Convention on Psychotropic Substances*). Such extensions, on the other hand, may equally encompass formerly floating subjects, like linking migrants, terrorism and drug traffic. Neither migrants nor terrorists are in a direct relation to drugs but via discursive association they become part of the antagonized chain of equivalence (for instance, claiming that the money gained via drug trafficking is used to finance terrorism). However, extending or emphasizing proximity, risks strengthening and undermining the coherence of the antagonized chain of equivalences at the same time. Hence, what counts for *chain A* also counts for *chain Z* – the wider a chain and the more global and heterogeneous the Other, the more the identity of the antagonized force becomes difficult to determine (Laclau 2005: 96–9). Again, this ambivalence of the identified strategies highlights the relationship between the logic of difference and equivalence: they are not mutually exclusive, but subvert each other and never one dominates to the full. To sum up, the supplementary dimension of productive hegemonic strategies consists of five strategies:

*   Extending the antagonizing chain of equivalence
*   Referring to a subject's agreement with the general equivalent
*   Simultaneously emphasizing and downgrading the particularity of a subject of *chain A*
*   Crossing the antagonistic frontier in order to strengthen *chain A*
*   Enlarging the antagonized chain of equivalence

Differential articulations and counter-hegemonic strategies

As referred to above, demands can appear in two forms. While productive hegemonic strategies encompass demands that are linked via equivalential relations, the second type of demands – differential demands – subverts these relations. Differential demands neutralize the equivalential potential of demands by separating the links between chains of equivalence; hence, they disperse the articulations pertaining to the general equivalent. Contrary to equivalential articulations, the nature of differential articulations makes it impossible to depict what they 'all share' because they do not refer to a common aim but deny exactly the existence, importance or relevance of such a goal uniting subjects in a chain of equivalence. Hence, the only characteristic shared is their aim to neutralize the equivalential potential of the subjects in a chain of equivalence.

More practically, differential articulations centre on *dissent*, for instance when it is stated that 'the contemporary increase in acts of violence [. . .] was due to the indifference or complicity of certain States' (UN Sixth Committee 1972p: 475). They equally address *conflict* between subjects:

> The economic powers which exercised domination throughout the world by means of multinational cartels and trusts were trying to prevent individuals from thinking, and thereby to head off any challenge to their exploitative policies. For them, drug addiction was an ideal solution.
>
> (United Nations 1991: 12)

Moreover, differential articulations request to *deny the importance of the general equivalent* and *request for recognition* and *the perseverance of (national) Sonderwege*: 'the Assembly's agenda contained other problems [. . .] whose solution was even more important for the prestige of the United Nations than international terrorism' (UN Sixth Committee 1972j: 327) or 'the provision concerning local inquiries infringed national sovereignty and was therefore unacceptable' (United Nations 1964a: 85). Another way to disperse the equivalential potential of demands is to *reject the common and/or ultimate goals*: 'The illicit traffic was virtually non-existent and drug addiction was not a serious social problem' (United Nations 1964a: 10).

Of similar importance is the realization of particularities of the Other. Formulations *criticize or differentiate the unified picture of the Other*, as, for example, when it is claimed that 'coca leaf was not a narcotic, nor was it used for narcotics production' (United Nations 1991: 154). Some formulations claim the *similarity of an antagonized subject with the Other:* 'the majority of Member States supported that legitimate violence because their own countries had their origins in revolutionary and national liberation struggles'(UN Sixth Committee 1972h: 308). Such formulations also tend to *defame* any attempt to point out similarities as a strategy to dishonour these subjects: 'Resistance to terror, however, was not terrorism. The anti-colonial liberation struggle was legitimate because it was founded on the right of peoples to self-determination' (UN Sixth Committee 1972c: 252). This demand is frequently raised in conjunction with formulations *requesting to stop associating the Other with the subjects fighting the Other*. The examples show that differential articulations share the aim to disperse and break up equivalential bonds by demonstrating their fragility. And these on 'both sides of the frontier' as equivalential chains of the antagonizing force are just as much targets of subversion as their antagonized chains.

Associating differential articulations with the three counter-hegemonic strategies of the basic dimension (*Particularization, Breaking off the chain* and *Weakening the antagonistic frontier*) pays tribute to their potential to subvert equivalential relations. The various subjects of a chain are particularized by re-inscribing their differential character and the links between them are broken off. Consequently, the antagonistic frontier, the dichotomization of the discursive space is weakened and the divisions are relegated to the margins of the discourse. One important corollary of breaking off the chain of equivalence consists in re-establishing the autonomy of the subjects formerly bound by the chain (as a subject can only operate within the chain's parameters). This leads to the first counter-hegemonic strategy of the supplementary dimension. Through the strategy *Autonomization of subject of chain A* subjects regain their autonomy and can work towards the realization of their demands in a different context. Autonomy beyond a certain limit leads to the dominance of the logic of difference and lets the equivalential camp collapse (Laclau 2005: 129–30).

An equally radical movement is circumscribed by counter hegemonic strategy *Stressing the particularity of subject of chain A explicitly at the expense of the general equivalent*. While at first glance, this strategy seems to restate basic counter-hegemonic strategy *Particularization*, the supplementing strategy hints at the 'how to' of the moment of particularization. Protecting the particularity of a subject may be considered incompatible with its agreement to the general equivalent. Consequently, either the general equivalent has to be adjusted or the subject has to be protected by, for instance, being disassociated from the chain.

The crossing of an antagonistic frontier is central to the supplementary dimension of counter-hegemonic strategies. The importance of a frontier's stability for a chain of equivalence has been outlined; accordingly, one of the main aims of the strategies obstructing hegemonies is to weaken and displace this frontier (it has also been stated that counter-hegemonic strategies are not aiming at eliminating the frontier). While productive-hegemonic strategies cross the frontier to strengthen the antagonizing chain, crossing the frontier in counter-hegemonic strategies is about denying its course.

Thereby, the counter-hegemonic strategy *Crossing the antagonistic frontier in order to weaken it* splits in two movements. First, a subject of *chain A* can present its particularity as being part of *chain Z*. The frontier between the antagonized and antagonizing force is blurred by demonstrating that it does not consistently separate the collective Self from the antagonistic Other but transfers 'parts of the collective Self' to the Other. Hence, the frontier is misplaced in the eyes of the concerned subject and should be moved to no longer include the particularity of this very subject (sub-strategy *Protect particularity of a subject by articulating its particularity as part of chain Z*). A second, more subtle movement aims at breaking off the apparently coherent construction of the force as the antagonized one. Differentiating the antagonistic Other by pointing out specific particularities of it or denying the adherence of discursive elements to *chain Z* equally weakens the frontier. This operation is circumscribed by the second sub-strategy called *Underscore particularity of a subject of chain Z*. Both movements not only show again that the more global and heterogeneous the Other, the more difficult the identity of the antagonizing force becomes to determine – but imply that this difficulty applies equally to the construction of the Other.

The last counter-hegemonic strategy entitled *Attempts to disarticulate floating elements of chain Z* stands in intimate relation with the supplementary productive hegemonic strategy aiming at *Enlarging the antagonistic chain of equivalence*. Where the latter extends the antagonized chain by adding new discursive elements and subjects, the former explicitly denies these relations. Thus, terrorism and migration cannot be automatically associated, nor can one bring terrorism and specific cultures, traditions or religions together. The attempt to disassociate floating elements or subjects that have been linked with the antagonized Other weakens not only the frontier but also the coherent construction of *chain Z*, and, thereby, ultimately of *chain A*. To conclude, the supplementary dimension of counter-hegemonic strategies consists of four more strategies:

- Autonomization of subject of *chain A*
- Stressing particularity of a subject of *chain A* explicitly at the expense of the general equivalent
- Crossing the antagonistic frontier in order to weaken it
    - Protect particularity of a subject by articulating its particularity as part of *chain Z*
    - Underscore particularity of a subject/element of *chain Z*
- Attempts to disarticulate floating elements of *chain Z*

We now dispose of 15 hegemonic strategies distinguished in productive and counter-hegemonic according to their role in the process of the construction of a hegemonic regime of practices at the international level.[7] While the former strategies are conducive to such a regime, the latter are detrimental to it. Each strategy type is divided into a basic and a supplementary dimension, and while only the basic dimension can trigger hegemonies alone, the supplementary adds a number of discursive strategies that are necessary to capture the breadth of a hegemonic regime and to analyze the wealth of the empirical material satisfactorily. With the help of these analytical tools, we are prepared to 'open the black box' of hegemonic regimes empirically in order to find out about the processes leading to their spread in the international discourses on terrorism and drug prohibition.

Analyzing discourses on international terrorism and drug prohibition

Before starting with the actual analysis of the two discourses, a few methodological remarks are in order. In general, the starting point of a discourse analysis is debatable, since the selection of sources is a delicate matter in discourse analysis (due to the openness of discourses, various types of data might be interesting and equally relevant). Nevertheless, one needs to start somewhere and determine the corpus of data and a lot of the contentious potential of one's starting point can be mitigated by explaining each choice for each source. By maximizing the transparency of my methodological decisions, I attempt to ensure the plausibility of my findings and to bring some methodological rigor to the poststructuralist enterprise in IR.

While the field of international security is vast and diverse, I have decided to analyze the *discourses on international terrorism* and *drug prohibition*. For more than five decades, both have been perceived as a threat not only to a single nation-state but increasingly to international peace and security. The two issues have been on the contemporary international policy agenda for roughly 50 (drugs) and 40 (terrorism) years respectively, which represents a sufficiently long period to carry out a meaningful discourse analysis. The different time periods chosen for the two case studies are justified with reference to the decisive framing periods of both discourses. While the international drug prohibition discourse was essentially framed from 1961 to 1988, the framing of the international terrorism discourse is still underway. Drug prohibition goes as far back as the early twentieth century but it was only in the 1960s and 1970s that drugs were constructed as an existential concern for the international community. In 1961, states agreed on the *Single Convention on Narcotic Drugs*, replacing the former patchwork of six conventions. Since that time, two further conventions have been adopted: first, the 1971 UN *Protocol on Psychotropic Substances* and, second, the 1988 UN *Convention Against Illicit Traffic in Narcotic Drugs and Psychotropic Substances*. Furthermore, the Single Convention has been amended by the 1972 UN *Conference to Consider Amendments to the Single Convention on Narcotic Drugs*. Except for these conventions, no equally important attempts can be identified, which justifies their selection for the present analysis.[8]

When airplane hijacking was first constructed as a major threat in the 1960s and early 1970s, terrorism entered the international agenda. In the ensuing years, three sectoral conventions were adopted meant to improve international responses to terrorism: UN *Convention on Offences and Certain Other Acts Committed on Board Aircraft* (1963); UN *Convention for the Suppression of Unlawful Seizure of Aircraft* (1970) and the UN *Convention for the Suppression of Unlawful Acts against the Safety of Civil Aviation* (1971). After the terrorist attacks on the Olympic Village in Munich on 5 September 1972, the UN launched a more general approach to terrorism in an attempt to agree upon a comprehensive convention on terrorism and finding an internationally approved definition of terrorism. These debates and conventions marked the beginning of a number of sectoral conventions in the following years. Although the negotiations on a general convention failed in 1979, they were resumed in 1999, three years after the General Assembly (GA) re-established the *Ad Hoc Committee on terrorism*.[9] So far, these two rounds have been the most important attempts to internationally define terrorism and legitimize subsequent counter-measures.[10] In contrast to the drug case, the choice of documents on the international fight against terrorism proves to be less systematic as a number of different bodies of the UN have been involved. Next to the General Assembly of the UN, the *Sixth Committee* and the *Ad Hoc Committee on terrorism* have worked on a comprehensive convention on terrorism.[11]

Although the study of terrorists' leaflets or detective novels on organized crime might be equally conceivable, the UN is particularly well suited for the present purpose. While some might object that the UN is not the forum for authoritative decisions on terrorism and drug prohibition, it is a central venue within which key discursive agents struggle for a global consensus via voicing their vision of what the world should look like if terrorism and drugs no longer existed. In this sense, the UN is an ideal place for analyzing the attempts of constructing not only an Other but also a Self. Furthermore, the UN-debates represent central sources of both discourses. Fighting drugs and terrorism are elite-led projects and within the UN-discourses elites provide the overall vision and justification for anti-drug and counter-terrorist practices. Thereby, the UN is represented as the central forum for legitimizing and initiating global instruments against international terrorism and drug abuse – practices that have far-reaching effects on the rest of the population and on antagonized Others.[12] Still, while UN documents make up for the lion's share of the present database, there are a large number of documents from various other sources like the EU, Europol, the INCB, international NGOs as well as various national sources such as newspapers, reports and documents from government representatives.

However, in order to widen the perspective the study pursues an intertextual approach to the official discourses. In this understanding, each text is 'simultaneously unique and united' (Hansen 2006: 55). Indeed, every text is located in a wider universe of other texts, making references to previous texts – whether implicitly or explicitly – and in doing so, each text turns into a single interpretation of the reading of previous texts while at the same time being the product of earlier texts. Julia Kristeva called this process *intertextuality*: for her, any text is 'constructed as mosaic of quotations; any text is the absorption and transformation of another' (Kristeva 1980: 66). While this implies that each of today's texts wears the stains and marks of previous texts, it also directs our attention to the construction of meaning via juxtaposition to past meanings. Most importantly, the new textual product not only delivers a new interpretation; by drawing on former texts it also builds its own authority on quoting them. The new text gains legitimacy by referring to the older texts, by reconstructing and reproducing their authoritative status. In consequence, rather 'than seeing new texts as depending on older, one should therefore see the two as interacting in an exchange where one text gains legitimacy from quoting the other and the other gains legitimacy from being quoted' (Hansen 2006: 57). On a conceptual level, this understanding implies that neither a quote of an original text is a complete 'true' reproduction of the latter, nor does it mean that the original text's meaning will be left untouched but it will be read and re-written through new lenses, new texts.

On a more practical level, intertextuality offers the advantage of making choices between text genres without excluding other types. Analyzing mainly the UN debates by no means implies that insights and knowledge present in other text genres are absent. On the contrary, as the analysis will show, the UN discussions are full of references to other texts and discourses, which bring in texts from a variety of genres as well as different types of authors (such as scientists, journalists, intellectuals etc.). Indeed, focusing on the UN debates does not rule out attention to and inclusion of institutionalized practices, since they are represented and contested in the debates. Choosing material to account for the institutionalization of hegemonic anti-drug and anti-terrorist practices followed the rationale of selecting *international measures of cooperation*, i.e. only those measures are of interest that have been agreed upon as part of the respective conventions or reaction to the debates (at an international or regional level) and are carried out within the study's period of investigation. It should be noted that these measures fall especially in the realm of police forces and intelligence services; only in the last decades did the military begin to play an increasingly important role.[13] Overall, I have analyzed 486 documents (280 documents of the drug discourse; 206 documents of the terrorism discourse).[14]

As a corpus of that size makes it necessary to think about a way to get a systematic handle on the data, the computer program MAXQDA is used in the process of analysis. Of course, applying computer software does not contradict poststructuralist discourse theory *per se*: '[S]oftware is not now, if it ever was, something that is relevant only to "positivist" or "quasi-positivist" approaches' (Weitzman 2000: 804). For instance, in the late 1960s, Michel Pêcheux, one of the pioneers of French discourse analysis, introduced the '*Analyse automatique du discours*' on which a whole tradition of software used in France was later based (Pêcheux 1969; Angermüller 2005).

Applying MAXQDA allows systematizing the amount of empirical material to document the research process comprehensively and thus ensure its transparency and plausibility. The program simplifies the practical organization of the material and the analytical work since it allows for an instant verification of decisions directly at the relevant text lines and allows for revising and adapting if necessary (Diaz-Bone and Schneider 2003: 485). With its functions of analysis, such as searching for co-occurrences or intersections of codes, MAXQDA provides the main tools necessary for the coding process in a poststructuralist discourse analysis.[15] As the codes are the references to a certain discursive order in the data, they need to be assembled according to empirically reconstructed practices. On this basis, empirically condensed and plausible statements about the outlook and constitution of the discursive order in which this study is interested are possible (Diaz-Bone and Schneider 2003: 474). Hence, to apply MAXQDA in the present context is warranted because it demonstrates recurrently the linkages between the theoretical premises to which the codes refer and in how far they allow reconstructing specific patterns and meanings.

Putting the pieces together

With the characterization of the different hegemonic strategies operating 'inside' of hegemonic regimes and the depiction of the methodological procedure, the present section concludes the book's theoretical part by briefly summarizing what has been said so far on hegemonies and collective identities at the international level, on identification and antagonism, on the logic of equivalence and difference. The chapter closes by delivering an overview on the two dimensions of productive and counter-hegemonic strategies.

Crucial for hegemonic orders to emerge is the moment of discursive closure. Since a discourse is a structure penetrated by contingency and temporality, ultimate fixation of meaning is impossible; however, partial fixations are probable. In order to partially fixate meaning, discourses establish boundaries by relating to elements of an Other which cannot be incorporated in the discourse. The establishment of discursive limits serves to exclude otherness that, at the same time, constitutes and negates the discourse and the subjects present in the discourse. Constructing international terrorism and drug abuse as threats employs a particular language that brings about radical differences and, thereby, confers a specific meaning to both phenomena. In this process, at least two identities are created, an Other and a Self.

Yet, one effect of excluding that what a subject is not consists in the homogenization of inner differences. Internal differences are one type of difference emanating from the constitutive split of each subject. At the same time, homogenization of internal differences is an effect of hegemonic operations establishing a chain of equivalence via the logic of equivalence. In hegemonic operations, differential subjects are universalized (by identifying with a common signifier and by outlining the 'something underlying them all' – the general equivalent), an antagonistic frontier is constructed and one particular signifier takes up the task of representing the equivalential chain as a whole – the tendentially empty signifier. These operations create not only a common enemy but also a vision of what the world would look like without being threatened by the enemy. This vision can induce the linking of various political forces into a common project, provided they share a consensus about their commonalities as much as about the character and the quality of the Other, terrorism and drugs.

The signifier representing the chain of equivalence is empty because of the impossibility of signification as such (no signifier can represent a subject or a chain of subjects in its/their entirety) and the respective particularity has to be emptied from its particular content to represent a chain. It is also tendentially empty, since no signifier can be completely emptied from its particular content; it is a question of degree, but the lesser the particularity of the signifier, the emptier it is, the better it is able to represent the chain of equivalence and to organize the discourse by establishing a horizon of closure of the discursive system.

The homogenization of the subjects in an equivalential chain via the logic of equivalence leads to an incomplete surrender of every subject's particularity, underlining what they all have in common. However, homogenization is not unopposed. Identities are understood as always failed identities, since at the root of every subject prevails the experience of a lack. This implies that to identify does not eliminate the lack, since every signifier fails to represent a subject in its entirety. The residue that cannot be represented refers to the constitutive split of any subject: it is divided in a universal and particular part. While the universal symbolizes the missing fullness of each subject that cannot be achieved, the particular part includes that each subject construct itself as a particularity, as different from other subjects. Precisely this differential remainder represents inner differences that have not been mitigated and continue to disturb the process of homogenization. These internal differences have been encompassed by the concept of *heterogeneity* representing essentially (but not only) the differential remainder of each subject. Heterogeneity agitates an already established hegemonic order at the international level or subverts the attempts to construct one (i.e. a hegemonic project).

To address how hegemonic projects and hegemonies are successful, I introduced the notion of strategy, explaining that hegemonic operations are enacted in and related to specific type of strategies: productive-hegemonic strategies promoting and counter-hegemonic strategies subverting the spread of a hegemonic regime at the international level or the transformation of a hegemonic project in a 'full-fledged' hegemony. Therefore, hegemonic strategy is a mode of dislocation which seeks to break up a structure of discursive elements in order to rearrange it into something 'better'. Hence, hegemonic strategies are a specific arrangement of discursive elements and subjects based on power calculations to form discourse coalitions and structured around specific objectives, intentions and aims. At the same time, they are always failing strategies.

In light of what has been said on successful hegemonic operations, productive hegemonic strategies have been developed in intimate relation with the logic of equivalence, whereas counter-hegemonic strategies are based on the logic of difference, which turns them equally into strategies of heterogeneity. While the basic dimension of each type is represented by the threefold nature of the two logics, the supplementary dimension has been established in direct exchange with the concrete discourses on terrorism and drugs. The practical reconstruction of both strategy types works via equivalential and differential articulations in both discourses. The following delivers an overview of the different strategies of both types.[16]

A. Productive hegemonic strategies
    Basic dimension
    –   Universalization
    –   Establishing an antagonistic frontier
    –   Representation

    Supplementary dimension
    –   Extending the antagonizing chain of equivalence
    –   Referring to a subject's agreement with the general equivalent
    –   Simultaneously emphasizing and downgrading the particularity of a subject of *chain A*
    –   Crossing the antagonistic frontier in order to strengthen *chain A*
    –   Enlarging the antagonized chain of equivalence

B. Counter-hegemonic strategies
    Basic dimension
    –   Particularization
    –   Breaking off the chain
    –   Weakening of the antagonistic frontier

    Supplementary dimension
    –   Autonomization of subject of *chain A*
    –   Stressing the particularity of a subject of *chain A* explicitly at the expense of the general equivalent
    –   Crossing the antagonistic frontier in order to weaken it
        –   Protect particularity of a subject by articulating its particularity as part of *chain Z*

  –   Underscore particularity of a subject/element of *chain Z*

  –   Attempts to disarticulate floating elements of *chain Z*

Having developed a number of hegemonic strategies, exposed the details on their practical identification, delimited text corpus and issues, chapter two has made use of a continuous exchange between theoretical framework and empirical material. As the locus of merging theory and concrete material, it presented a poststructuralist framework and method of how to analyze the discourses on drugs and terrorism. The subsequent chapters will not only reconstruct the different hegemonic strategies but will apply the procedure of practical identification of various types of articulations and tendentially empty signifiers.

3   International drug prohibition

Constructing the 'drug-free world'

While the 'black box' of hegemonic orders has by now been 'opened' at the international level in theoretical terms, chapters three and four respectively advance the theoretical reflections to the empirical context. By carrying out a fine-grained analysis, the following two chapters provide for one of the two central contributions of the present study, i.e. to offer a change of perspective on the international efforts to counter drugs and terrorism. Whereas chapter three analyses the discourse on drug prohibition, chapter four centres on terrorism. In order to allow for comparison of the two discourses (which follows in chapter five) both parts are structured in the same manner. First, they aim to reconstruct the process by which drugs and terrorism have been constituted as a major international security threat; second, how a Self has been established representing the 'drug-/terrorism-free world' and opposing the drugs/terrorist Other; and, third, the chapters shed light on how specific practices flowing from these constructions have been institutionalized as counter-measures.

Drugs as an existential threat to international peace and security

The historical roots of the contemporary interpretation of drugs

We presently witness a specific interpretation of what the drug problem is about, how it should be conceived and how it should be fought. Drugs, however, have not always been construed as a problem and today's interpretation did not evolve naturally. Drugs were gradually construed as presenting a danger, they have not been a problem but *became* one: today's perspective on narcotics is/was a matter of conflict, as interested parties struggled to define or prevent a definition of drugs as something international action should do something about (Gusfield 1981; Driscoll 2000: 12). For that reason, the familiar interpretation of drugs (understood mainly as psychoactive or mind altering substances) as illicit and their use as deviant has been developed over the course of the last decades. We take both more or less for granted and do not really question. Indeed, drug prohibition dating back to the early twentieth century became structured by a series of three international drug treaties under the aegis of the UN. Almost every state in the world has signed these treaties accepting legal constraints regarding the production, sale, possession and consumption of drugs. Today, these countries criminalize not only the production and sale of cannabis, cocaine and opiates and some other psychoactive substances, they are equally 'holding criminal simple possession of small amounts of the prohibited substances' (Levine 2003: 145). The attempts to universalize a specific understanding and, as a corollary, its norms and legal sanctions regarding trade and consumption have resulted in a 'global drug prohibition regime' as Ethan Nadelmann termed it (Nadelmann 1990).

A series of events in the nineteenth century paved the way for the dominant interpretation of drugs as illicit. First, Britain's strong interest in controlling the global opium trade – which was at that time the main drug substance – ignited two 'opium wars' between the colonial power and China (from 1839–42 and from 1856–58). Both wars strengthened British global dominance in exporting opium from British India to China during the following years.[1] Second, a number of important chemical and medical innovations, which made modern drug consumption possible, raised levels of concern regarding the potentially damaging effects of drugs. In 1805, morphine was isolated from opium, followed by the advent of hypodermic injection in 1843, the synthesis of cocaine from the coca bush (1855) and the synthesis of heroin from morphine after 1874 (Nadelmann 1990: 504; Elvins 2003: 27).

Whereas Britain made no significant attempts to call for a global banning of opium, the endeavour was later launched by the US-Americans. US acquisition of the Philippines in 1898 and a growing moral panic over drug use within the United States around the same time fuelled a specific view on opium and its trade. Drugs that had been consumed by the inner circles of society – lemonade and alcoholic beverages or sprays contained constituents of the coca bush; white women calmed their nerves (or relieved their depression) with opiates; doctors or pharmacists used the morphine meant for subscription – became more and more associated with outsiders. This association was intermingled with explicit racial discrimination at the turn of the twentieth century and mixed up with moral judgements and political opportunism: Chinese immigrants smoke opium to incite white women; Blacks in the South consume cocaine to resist and attack white society; Mexicans smoke marijuana and become violent and so forth. According to the dominant reading in the literature on drug prohibition, the US interpretation of drugs and its efforts at home and abroad have been driven by fears of deviant drug use, moralistic abhorrence of the recreational use of psychoactive substances other than alcohol and tobacco, a sense of righteousness as well as a compulsion to proselytize (Nadelmann 1990: 504–8; Boekhaut van Solinge 2004: 16). Successively, this new stance met with the interpretation of drugs as illicit and their use as deviant. Since from the outset, drugs and their trade have been conceived of as an international problem, the United States initiated the convening of an international opium commission which met in Shanghai in 1909 (Musto 1999; Elvins 2003: 28; Briesen 2005: 13).

Representing the first significant multinational meeting in the field, the commission recommended a legal basis for the homogenization of the various domestic drug policies on a global scale. Shanghai was followed by a number of international meetings, and with the *International Opium Convention of 1925* in Geneva, the drug question became a permanent feature of international relations. With the successful negotiation of the *Convention On the Limitation of the Manufacture of Narcotic Drugs* (1931) the still dispersed efforts coalesced into coherence as the agreement delineated the boundary between licit trade and illicit drug traffic. The *Conference for the Suppression of the Illicit Traffic in Dangerous Drugs* of 1936 in Geneva called for harsher penal measures against illicit drug traffickers. Following the creation of the United Nations in 1945, three further protocols (1946, 1948 and 1953) were adopted that were meant to close loopholes in the at that time regulatory system, gaps mainly relating to the increasing number of synthetic drugs. Throughout these years, the call was heard for a universal convention serving as an umbrella for all existing conventions consolidating and extending international drug control. After two failed drafts, the third draft of a *Single Convention on Narcotic Drugs* was accepted as a basis for negotiations which began in January 1961.

The convention of 1961 and the way to the 1988 agreement

Obviously, the conference in Shanghai set in motion a series of conventions against drugs 'and since then, through multilateral treaties and their international obligations, members of the international community have attempted to control the growth, processing, trafficking and consumption of a category of drugs collectively known as narcotics' (Bewley-Taylor 1999: 2–3). The United States played a decisive role in the evolution of the global drug prohibition regime. Quite clearly, the early attempts of the US to convince the rest of the world to accept their interpretation can be regarded as productive hegemonic strategies to spur the development of a chain of equivalence and to transform a hegemonic project into a hegemony aspiring to heal the world from drugs. When negotiations of the Single Convention began in 1961, the interpretation of drugs and their use as deviant and morally abhorrent had already been present in the discourse and began to supersede alternative meanings.

The *Single Convention on Narcotic Drugs* opened up a new era of international drug prohibition.[2] The convention centralized all previous treaties and protocols into one coherent text.[3] It obliged states

> to limit exclusively to medical and scientific purposes the production, manufacture, export, import, distribution of, trade in, use and possession of drugs, eradicate all unlicensed cultivation; suppress illicit manufacture and traffic; and cooperate with each other in achieving the aims of the convention.
>
> (Bewley-Taylor 1999: 7)

The convention put under control not only several substances that are pre-made, such as heroin or cocaine, but also raw products and their cultivation (for instance, the cultivation of cannabis experienced a number of restrictions for the first time). It defined illegal drugs with the help of the concept of 'schedules of control'. Introduced in the 1931 agreement, the *Single Convention* expanded the number of schedules from two to four. A long list of incriminated substances figures in its annex. By providing one single document, the *Single Convention* established the current system of drug prohibition, as it promoted the regime's universality. Regarding illicit drugs as 'a danger to mankind' (United Nations 1964a: 300), the convention perpetuates the (US-) prohibitive approach to drug control and a hegemonization of the meaning of drugs as illicit becomes possible. The ensuing analysis will show how the consensus on prohibition installed the bedrock of the system on global drug prohibition and how it spread.

Treaties like the 1971 *Convention on Psychotropic Substances* and the 1972 *Conference to Consider Amendments to the Single Convention on Narcotic Drugs* consolidated the prohibitionist system and extended it to include synthetic drugs which have been successively regarded as dangerous to humankind as natural drugs. A large number of synthetic substances have been added to the lists of 1961. During the 1980s, the growing drug traffic alarmed the signatories and spurred the elaboration of a convention explicitly dealing with trafficking, as this had not sufficiently been done by former agreements. With the 1988 UN *Convention Against Illicit Traffic in Narcotic Drugs and Psychotropic Substances*, efforts against drugs now covered the most important aspects of the phenomenon. The 1988 convention criminalizes acts such as illicit trading in precursor chemicals, international drug trafficking, and laundering of money and assets. Parties are required to offer mutual legal assistance, share information, cooperate in law enforcement efforts, and enact 'appropriate measures' for the eradication of illicit cultivation. The treaty also includes a limited extradition clause. While the early conventions and protocols only requested application of criminal policy measures to the supply side of the drug problem, the 1988 convention tightened the system by including more cohesively the demand-side. Article 3(2) requires the signatories to make the possession of any drug for personal consumption a criminal offence under their laws – this 'amounts in fact to a penalization of personal consumption' (United Nations 1998: 80).

Today, the acceptance of the global drug prohibition regime under the aegis of the UN is without a doubt worldwide: currently (October 2010), 184 states were parties to the 1961 and 1988 conventions whereas 183 states are parties to the 1971 convention.[4] Although the present analysis ends with the 1988 agreement, the involvement of the UN in the expansion of international drug control continued with the 1998 UN *General Assembly Special Session on Drugs* which confirmed the organization's commitment to and expansion of its ingrained policies against the 'evil' drugs. Furthermore, with the eve of the 1990s, the EU began to develop its own anti-drug policies with the establishment of successive European action plans and strategies to fight drugs and the creation of the European Monitoring Centre for Drugs and Drug Addiction in Lisbon in 1993 (Boekhaut van Solinge 2002; 2004; Elvins 2003).

However, historically speaking, today's acceptance of global drug prohibition is a rather recent development. Throughout history, individuals have always used drugs to satisfy their desire, to change their state of consciousness. Drugs have been consumed in various societies for hundreds, thousands of years. Drug consumption played an important socio-cultural role (i.e. for medicinal, ritual or recreational purposes) and, as a result, the meaning of drugs has been constantly adjusted (Weil 1986: 1; Bewley-Taylor 1999: 1–2). Hence, society's reactions to the consumption of drugs are in a state of flux – and this allows considering the current view of drugs as illicit and their use as deviant, with efforts to internationally control these substances as one possible reaction among others to the phenomenon.

Yet, if drugs were once an accepted or tolerated part of human life, how did they become prohibited? How did the interpretation of drugs as dangerous, evil, and criminal become dominant and lead to an excess of practices banning drugs to the margins of society? Current writings offer different stories. While some explain the evolvement of an international drug prohibition by outlining the importance of particular individuals in its historical development (Bruun, Lynn and Rexed 1975; McAllister 2000; Briesen 2005), others investigate prohibition from the vantage point of norms and epistemic communities (Nadelmann 1990; Elvins 2003). A further number of authors draw on theories of security cooperation in IR, such as regime-theory (Bewley-Taylor 1999) or consider a mixture of political and economic considerations of external and internal nature as explanatory factors (Levine 2003; Boekhaut van Solinge 2004). All works agree that the United States played a central role in the global stance on the drug problem, as they have been able to spread their interpretation of drugs as illicit and their use as deviant to the rest of the world (Friesendorf 2007). According to the literature, we witness such a strong international political consensus over the illegality of drugs 'that it has become difficult to discuss alternatives or to evaluate current international policy' (Boekhaut van Solinge 2004: 18).

While there is disagreement in the literature on how this consensus has developed and why it prevails, the analysis will show that focusing on the construction of hegemonic orders elucidates the mechanisms behind the consensus in a field where moral and emotional considerations are much more involved than in other areas of international security cooperation. Current literature is rather silent on this point. There is a lack of critical engagement on the question of how the consensus in this field was able to overcome important national and cultural differences in the interpretation of what should be classified as a drug, and which measures are appropriate. Consider only the different meanings associated with alcohol in Muslim countries (forbidden by the Koran), cannabis in Africa (part of cultural recreation) or coca in Latin America (part of indigenous medicine) either disregarded by the dominant definition of illicit drugs or under the restrictions of the regime. To accept this interpretation means to abandon deep traditions and aspects of cultural and/or religious identity and to subscribe to a meaning of drugs that stemmed from a foreign (read Western) understanding. Analyzing the hegemonic strategies of how the consensus on drugs as illicit emerged addresses how countries with a different understanding of drugs came to accept a consensus that contradicts integral parts of their culture and identity and how it persisted for a number of decades (and still does).

To sum up, the 1961 agreement globalized a specific interpretation of drugs (illicit and deviant) and installed it as the only possible one to defend. While the 1961 convention paved the way for a strong international political consensus over the illegality of drugs, making it difficult to discuss alternatives to current international policy, this consensus has been consolidated in a number of treaties, with the 1988 convention 'finalizing' the consolidation and expansion of the global drug prohibition regime. To explain what this consensus is exactly about, how it has been created and how it persists, how the association between drugs and illegality, between drugs and their *ab*use has become an international problem, is the task of the next sections.

Constructing the evil Other – establishing an antagonistic frontier

In chapter two I argued that equivalential articulations outline a common reference point of differential subjects and construct them as equivalent with regard to this point. At the same time, this common reference point implies to overcome the lack that is at the root of the equivalent subjects. Yet, subjects can only eliminate their lack if they project it onto something represented as external. In hegemonic relations, this external is constructed in an act of power as a negated entity, as a threat to the subjects related by equivalential articulations. Therefore, the discursive space is dichotomized and an antagonistic frontier is established. Referring to the construal of the Other, to a common external, we aim to reconstruct productive hegemonic strategy *Establishing an antagonistic frontier* of the basic dimension.

To locate articulations constructing an antagonistic Other in the international discourse on drugs is a rather easy task. Building from the outset on a seldom questioned illegality of drugs, the discourse is abundant of articulations constituting drugs, the internationally organized drug dealers or the individual drug dealer as antagonistic Other. Drugs as the antagonistic Other are the *common* enemy, the global threat. It is necessary to 'abolish that evil', as this implies to eliminate 'a source of danger to the health of the whole world and benefiting all mankind' (United Nations 1964a: 6). Drugs are a 'social evil', they 'had become a scourge of humanity' and are posing a serious threat to 'the political and economic stability of the *international community* as a whole'. Hence, 'to isolate the common enemy' and to fight drugs a 'world alliance of forces was needed' (United Nations 1973b: 20; 1991: 3, 107, emphasis added).

Although not all texts necessarily construct drugs as a common enemy 'through a slavish juxtaposition of Self and Other' (Hansen 2006: 44), drugs are frequently contrasted to the international community. The repeated co-occurrences of the codes of the Other and of a potential collective Self, the international community, forcefully underline this opposition: in 252 documents they co-occurred 1548 times. Drugs are perceived as a contradiction to all goals and interests shared by subjects in favour of an international drug control and, most importantly, they are deemed responsible for the lack the world is experiencing. Their elimination will heal the blockage of the world's identity as a peaceful and safe place for humanity. This construction draws an antagonistic frontier between the subjects aiming at a drug-free world and the Other standing in the way of the realization of this goal. Overall, a sharp and homogeneous picture of the antagonistic drugs Other emerges.

Yet, the characterization of 'drugs' or 'the drug' as antagonistic Other experiences certain shifts, as it is written into a discursive terrain already partially structured through previously articulated interpretations and identities (as the depiction of the historical background has shown). Drugs are evil, illegal and endanger the world in its entirety; they represent a huge financial market and are related to illness and other serious crimes. However, there is 'an inevitable conflict between the need to protect human beings from the evils of narcotic substances and the advantages of their use in the fight against sickness and pain' (United Nations 1964a: 11). To acknowledge the beneficial side of drugs – for instance, how morphine eases pain – refers to the paradoxical nature of drugs and adds shades of grey to the dark and sharply framed picture of the antagonistic Other. Allowing a certain diffuseness to enter this picture implies varying degrees of otherness – and this endangers the homogeneity of the antagonistic Other and, thereby, one element crucial for the establishment of a hegemonic order.

At first glance, the request to exempt *indigenous or traditional use of drugs* from the remit of international drug control seems to contribute some of the grey shades, since it disturbs a homogeneous construction of the antagonistic Other. By denoting indigenous use as 'a traditional, although diminishing, practice in some countries' that should only be allowed 'where there is historical evidence of such use', delegations in particular from South America demanded its exemption which was allowed by the 1961 Single Convention (United Nations 1964a: 179; 1991: 307). However, the antagonistic frontier is upheld by trivializing the use and associating it with an undeveloped, uncultivated and minor, mostly oppressed part of the population (the 'Andean communities'). To link the traditional use with the indigenous people denotes this use as backward practice, which has so far escaped any attempts of modernization. Progressive, modern people are not endangered by this practice, as they have freed themselves from the traditions, culture and rites that obstruct enlightening modernization and economic development. Moreover, the indigenous use of drugs is downgraded *simultaneously* with the 'conviction that the only solution to the problem for the international community was to curb all stages in the illicit process', i.e. with an agreement with the general equivalent (United Nations 1991: 15). Particularly, the simultaneity with which both elements are articulated leads to the identification of productive hegemonic strategy *Simultaneously emphasizing and downgrading the particularity of a subject of chain A*.

In 1988, the areas of grey vanish. The image of drugs as solely bad or dangerous is re-inscribed into the discourse. In particular, references to the 'changing nature of drugs' strengthen this unified construction. It provides for an interpretation of drugs as an enemy adapting its means on the spot, reacting and anticipating the measures from the international community or a single state. While such characterization increases the dangerousness of the drugs Other, it also legitimizes an ongoing and broadened international control of drugs (United Nations 1964a: 42, 60; 1991: 10). As such, these articulations reformulate the antagonistic frontier by re-inscribing it in the discourse, not only to stabilize the border but also to associate new elements with the drugs Other; therefore, they signal supplementary productive hegemonic strategy *Enlarging the antagonized chain of equivalence*, which extends the antagonized chain by adding discursive elements and subjects. In sum, the strategy reinforces the drawing of the antagonistic frontier, a movement encompassed by the basic strategy *Establishing an antagonistic frontier* of productive hegemonic strategies.

Productive hegemonic strategy *Enlarging the antagonized chain of equivalence* also looms behind the call for controlling the 'new danger synthetic drugs' which associated formerly floating elements with the antagonized chain. Although not part of the schedules of substances to be controlled by the 1961 convention, frequent references in the debates are made to the 'real problem of the future': synthetic drugs (see for many references United Nations 1964a: 6, 7, 28, 193). In reaction to this 'new danger', the 1971 *Convention on Psychotropic Substances* explicitly added synthetic drugs to the remit of the emerging international drug regime.

Individualization within the discourse on the Other

Characterization of the antagonistic drugs Other would remain pale without a constant process of individualization within the discourse. Specific individuals, subjects and organizations are recurrently associated with drugs and deemed responsible for the international drug problem. Thereby, the dangerousness of drugs is enormously increased by naming subjects and associations who make their living from the drug trade or are victims of a drug's addictive potential. Moreover, such individualizations generate the necessary suitable 'targets' for a 'war on drugs'. Three types of individuals and organizations are recurrently associated with drugs: first, the internationally operating drug mafia or organization responsible for international drug traffic; second, the internationally operating drug dealer; and, finally, the individual drug dealer, the individual drug cultivator and – although contentious – the drug addict.

Without a doubt, destroying *international drug organizations* is a central target of anti-drug policies. One has to cope with the 'ringleaders of the drug traffic' or 'gangs of traffickers', who are intelligent and powerful 'rings of smugglers, who had vast financial resources and ever more rapid and effective means of telecommunication and transportation' (United Nations 1964a: 15, 121; 1973c: 65). The drug organizations are the profiteers from 'scientific and technological development to devise new drugs and new smuggling techniques' armed with 'advanced weapons' (United Nations 1991: 7, 12). While in the 1960s disagreement arouse on what the term 'drug trafficking' ultimately includes; yet, by demonizing the drug organizations, articulations in 1988 have shaken off the more moderate tone of the earlier years (United Nations 1991: especially 43). Operating illegally, 'carried on through their networks extending to many parts of the world' and via their 'tentacles [which] now infiltrated all regions of the world' (United Nations 1991: 17), these organizations exploit innocent people for monetary gain through their 'diabolical machinations of drug trafficking' without accepting any 'political, ideological or moral boundaries' or 'national borders' (United Nations 1991: 2, 10). As they 'threatened to destroy the very foundations of human society' and induced not only adults 'to commit every possible type of crime' but also involved children, drug traffic 'was held to be an inhuman act' and, therefore, the 'international community stigmatized [it] as a crime against humanity' (United Nations 1991: 2, 39, 171, 207). In 1988, the president of the conference summarizes this stance:

Illicit drug trafficking was not a new phenomenon, but since 1945 it had acquired an international dimension and had begun to affect international economics and politics. Requiring transnational finance and offering high returns, it benefited from the participation of new agents such as banks and corporations and necessitated the creation of illegal machinery for recycling profits, thus involving large sections of the population in its activities. Drug trafficking had a highly structured world of its own – a horrifying one of crime, violence, corrupt deals and moral seduction.

(United Nations 1991: 3)

In this world, the 'international drug barons wielded an immense power', since 'they were the kingpins of the international traffic' (United Nations 1964b: 121). Referring to the 'participation of new agents' in the drug trade shows how these barons no longer only rely on guns for hire and brute force but discover the opportunities of the international financial architecture. On their payroll are now 'individuals who channelled funds derived from the illicit traffic' and white-collar crime becomes associated with drug trafficking (United Nations 1964b: 121; see also United Nations 1991: 13, 84). Again, this is an association of new discursive elements, since prior to the 1980s this type of crime was not contextualized within the overall drug problem, and signals again the supplementary productive hegemonic strategy *Enlarging the antagonized chain of equivalence*. As the barons are 'very rarely brought to justice', a picture of a dark universe is painted in which the wolfish nature of man reigns and only the fittest is able to survive (United Nations 1964b: 121). It is a barbaric universe radically opposed to the enlightened world, a dark universe promoting the greedy nature of man – it is all that the enlightened world considers inhumane and corrupt; it is everything that the enlightened world is not. In view of this danger, it is only the harshest, ultimate instrument civilization has at its disposal, i.e. only a war can preserve civilization from the dangers of drugs and the associated subjects and organizations, from a 'drug holocaust' (United Nations 1991: 9).

Individualization is further pursued with respect to the single *drug dealer*, *drug cultivator* and *drug addict*. Individual drug dealers are 'peddlers' or 'notorious smugglers'. They are the ones who physically transport the illegal substances from one country to the other (for instance, they steal legal drugs from pharmacies and fuel them into the illicit market) and should be subjected to 'severe penalties' (United Nations 1964a: 2, 43). While the individual drug dealer was the central subject associated with the drugs Other in the 1961 debates, the dealer was mentioned less often in 1988, since the focus shifted more towards the international operating drug 'barons'. However, individual dealers are still *persona non grata*, they are 'sophisticated gangsters who operated the drugs traffic' and 'ruthless mercenaries who encouraged the use of drugs for the worst possible purposes' by 'sparing no effort to build up their trade' (United Nations 1991: 22, 48, 27). At worst, dealers – and this also counts for the drug 'barons' – 'paid no attention to country, religion or flag' (United Nations 1991: 28); they are outsiders to the modern world, within which the adherence to religion or country signifies one's allegiance to a specific culture or state of mind and classifies a person. As Tsvetan Todorov once said, knowledge about the Other (regardless whether false or correct) can lead the Self to adopt a more positive stance towards and put a positive value judgement on the Other (Todorov 1992: 185). Those who do not disclose their identity – who do not want to be known – have something to hide, presumably their dark business which runs counter to the values and rules of the civilized world. They hinder the Self to know and judge them, thus, the safest way to deal with such individuals consists in classifying them as antagonistic Others. Accordingly, those who do not reveal their belonging, their roots or refuse to do so are all categorized as antagonistic Others threatening the modern, civilized world.

Though rarely mentioned, the individual drug *cultivators* represent an interesting case, since their make-up shows how hegemonic practices are institutionalized. One should keep in mind that the farmers are actively involved in the production of drugs, ensuring with their work the continuous supply of narcotics worldwide. However, they are portrayed as those who are exploited by traffickers and 'drug barons [. . .] in order to promote the cultivation of illicit crops, thereby hindering social progress' (United Nations 1991: 14). The cultivators of poppy in Afghanistan or of coca in Columbia are the victims, not the beneficiaries, of the drug trade. It is argued, therefore, that they are outside the remit of international drug control. Despite this assurance, we will see below how farmers and their families are still targets of international anti-drug measures, which makes them victims in a double sense.

Without a doubt, the most contentious subject in the discourse of drugs is the *drug addict*. While in 1961 addiction has been considered as a vice of societal outsiders only, 27 years later, delegations construct addiction as a problem that can be encountered at any level of society regardless of profession, education, income, etc. (United Nations 1964a: 110; 1991: 6). Three interpretations of the addict and addiction can be discerned. Whether addiction and the addict are considered, first, as a vice with epidemic quality and as a criminal aiming to spread her habit, second, as a medical, psychological problem and not as a correctional one or, third, as victim of circumstances who should resume a normal life, depends on the stance towards the individual drug addict (see United Nations 1964a: 107, 11, 13; 1991: 6, 17). While the first conceives of the addict as evil as drugs or as drug dealers, according to the latter understandings the drug addict is considered as a non-antagonistic Other.[5]

Overall, constructing drug addicts as criminals is much more frequent than the more moderate interpretations, since it serves to darken the antagonistic Other. Drug addicts need to obtain money to satisfy their vice, spread their 'morbid habit' and most often become – if not already – a drug dealer (United Nations 1964a: 104). Using drugs 'produces anti-social behavior which was threat to the whole community'; thus, addicts are 'both liars and active proselytizers' and ceased to be normal human beings (United Nations 1964a: 60; 1973d: 183). They are 'psychopaths' who experience a deterioration and destruction of their character, mind and body, who 'doomed their family to poverty and ignorance' (United Nations 1964a: 107). Most dangerously, they undermine the fundaments of society by, for example, spreading not only their habit but also illnesses such as aids (United Nations 1991: 3, 9, 11). Accordingly, only treatment in closed institutions can guarantee their re-entry into society and re-activate their role as a useful member (United Nations 1964a: 107). A longer quote from the 1961 debates illustrates exemplarily the construction of the drug addict as an antagonistic Other:

> There were many specialists on the subject in the United States and they had learned from experience that those ends could be achieved only if drug addicts were confined in surroundings where they were progressively deprived of their drugs – in other words, in a closed institution. There was nothing punitive about a method of treatment which consisted in reducing the addict's opportunities for obtaining drugs. The isolation of susceptible persons from pathogenic agents was one of the most time-honoured practices in public health. Drug addiction was contagious in the sense that the addict tended to convert others to his morbid habit, and it was therefore essential in his case to use the recognised public health method of quarantine. Treatment in liberty had failed wherever it had been tried [. . .].
>
> (United Nations 1964a: 103)

This image of drug addicts is completed by frequent references to migrants, linking these with addicts, since the latter are mostly described as foreign immigrants to a country (United Nations 1964a: 104). Of course, these linkages are reminiscent of those at the turn of the twentieth century, when Chinese and Mexican immigrants in the United States were associated with opium and marijuana and were accused of becoming violent and sexually aggressive.

Still, not all articulations subscribe fully to the picture of the antagonistic drug addict. Articulations depict the addict as a sick person in 'need of medical care' (United Nations 1964a: 106; 1991: 12) and as a 'victim' of her own circumstances with a right to rehabilitation (United Nations 1964a: 105; 1973d: 17; 1973b: 53; 1991: 9, 12–3). While rehabilitation will make her a 'useful citizen' again and let her 'resume a normal life', she does not necessarily need to receive therapy in a closed institution. In this respect, opinions vary on the methods of treatment to be used (United Nations 1964a: 104, 6, 7, 8). These articulations portray the addict as a sort of fallen member of society who is, despite her faults and sins, still welcome in the community of those who obeyed the rules of society by not consuming drugs. The addict has not been able to lead the decent life she would have normally led for a number of reasons. Exactly this kind of differential articulations attempt to weaken the antagonistic frontier. If the drug addict is initially a member of a society that aims to become a drug-free society, the addict cannot be part of the antagonistic Other threatening the international community. If the drug addict is part of the Self at the international level, she needs to be rescued and re-constituted as a non-antagonistic Other.

In this interpretation, addiction is the vice, the culprit while the person that is addicted to drugs can be separated from it. Isolate the person from addiction and you get back the individual that can return to society. Addiction is the '"parasite" (or demonic possession) that desperately wants to stay in the body and damage its "host"' (Driscoll 2000: 14). However, addiction to drugs does not come without a cost for the addict. Addiction is comprehended as a 'disease of will' since 'an addict who had given up his morbid habit might easily resume it', which means that the individual is responsible for her disease because she does not sufficiently struggle to resist the 'overpowering desire to continue using drugs' (United Nations 1964a: 104–5; 1991: 12). This strong moral component leaves the addict in a double bind: she is 'responsible for a condition which was somehow also the proper province of medical intervention [. . .] but failure to achieve cure was a failure of personal responsibility, not medical science' (Berridge and Edwards 1981: 155–6). Such conceptualizations attempt to deteriorate the antagonistic frontier, operations which are addressed by counter-hegemonic strategy *Weakening of the antagonistic frontier* of the basic dimension. Figure 3.1. illustrates this movement in the discursive space.

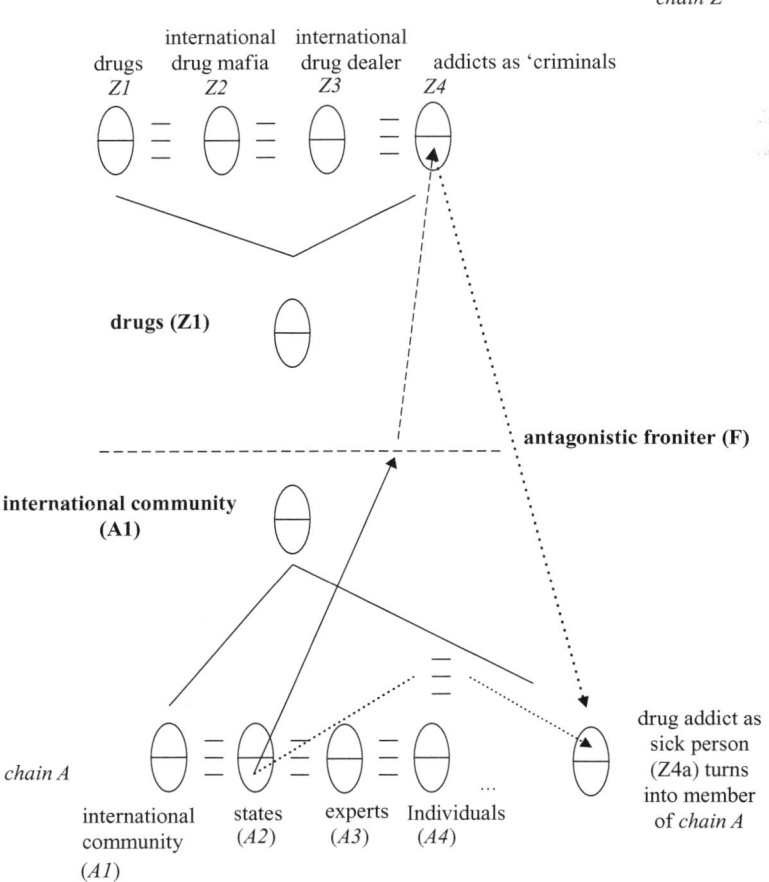

Figure 3.1 Counter-hegemonic strategies in the international discourse on drugs

The arrow from *A2* (for the moment this could be any subject) towards the antagonistic frontier indicates the movement of counter-hegemonic strategy *Weakening of the antagonistic frontier*, which produces a differentiation between the addict and the remainder of the antagonized chain of equivalence (*chain Z*) – signalled by the dashed arrow. The attempt to integrate the drug addict – interpreted as a sick person (therefore *Z4a*) – into the antagonizing chain (*chain A*) is denoted by the fine dotted arrows.

Still, drug addiction rarely happens unexpectedly. The attempts to construct the drug addict as non-antagonistic Other are embedded in the discussion of the *underlying causes* of not only addiction but of the entire drug problem. These articulations need to be considered as a further challenge and weakening of the antagonistic frontier, since they are criticizing and differentiating the picture of the antagonistic Other, and thereby challenge its homogenous construction. In 1961, economic, cultural or social conditions were thought to be responsible for drug addiction and trade: for example, when delegates hoped 'that after the Single Convention had been approved, the *international community* would turn its attention to removing the social conditions which were the fundamental cause of the narcotics problem' (United Nations 1964a: 13, emphasis added). This changed until 1988, when the 'decay in spiritual values' was made responsible for the world's drug problem and the latter 'phenomenon revealed a crisis of civilization and showed the need for improvement of the moral condition of society in general' (United Nations 1991: 9, 11). The demand to 'take the underlying causes of the drug problem into account' underscores the particularity of a subject of the antagonized chain of equivalence.[6]

However, references to the underlying causes are ambiguous and cannot be clearly considered as counter-hegemonic strategy. This can best be illustrated with regard to the question on the 'sources of the drug traffic'. In the course of the debates, delegations accused each other of involvement in drug traffic. During the 1961 discussions, such accusations were directly raised either by explicitly naming various countries and reproaching them as being not active enough in the fight against drugs or by pointing towards specific regions as lagging behind the actual standard of drug control (United Nations 1964a: 14, 21, 42, 56, 8, 106). In the ensuing years, the divide was almost always drawn between drug producing and manufacturing/consuming countries and coinciding roughly with the divide between 'developed' and 'developing' countries when, for example, Peru, Bolivia or Nigeria emphasized 'that the root of the problem lay with the consumers rather than the production' (United Nations 1973b: 12; 1973d: 45; 1991: 3, 5, 12, 26, 47, 297).

These articulations attempt to disassociate subjects that are integrated in the antagonizing chain and, by accusing them of being the source of drugs, try to associate them with the drugs Other. In this respect, it seems counter-intuitive to consider the accusation as a productive hegemonic strategy. Still, to accuse other countries of being a source of drug traffic rearticulates forcefully the precise location of the antagonistic frontier separating the chain of subjects prepared to fight drugs from those subjects that spread drugs for their profit. Whoever can be linked in any way to drugs – through insufficient control and fight against consumption and trade – is suspected to be at minimum no longer actively engaged in international drug control and at maximum to 'collaborate' with the Other. In consequence, countries wishing to get rid of this suspicion either articulate their 'genuine' interest in the control of drugs and unambiguous support of the ultimate and common goals by pointing out their abhorrence of the common enemy. Or they refuse the reproaches and at the same time praise themselves for their efforts in drug control (the latter argumentation was much more prominent in 1988) (United Nations 1964a: 16, 41, 55–6, 182; 1991: 301–2). Again, the frontier is rearticulated, partially fixed at its former place and thus strengthens the hegemonic order. Since the accused subjects struggle to deliver 'true' proof of their subordination to the ultimate and common goals, the coherence of the chain is reinforced. Both movements are clearly the aim of the supplementary productive hegemonic strategy *Crossing the antagonistic frontier in order to strengthen chain A.*

Yet, it should be noted that speaking of the weakening of an antagonistic frontier does not imply to *eliminate* it. Rather, these demands attempt to weaken the frontier in their actual outlook, i.e. at the divide where the current hegemonic order constituted it. They try to move the frontier to the margins of the discursive space, since this allows including parts of society that have been excluded by the current frontier. Furthermore, the identified Others are intimately interwoven and intermingled: the international drug mafia is led by the internationally operating drug baron who depends on the individual drug dealer who, in turn, supplies the individual drug addict or is herself a dealer-consumer. Exactly this manner of constructing intimate links between the various subjects of the drugs Other that threaten an international community and its objective of creating a drug-free world illustrates that an antagonized chain of equivalence (*chain Z*) has been constituted. This splits the discursive field into those that fight drugs and those that consume, deal, trade and profit from them (whether in monetary or physical terms). Hence, despite the identification of varying degrees of otherness – best example the contentious meaning of the drug addict – we can conclude that a homogeneous antagonistic drugs Other has been reconstructed. The retraced counter-hegemonic strategies are neither strong nor frequent enough to differentiate the unified picture of the antagonistic Other in the discourse on drugs.

Constructing the 'good' Self – International community vs. drugs as Other

'The something that underlies us all' – universalizing subjects

'If there were no drug addiction, narcotics control would not be necessary, illicit traffic would not exist and there would scarcely be any reason for the historic Conference' (United Nations 1964a: 103). There can be only one goal to eliminate the world's lack: to free humankind from its 'bondage to narcotics' (United Nations 1964a: 6). Facing the threat, 'the international community was ready to reach an agreement for the purpose of dealing with a scourge that was now affecting humanity at large' (United Nations 1991: 11). Humanity and the international community are constructed as suffering from drugs and their effects, and as long as narcotics are abused the world will not be a peaceful and healthy place for humankind. Clearly, here looms the above-mentioned interpretation of drugs as illicit and their use as deviant and in the 1971 and 1988 debates this lack is rearticulated. None could 'remain indifferent to the dangers threatening the international community' or ignore 'the seriousness of the threat posed by narcotics traffickers to the political and economic stability of the international community as a whole'. In consequence, it is necessary to 'create a society free from drug abuse and [. . .] illicit traffic' (United Nations 1973b: 8; 1991: 5, 107).

The articulation of this lack is embedded in a range of demands aimed at healing the lack through the realization of a drug-free world. Two types of highly interwoven demands can be distinguished: those that pertain to a *common and ultimate goal* or to *common interests* and demands that request specific *means* to realize these goals or interests. These demands can be conceived of as *equivalential articulations*, i.e. as articulations that universalize differential subjects to form a chain of equivalence – precisely this operation is encompassed by the basic productive hegemonic strategy *Universalization* of subjects.

According to the first type of demands, the lack can be surmounted only if the international community aims at prohibiting and ultimately at abolishing drugs. A prohibition would imply 'in fact eliminating a source of danger to the health of the whole world and benefiting all mankind', which ultimately leads to – as already quoted above –the freedom of humanity from its 'bondage of narcotics' (United Nations 1964a: 6). This ultimate goal of a *drug-free world* is combined with the more 'middle-ranged' common goals of an *international drug control* and a *convention* that 'had to be universally acceptable' and 'applicable' in order to become 'an effective instrument serving the interests of the entire world' (United Nations 1964a: 6, 4, 11). 'The principle of universality was essential to the Convention since drug addiction could not [be] contained by national boundaries' and 'universality has always been the goal of narcotics control' (United Nations 1964a: 12, 158). The importance of a universally acceptable convention as a common goal is forcefully underscored by the frequency of its appearance: it occurred 295 times in 252 documents.[7] If universality seems to be too hard a goal, 'the number of countries acceding to the Single Conventions should be as close as possible to the *ideal of universality*, which was essential to satisfactory international action' (United Nations 1964a: 5, emphasis added). Especially since only a universally accepted convention can ensure the creation of a global drug free society.

The common goal of a convention with universal acceptance is voiced throughout the 1970s and 1980s as the ultimate goal of making 'the world a safe and healthy place for future generations' (United Nations 1991: 43). The ideal of a drug-free world and an international community that was able to overcome the drug problem is constantly re-inscribed into the discourse. Yet, in particular the 1988 debates add an apodictic tone of urgency to the emotional atmosphere of moral abhorrence in the 1960s exacerbating the frontiers drawn in the discourse. '[T]he recent dramatic growth in the illicit traffic in narcotic drugs called for concerted action by the international community' and the convention is an 'instrument capable of eliminating the curse of drug trafficking once and for all' since humanity needs to be freed 'from the *drug holocaust* threatening it' (United Nations 1991: 5, 27, 9 emphasis added). The undisputed necessity of an international drug control allows considering it as the *general equivalent* that all subjects present in the discourse are meant to share; it is 'the something that underlies them all'.[8] The overall frequency of 1196 hits support this conclusion, particularly the high co-occurrence of the codes of the international community with the international drug control (957 hits).[9]

Demands voicing ultimate and common goals are substantiated by referring to a common interest or the interest of mankind and/or the international community. In 1961, a universally acceptable convention can only be drafted 'if the interests of all countries were respected' (United Nations 1964a: 12). The interests of each country have to be either disregarded or adjusted to the common interest in the interest of humankind. For the sake of international drug control '[e]ach State should be prepared to surrender a part of its sovereignty' and '[p]olitical and economic considerations should be set aside in favor of the interests of public health and morality; otherwise the Conference might fail to achieve its fundamental purposes' (United Nations 1964a: 45, 56). Hence, the common interest is intimately linked with the general equivalent, as the latter consists of establishing this very control.

National interests are interpreted as in line with the ultimate goal and common interest when representatives assure that the convention is not only in the interest of a particular country but 'a contribution to the health and welfare of mankind' (United Nations 1964a: 10). The same happens when representatives invoke that 'no country could say that it was wholly safe from [drugs]' (United Nations 1973b: 15), and, therefore, no alternative to international drug control exists. And to assert that 'progress in the control of narcotic drugs would only be made if the international and humanitarian aspects of the problem were given precedence over national interests' explicitly places 'the interests of mankind as whole above all national and private interests' essential to achieve the ultimate goal and to eliminate the lack the world is haunted by (United Nations 1964a: 10–3).

When states declared that 'the only solution to the problem was for the entire international community to curb all stages in the illicit process, from production to consumption' and that 'the aim of the Convention was to provide the international community with a new global instrument, sufficiently rigorous to reach drug traffickers wherever they were', it becomes obvious that the common interest is still linked to the general equivalent – international drug control – in the 1980s (United Nations 1991: 15, 26). However, in 1988 statements become more and more explicit – just as references to common and ultimate goals experience a shift towards extreme formulations (like the 'drug holocaust'). For instance, the 'competing claims of what were perceived *not always correctly*, as the best interests of individual States, regions or groups of countries' should be set aside and delegations 'be wary of over-emphasizing individual interests and keep their sights fixed on the overriding aim' (United Nations 1991: 2, emphasis added).

Of course, parts of the convention 'might impinge upon certain aspects of sovereignty, but in light of the growing danger to all societies from the drugs abuse, they could, on the contrary, be shown to reinforce sovereignty in its most fundamental sense' (United Nations 1991: 2). The individual interest – to keep sovereignty untouched – can be better accomplished by ceding sovereignty in the first place, but by empowering the states to pursue drugs on the basis of a strong convention, sovereignty is reinforced by the convention. Particular interests need to be considered from the standpoint of the international community's common interest. Such a perspective culminates in the assertion that 'the new convention [. . .] was in full conformity with the needs and interests of all countries and peoples of the world' (United Nations 1991: 11). The particular interests of states were acknowledged as a valid, though avoidable, objection to a common interest or the interest of mankind in the 1960s but their validity is doubted at the end of the 1980s.

The skeleton of ultimate and common goals and interest is embedded in demands articulating specific means to achieve these goals and interests. One main instrument can be identified: cooperation. It is frequently invoked, i.e. in 252 documents, 381 segments are assigned to the codes of cooperation. 'Without the international co-operation' initiated by the 1961 convention, 'the situation would have been catastrophic' (United Nations 1973b: 1). Hence, cooperation plays a central role and exhibits intimate links to the general equivalent, the ultimate goal and the common interests, since 'where co-operation and humanitarian aims were primary considerations, political considerations should be forgotten' (United Nations 1964a: 160). '[T]he Community wished to appeal for wider and strengthened cooperation' as 'the recent dramatic growth in the illicit traffic in narcotic drugs called for concerted action by the *international community*' (United Nations 1991: 8, 5, emphasis added).

Throughout the years, cooperation is considered as the *only* means to effectively fight and control drugs. It stands in implicit and explicit relationship with the international community and the ultimate goal, for example, when it is stated that 'whole mankind' is threatened by drugs or delegations cooperate to improve 'the lot of humanity'. Moreover, delegations consider effective cooperation as necessary to spur a *consensus* against narcotic abuse and vice versa. When it is claimed that 'all countries were aware of the evils of that traffic, which was spreading throughout the international community, he [the representative] felt sure that a clear *consensus* would emerge' and 'if the struggle against the illicit drug traffic was to continue, it was essential to show mutual understanding', this consensus is the product of a growing awareness of the drug problem (United Nations 1964a: 7; 1991: 9, emphasis added). Yet, how should international cooperation be realized in the fight against drugs and exactly how should states cooperate? On the one hand, the coordination of cooperation should be carried out by the United Nations system, with its different bodies dealing with drug control. On the other hand, states agree to restrict the supply side through control of cultivation, eradication, and trade or through cooperation of enforcement agencies, for instance, in the issue of extradition, confiscation of proceeds derived from drug related offences or money laundering (United Nations 1964a: 14, 29, 122–8; 1991: 1–2, 10). Hence, cooperation is considered essential to establish a consensus over the common drug problem, which, in turn, paves the way to realize the common and ultimate goals.

The reconstruction of ultimate and common goals and interests and cooperation as a means to realize both brings us to question what kinds of subjects are constructed in the discourse. Two types can be distinguished: first, nation-states, and, second, individuals endowed with special competence relevant to the matter in question. First, states construct themselves for example as 'producer', 'manufacturing', 'transit' or 'consumer' countries or construct other states as developing and developed countries (United Nations 1964a: 2; 1991: 6). They are characterized by invoking their position towards international drug control. For example, when the US claim that 'for more than half a century, the United States had been advocating the international control of narcotic drugs' or Sri Lanka considers its drugs laws as 'among the most stringent in the world', states construe themselves as longstanding promoters of international drug control (United Nations 1964a: 6; 1991: 233). Indeed, by referring to their long experience in dealing with drugs, states try to present themselves as having both authoritative knowledge about the drug problem ('for more than half a century') and the authority to decide how to respond to the problem ('international control' and 'most stringent' drug laws).

Most importantly, we can trace that states identify with the signifier of the international community. For instance, when states refer to their 'conviction that the only solution to the problem was for the entire international community to curb all stages of the illicit process [. . .] on the basis of shared responsibility and equal participation by all' they consider the international community as central addressee for the international handling of drugs (United Nations 1991: 15). Moreover, 'as a member of the international community' each state is reminded of its 'duties and obligations' towards the community (United Nations 1991: 13). Thereby, the lack of each state is paralleled with the lack of the community, of humanity, of the world: states can only be safe when drugs are eliminated, and as drugs are an international problem, a globe free of drugs turns each state into a drug-free territory as well. In how far the acts of identification with the signifier of the international community are of particular importance is discussed with regard to the moment of representation below.

Next to states, a number of individuals endowed with special competence – special in the sense of the respective discourse – can be identified and represent the second type of subjects. These encompass mainly any kind of expert in drug matters, such as scientists, doctors, pharmacists, bureaucrats of the respective ministries or individuals from the enforcement agencies and officials from diverse international organizations (UN, World Health Organization, Interpol or International Labour Organization officials). Experts are most often mentioned to strengthen an argument invoking scientific results. The results are presented as objective facts, which are non-debatable because their validity has been ensured by internationally respected standards of science. Making use of their expertise, for example, to classify drug addicts as criminals, since their scientific results have shown that a criminal disposition is endemic to addicts, brings about a specific vision on how to perceive of and deal with the drug problem. Only those experts have access to the debates that support international drug control and do not advocate alternative meanings such as decriminalization policies or controlled consumption. Such alternative expertise is referred to as non-acceptable and non-valid or, worse, non-scientific (United Nations 1964a: 18, 92; 1973b: 46; 1991: 10).

It is worth stressing that all subjects described so far acknowledge the 'righteousness' of the ultimate and common goals and interests, as well as cooperation as means to internationally control drugs (the general equivalent). Most importantly, this acknowledgement can be understood as acts of identification with a common enterprise spelt out by theses goals, interests and means. Overall, a dense web of equivalential articulations is revealed emphasizing what all participants in the discourse on drugs share and constructing the 'righteousness' of these aims. The main effect consists in the universalization of differential subjects, which allows reconstructing productive hegemonic strategy *Universalization* of subjects. Goals, interests and cooperation highlight what all subjects have in common, what they all share: the consensus to control drugs internationally. An equivalential bond is construed between those subjects that constitute themselves as in favour of the control and aiming at the ultimate goal of a drug-free world. Ultimately, a chain of equivalence (*chain A*) has been established confronting the antagonistic drugs Other (*chain Z*).

Representing the Self – constructing the international community as tendentially empty signifier

Reconstructing the last productive hegemonic strategy of the basic dimension *Representation* allows us not only to conclude whether a hegemonic order at the international level has been constituted in the field of drugs. With regard to the discourse on international drug prohibition, it also permits to fully satisfy the book's central argument: hegemonic regimes on the one hand aim at a homogenous, clear-cut interpretation of the antagonistic Other and on the other hand they successfully attempt to construct an unambiguous vision of the Self shared among subjects jointly opposing the Other. This vision is based on a political consensus between these subjects and therefore allows for enacting internationally accepted measures countering the Other.

Before analyzing the representation by the Self and its connection to the consensus on an international drug control (the general equivalent), let me briefly recapitulate what representation is about. As each subject of a chain of equivalence is marked by a lack, which the ultimate and common goals strive to fill, they project their lack onto something external, i.e. the antagonistic Other. In this moment – if a hegemonic operation is successful – one signifier is able to represent the chain in its entirety. Qualifying this movement as the 'core' of a hegemonic operation bespeaks of a culmination: one specific signifier now becomes the point of crystallization of a number of differential meanings, articulations and practices. It acts as a 'stand-in' for all those various meanings – and for the absent fullness of the entire chain. Yet, this task can only be accomplished by a signifier already part of the chain and emptied from its particular content. Of course, empty means *tendentially empty*, as signifiers always dispose of a remainder, of a particular content. Hence, to reconstruct productive hegemonic strategy *Representation* a tendentially empty signifier has to be located which represents the chain of equivalences between those subjects in favour of an international drug prohibition and those spreading drugs for profit.

The best way to approach the identification of a tendentially empty signifier consists of, first, identifying *nodal points* in the discourse and, second, applying the two theoretical conditions of *availability* and *credibility*. As any discourse is construed as an attempt to hegemonize the field of discursivity, to establish a 'centre', these discursively constructed 'centres' consist of nodal points (or in the Lacanian vocabulary a *point the capiton*).[10] It is the point of a partial fixation of meaning and the site of a particular discursive concentration. It creates and sustains the identity of a discourse by constructing a knot of definite meanings, i.e. it attempts to 'close' the discursive system. According to Žižek (2002: 95) 'the point de capiton is rather the word which, as a word, on the level of the signifier itself, unifies a given field, constitutes its identity'. Nodal points like 'God', 'Nation' or 'Party' are not characterized by a supreme density of meaning, but by a certain emptying of their contents. Exactly this feature facilitates their structural role of unifying a discursive terrain.

The allusion to 'a certain emptying of their contents' already indicates the intimate connection of nodal points and tendentially empty signifiers: a nodal point is at the same time an empty signifier and vice versa. Both create and enable the identity of discourses because they partially fix meaning. Why then two concepts? It is necessary to keep them distinct for theoretical and analytical clarity because nodal points refer to the articulating function, whereas the empty signifier addresses the universal signification (Laclau 2004: 322). More bluntly stated, nodal points relate to the form of a discourse, as they are the product of the practice of articulation, while the empty signifier encompasses the quality of representation. To 'hegemonize' content would therefore amount to fixing its meaning around a nodal point. Moreover, in the empirical analysis it is not sufficient to identify a nodal point in order to locate a tendentially empty signifier at the same time. In the analysis, the identification of a nodal point facilitates the location of an empty signifier; however, neither it explains why this specific signifier came to signify the whole chain nor does it investigate the 'emptiness' of the empty signifier. This needs to be done by an empirical analysis, carefully separating but equally identifying these two concepts in the discourses. Now, how does one proceed to locate nodal points? Practically, a nodal point is 'likely to be apparent in a series of similar terms rather than the recurrent use of a single term' (Reyes 2005: 242). Thus, when searching for a nodal point, one should look for signs of over-wording, i.e. a proliferation of words having a presumably similar meaning that is extended across a wide range of policy fields (Fairclough 2000: 163).

In principle, nodal points can be identified via the sheer frequency of their appearance. This may seem at odds with a poststructuralist approach (to 'count' words or formulations), but if a nodal point – indeed, to be such a point! – should be a site of discursive concentration and structuration it is definitively necessary to encounter it frequently in a discourse. Still, it is important to keep the interconnectedness of the nodal point in sight, since a large number of co-occurrences of a potential point with the rest of the codes hints equally at its quality as a site of discursive concentration. At the end of the coding process, the term(s) or formulation(s) with the highest score *and* the highest number of co-occurrences counted as nodal point(s). Additionally, I paid attention to newly occurring terms and notions in order to draw conclusions about former elements in the discursive field. They are especially relevant tracing potential changes in the discourse, since they show the kinds of signifiers available at a given moment in time and demonstrate the creativity of the political forces involved in the articulatory practices (Howarth and Stavrakakis 2000: 21, footnote 35). The practical identification of nodal points serves to locate the signifier before speaking of a tendentially empty signifier. In this regard, frequencies and number of co-occurrences of a potential point with the remainder of the codes serve as the basis to draw conclusions on the content of the signifier and hint at its quality as a site of discursive concentration.

After the coding process, three formulations/words surfaced as potential nodal points in the discourse on drugs: international community, international drug control and drugs.[11] Table 3.1. displays their frequency in the discourse.

On the one hand, the high score of 'drugs' can be explained with reference to the topic of the discourse, since the debates centred on the fight against drugs. On the other hand – and more importantly – 'drugs' represent a nodal point, as they are the *antagonistic drugs Other* that has to be fought. The high score of 2904 hits is underlined by the co-occurrences of 'drugs' with the remainder of the codes: in 252 documents, 'drugs' have been 3649 times in direct neighbourhood with all other codes (overall 313 codes) in the discourse. This result underlines what has been said on the basic productive hegemonic strategies *Universalization* and *Establishment of an antagonistic frontier* in the discourse on drugs. Next, we need to consider the nodal point that potentially signals and represents the tendentially empty signifier of the antagonizing chain of equivalence. 'International drug control' has already been identified as the general equivalent. While this conclusion does not rule out its function as a nodal point, the question remains who should be responsible for the control. Potentially, the 'international community' appears to be the bearer of this control; still, the decision whether the community represents, first, the agent responsible for the control (which would already hint at its function as the tendentially empty signifier) and, second, a nodal point needs to be supported by its co-occurrences with the remainder of the codes and the ones of 'international drug control'. With all 313 codes, 'international community' co-occurred 4330 times and has been 957 times in direct neighbourhood with 'international drug control'.

Table 3.1 Frequency of potential nodal points in the international discourse on drugs

Terms	Hits
International community	902
International drug control	1196
Drugs	2904

Table 3.2 Co-occurrences of 'international community' in the international discourse on drugs

Co-occurrence with	Hits
All codes	4330
Other codes	1548
International drug control	957

Particularly important are the co-occurrences of 'international community' with codes signalling the drugs Other (for instance, codes describing the internationally operating drug dealer or the structure of international 'drug rings'): it appeared in intimate connection with codes referring to the Other, overall 1548 times. These results confirm a recurrent juxtaposition of Other- and Self-descriptions.

However, what do these numbers explain? First, they allow concluding that 'drugs' function as a site of discursive concentration and can be considered as the nodal point structuring the chain of equivalence of the Other (*chain Z*). The same applies to the signifier 'international community', which represents a second nodal point in the international discourse on drugs (and being the tendentially empty signifier heading *chain A*). Furthermore, the frequencies indicate that the discourse on drugs is structured by a Self embodied by the international community and an Other embodied by drugs that are both highly interconnected within the entire discourse. Although I consider the numbers to touch the surface of the discourse only, they support the theoretical conceptualization of identity being based on difference.

Essential in this respect is to question in how far the international community satisfies the qualities of a tendentially empty signifier. Considering the two theoretical conditions outlined above (availability and credibility), the question of discursive *availability* of the international community is the easiest to answer. When delegates praise the community for having instituted a system of international narcotics control 'already much more effective than that of the League of Nations', it was not only present from the very beginning of the debates in 1961 but also entered the debates as a known reference point (United Nations 1964a: 12). In 1988, it was a matter of course to mention the community as the agent responsible for international drug control (see among many United Nations 1991: 6).

The condition of *credibility* needs to be investigated with regard to two points: first, how the above-described subjects (especially states) identify with the signifier of the international community. Second, one needs to scrutinize how the international community is related to the general equivalent, i.e. the international drug control. With regard to the first point, the international community is 'alarmed' and 'conscious of the increasing dangers posed by the illicit traffic' and 'the world community's determination to combat drug-related crimes with the utmost vigour' is a 'historic task' which 'marked a turning point in the struggle by the international community against crime in general and illicit traffic in narcotic drugs and psychotropic substances in particular' (United Nations 1991: 13, 7, 203, 7, 39). Since drugs are a 'risk to the community', they affect 'humanity at large' and have 'devastating effects [. . .] on the lives of working people throughout the world', it is the duty of the international community to safeguard 'the integrity of the world's societies' and preserve 'the cultural and ethical values dear to all delegations present' (United Nations 1964a: 16; 1973b: 87; 1991: 11, 3, 2). Living up to its task, the international community reminds each state of its 'duties and obligations [. . .] as a member of the international community' and considers them 'under a moral obligation to make the Convention an effective instrument serving the interests of the entire world' (United Nations 1964a: 6; 1991: 7). These quotes invoke a close relation of the international community to humanity, presenting the former as the safeguard of the latter, exclusively engaged to the protection and well-being of humankind. Numerous references of this kind indicate the various acts of identification of the Member States with the signifier of the international community. The international community qualifies as the point of culmination – the genius loci – representing those subjects united in their desire to fight drugs and in their need to be protected from this global problem, since states cannot cope with drugs unilaterally. While this characterization of the international community is present from the 1960s on, the explicit references to the community are much more frequent in the 1971, 1972 and 1988 negotiations. In 1961, the allusion to the community can be successfully inferred from its link to humanity and its synonyms.

Second, the credibility of the international community as a potential tendentially empty signifier needs to be analyzed with respect to the general equivalent of international drug control. The quotes cited so far have shown that the international community is considered the ideal place for this control, as the drug problem is an international one and not only threatens specific countries but humanity at large. Furthermore, international drug control needs universal support and acceptance to be effective, since the ultimate goal of a drug-free society can only be accomplished at an international level.[12]

As such, the international community symbolizes a perfect – though absent – community within which humankind can live a peaceful and healthy life free of drugs: without drugs, traffickers who are only interested in their economic profit regardless of the damaging effects of drugs on other human beings would not exist; without drugs, no one would require therapy in a closed institution; without drugs, small farmers in developing countries could not be exploited and condemned to live in poverty. By eliminating drugs, the world could overcome the lowly spheres of addiction and human greed. Indeed, a perfect community could materialize as the realization of ultimate and common goals and interests. A community that incorporates the values dear to all countries and, in that way, does justice to the individual and humanity at the same time. Of course, a perfect drug-free community still does not exist but as the international community *symbolizes* such a perfect society, the former brings the latter into the discourse and thus represents a particularity that cannot be represented: the absent but imaginary fullness of the discourse. And as the imaginary fullness can never be achieved (as no discourse can ever be entirely fixed), the international community incarnates it. It represents the incorporation of all goals and interests and embraces all subjects in favour of international drug control, since the international community has been nearly emptied from its particular content. It is, for instance, much more than being only a community of states, the community stands for humanity at large.

Being explicitly juxtaposed to the common drugs Other and the corresponding chain of equivalence Z increases the credibility of the international community as tendentially empty signifier. In an already sedimented terrain permeated by relations of power, the international community ensures its credibility of representing successfully the entire *chain A* by being the only signifier that is coherently and constantly juxtaposed to the common Other.

Summarizing what has been said, the international community comes to represent the tendentially empty signifier in the discourse on drugs, i.e. represents a chain of subjects engaged in the international drug control to create a drug-free society. This allows, furthermore, concluding that the basic productive hegemonic strategy *Representation* has been identified in the international discourse on drugs; thus, the essential moment to indicate the success of the hegemonic project of international drug control is present. It equally bespeaks of the project's success that it has been able to recruit a large number of different subjects (see the number of parties to the treaties) and establish a consensus on the necessity of internationally controlling and fighting drugs. In light of a great number of clearly identified productive hegemonic strategies, the central finding of chapter three states that a hegemonic order denoting drugs as illicit and their use as deviant was established as early as the 1960s and has been continuously re-inscribed over the following years. The hegemonic order is based on a consensus, which stipulates international control and fight against drugs and considers drugs as antagonistic Other. The Self aims at a peaceful world free from drugs and the elimination of everything in the way to achieve this vision. And it is the international community that represents this Self, unifying the subjects in favour of an international drug prohibition. Figure 3.2. visualizes the construction of the hegemonic order in the discourse on drugs.

The international community and the states, experts and further individuals represent the differential subjects, which are articulated in a chain of equivalence (*chain A*). The international community represents the tendentially empty signifier, and the antagonistic frontier F is drawn between the international community and the antagonistic drugs Other. The antagonistic force $Z1$, drugs, and the international drug mafia ($Z2$), internationally operating drug dealer ($Z3$), the individual dealer and the addict as a criminal ($Z4$) stand for the subjects of the antagonized force and form the antagonized chain of equivalence (*chain Z*). While not reconstructed in detail, drugs as $Z1$ are meant to take over the same task as the international community and represent the antagonized chain. Of course, the arrangement of the antagonized *chain Z* is reconstructed from one position of the discourse, namely, from the position of the subjects of *chain A*.

Opponents of the consensus on how to fight drugs

Despite having reconstructed a clear-cut constitution of antagonistic drugs Other, an unambiguously shared vision of a drug-free world and a consensus on the necessity of international drug control, there are voices of dissent related to the inner

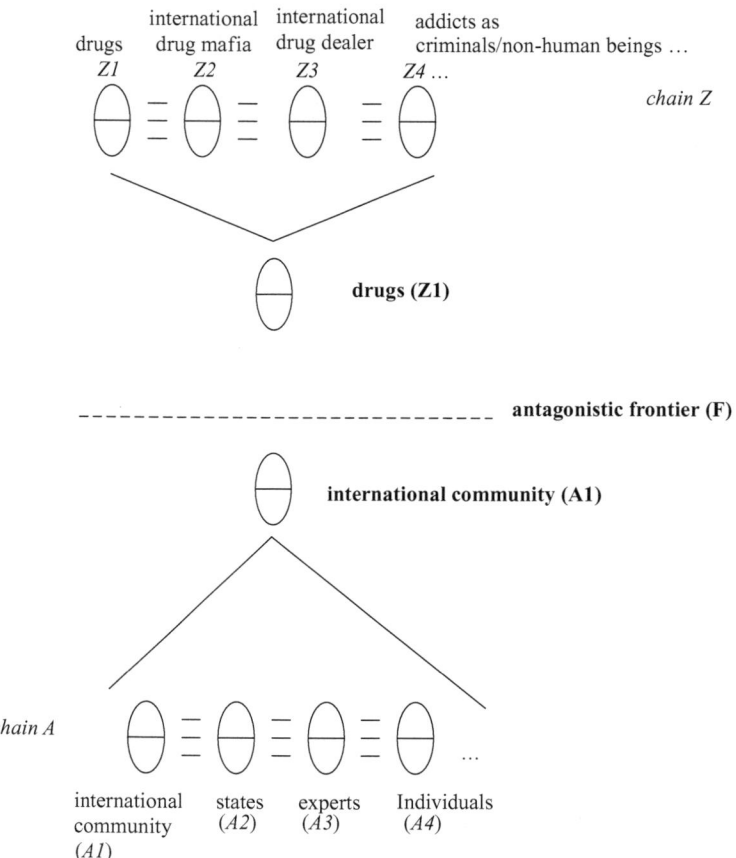

international international   addicts as
drugs   drug mafia   drug dealer   criminals/non-human beings …
Z1   Z2   Z3   Z4 …

chain Z

drugs (Z1)

-   antagonistic frontier (F)

international community (A1)

chain A

international   states   experts   Individuals
community   (A2)   (A3)   (A4)
(A1)

Figure 3.2 The construction of hegemonic order in the international discourse on drugs

mechanisms of the collective Self. They need to be addressed, since, in chapter two, the study voiced the aim to investigate whether internal differences (referred to as heterogeneity) are discernable *within* a hegemonic order at the international level. The current section attempts to reconstruct to what extent heterogeneity unfolds, what strategies are linked to it and in how far the differential remainder is conducive to or detrimental for the construction of a hegemonic order at the international level in the discourse on drugs.

To articulate dissent and conflict between subjects, to request the recognition of particularities and specific national ways (*Sonderwege*), to deny the importance of the general equivalent or reject the ultimate goal – such differential articulations refer to internal differences of the kind embraced by heterogeneity. Raising differences such as doubts of the 'genuine' engagement of other countries in international drug control, accusations of hypocrisy or pointing to differences between 'developing' and 'developed' countries in their ability to participate in international control create *dissent* and *conflict* between subjects (United Nations 1964a: 43; 1991: 218, 12).

In general, to doubt the engagement of other subjects or even to accuse them of being hypocritical is a re-inscription of these identities. Also, since a 'developing' state that points to the differences between 'developed' and 'developing' countries to justify one's resistance to specific elements of the control represents a rearticulation of the identity of this very state. Each of these subjects is rewritten by referring to parts of their differential identity. While a 'developing' state re-emphasizes its difference, its singularity in positive terms (as it describes itself), the accusers and doubters refer to the differential character of those not complying with the ultimate and common goals. Re-inscribing the differential character of a Self leads ultimately to the particularization of this very identity. This operation has been designated as basic counter-hegemonic strategy entitled *Particularization*.

The most interesting differential articulations are those requesting the recognition of *Sonderwege* – and here, the references to *national sovereignty* figure prominently (this is supported by the high score of the code 'sovereignty' including the sub-code 'respect of national principles': 222 hits in 252 documents). These articulations produce a strong moment of differentiation between the subjects linked by the antagonizing chain of equivalence. By invoking their national sovereignty and requesting respect of national ways of dealing with the drug problem, their particularity is evoked, which allows the subjects to consider themselves as different from the others in the chain. While some delegations appeal to their national sovereignty as a legitimate restriction in the control of the demand – 'the treatment of drug addicts [. . .] was primarily the responsibility of the national authorities' – others focus on their sovereign control of the supply side: '[e]ach State had its own legislation and enjoyed the sovereign right to make whatever use it saw fit of such [illegal] funds' (United Nations 1973b: 13; see also United Nations 1973d: 204; 1991: 79, see also 165). Some delegations interpret sovereignty in its most general sense with regard to international drug control:

> [T]he adoption of a restrictive list of producing countries or the establishment of mandatory limitations on producing countries [. . .] would be an act of intervention in the domestic affairs of such States, an infringement of their sovereignty and a violation of their right to dispose of their economic resources.
>
> (United Nations 1964a: 11)

In all these cases, referring to sovereignty is an act of differentiation. In general, the assertion of sovereignty involves implicit claims to represent an identifiable presence, to represent the will of a nation, of a people. By claiming to represent their will in a given territory, states experience a strong need for defining criteria differentiating the inside from the outside in order to avoid blurred boundaries, which endanger their sovereignty. Thereby, states ground their sovereignty also on their monopoly of the legitimate use of violence, which allows a state to formulate the above-mentioned criteria separating the inside from the outside (Connolly 1991: 64–6; Walker 1993; Doty 1996: 122). Exactly this general meaning of sovereignty spurs differentiation in the discourse on drugs and it is driven by self-descriptions of what determines sovereign nations (territorial integrity, independence and non-interference in domestic affairs).

It is entirely correct to consider the constant evocation of sovereignty as a way of particularizing subjects of the antagonizing chain. As sovereignty is discussed most often explicitly with regard to international drug control, the particularization of subjects is articulated at the expense of the ultimate and common goals and of the general equivalent. For instance, when '[a]ll governments recognised the necessity of *international control* and of uniform national measures, and if the Single Convention did not infringe *sovereign* rights, all countries would be ready to become parties' (United Nations 1964a: 9, emphasis added), supplementary counter-hegemonic strategy *Stressing the particularity of a subject of chain A explicitly at the expense of the general equivalent* is at play. Although the articulation of differences works at the expense of the general equivalent, it is very important to note that it does not imply a *denial* of the ultimate and common goals and interests.

Eventually, a number of elements, such as alcohol or tobacco, remained entirely outside the discourse and were considered to be outside the parameters established by the hegemonic drug regime. Nowadays, the dangerousness or harmlessness of both is widely discussed and scientific findings are called upon to prove or disprove the addictive potential and relation between tobacco, alcohol and illness. Whereas the interpretation of both substances as qualifying as non-drugs has come under pressure, the discourse on international drug prohibition is void of such references (only some explicit allusions to alcohol in the 1988 debates). However, among the participants there are still a great number of Islamic countries, which ban alcohol out of religious reasons. For those, the inclusion of alcohol on the lists naming proscribed drugs, i.e. defining it as an illicit drug, would be in accordance with the national interpretation of alcohol based on the Koran proscribing the consumption of alcoholic beverages. This complete neglect shows how the international discourse is dominated by a specific meaning attached to drugs – read Western interpretation – forcing subjects in the antagonizing chain to agree to a construction of an antagonistic Other that leaves out essential substances in their view and, thereby, contradicts integral parts of their national identity or culture. This is because, from an Islamic perspective, one would inevitably conclude that a drug-free world cannot be synonymous with a world within which the consumption of alcohol is still allowed. Moreover, the virtual absence of any references to alcohol in the 30 years of debates impressively shows that the parameters of the drug discourse have already been established with a particular view on what drugs are and which substances do not fall under the remit of the international drug regime.

To close, first, the simultaneous presence of productive hegemonic and counter-hegemonic strategies underscores the mutual subversion of the logic of equivalence and difference in a discursive field. With the re-construction of the hegemonic order at the international level, we concluded that the logic of equivalence prevails in the discourse on drugs; however, this did not exclude the logic of difference from operating. The reconstructed counter-hegemonic strategies, the internal differences (read heterogeneity) emphasize how the logic of difference dilutes what the logic of equivalence is attempting to fixate. Second, in the international discourse on drugs, heterogeneity has not been detrimental to the emergence of a hegemonic order. Its effects are mitigated and suppressed and a homogenization of the discourse has been achieved. The internal differences have not managed to disperse the equivalential subjects. While this conclusion is substantiated by the overall low frequency of the codes related to internal differences (sole exception: sovereignty), the unchallenged ultimate and common goals and interests and cooperation as means to achieve the goals are most revealing. In addition, with no denial of the general equivalent, of an international control of drugs, being voiced, the construction and persistence of the hegemonic regime in the field of drugs has not been opposed in the international discourse.

A hegemonic order at the international level was finally constructed in the discourse on drugs; it has been re-inscribed over a period of nearly 30 years. Attempts to constitute a homogeneous antagonistic drugs Other have been successful and the internal differences reconstructed (even those of detrimental character) have not disturbed the construction of the hegemonic order based on the consensus to internationally control drugs, or the unambiguously shared vision of a drug-free world represented by the signifier of the international community. In how far these constructions are used to justify a range of specific international measures to fight a 'war on drugs' will be discussed in the next section.

The institutionalization of the hegemonic discourse: justifying international measures against drugs

Identification with a new hegemonic order can be quite instable. However, over time, practices become routinized and the identity of the collective Self as much as the antagonistic construction of the Other are recurrently (partially) fixed and thus become increasingly stable. The stronger the authority of the hegemonic discourse and the tighter the ties of equivalence between the subjects identifying with the collective Self, the more likely the institutionalization of specific practices in accordance with the order. Thereby, representing an Other as an existential threat which endangers the entire globe, i.e. to securitize a security phenomenon as in the case of drugs (Buzan, Wæver and de Wilde 1998), proves on the one hand crucial to generate political support to institutionalize practices that would normally be opposed. As the analysis has shown, in the face of a declared existential danger it is much easier to justify the need for coherence of the civilized world – since without such unanimous support the threat, i.e. the antagonistic Other, the drugs will 'win the war'. Thus, a discourse demonizing and de-humanizing drugs and every individual or organization associated with it, proves to be highly beneficial for introducing, sustaining and justifying measures like a 'war on drugs'.

On the other hand, in this climate pushing through extraordinary measures is equally facilitated. Of course, in the formula of a 'war on drugs' a number of extraordinary measures coalesce since, as I have outlined, a war is the ultimate measure democracies and civilized states have at their disposal to eliminate an existential danger. Moreover, extraordinary measures during a 'war on drugs' cannot simply be tighter or more elaborated law-enforcement policies, these are for times of peace – extraordinary measures in wartime involve greater degree of violence. Furthermore, deploying a language of war not only justifies violence as a rationale for extraordinary measures but also has specific effects on contestation against the regime. In light of the institutional principles, norms, rules and values generated by hegemonic orders, which exclude alternative meanings and frameworks of behaviour, resistance to these measures can very easily be stigmatized as illegitimate, amoral and irrational. To this adds the universal appeal inherent to hegemonic practices. Thus, these practices attempt to neutralize challenges to existing social structures in a transformist way by providing incentives which tempt subjects to more actively accept and identify with the order (Gramsci 1971: 58–9). However, since the construction of an existential threat accords the securitizing agents the authority to carry out extraordinary measures, they also seek to suppress or defame public contestation, regardless whether resistance only questions the legitimacy of the measures or the construction of an evil Other in general. After the creation of a hegemonic regime it is very difficult to introduce or sustain alternative meanings into a discourse. Alternative knowledge is excluded when a specific socio-cultural knowledge dominates a discourse (in a similar vein Höhne 2001: 29–30). Thus, '[t]he power of discourse to materialize its effects is thus consonant with the power of discourse to circumscribe the domain of intelligibility' (Butler 1993: 187).

The above holds for the practices anchored in the hegemonic regime in the drugs discourse. Since the policies are presented as effective in attaining the ultimate goal – to free the world from drugs and to eliminate the danger threatening the existence of the world – the measures drastically thwart resistance to them. Indeed, how can one resist policies that will bring about a drug-free world? According to the regime, to deploy violence to eliminate drugs from the globe is unfortunate but necessary to reach the ultimate goal. Thus, the international foreseen measures against drugs commit its members to take a hard stance against drugs. Thereby, the *supply side* of the drug problem was crucial to the establishment and persistence of the regime. While in the 1960s, states recognized that drug traffic routes cross continents, in the 1980s they realized that not only the drug routes but also the money gained by the drug trade crosses borders. This money was difficult to trace, due to the increase of cross-border economic activities in the 1980s, and particularly the laundering of drug money appeared as an enormous threat to the states' economic stability. Apart from these supply-side measures, states are also obliged to take action against the *demand* for narcotics. However, as the analysis has shown, there are no clear prescriptions on how exactly to deal with drug addicts. This has led to a never-ending debate of whether it is permissible or not to pursue non-repressive policies towards drug consumers, as practiced in the Netherlands and Switzerland. Just as the measures stem from the particular interpretation of drugs as antagonistic Other, the critique that has been voiced towards this understanding calls for a different way of dealing with drug addiction and drug supply.

What kinds of measures are foreseen by the international drug regime? The United Nations as the 'foundation' of the universal system of drug control not only defines what an illicit drug is but also interferes with the policy-autonomy of Member States. The *Single Convention on Narcotic Drugs* established the International

Narcotics Control Board (INCB), an independent and quasi-judicial monitoring body for the implementation of all United Nations drug control conventions. The mandate of the INCB very clearly states its role as guardian of the treaties, since it ensures member state's compliance with the parameters of the hegemonic regime. Above all, it is the INCB which determines whether there is a need for change in the scope of control of Tables I and II of the 1988 Convention (both tables enumerate the substances which are classified as illicit drugs), and assesses whether specific chemicals should be placed under international control (in particular those which can be used for the production of synthetic drugs). In addition, the INCB 'identifies weaknesses in national and international control systems and contributes to correcting such situations' and it administers 'a system of estimates for narcotic drugs and a voluntary assessment system for psychotropic substances and monitors licit activities involving drugs through a statistical returns system'.[13] These very strict and encompassing definitions imply a limited range of manoeuvre for the signatory states with regard to the handling of drugs.

Next, we observe a great number of measures against the production and traffic of drugs, which vary in their importance throughout the regime's existence (due to the concentration of the regime on the supply-side). Two measures stand out: those against money laundering and the programs of crop eradication in producer countries. Since the late 1980s, there is a growing consensus that the fight against criminal finance is the best strategy against drug trafficking (Dorn, Murji and South 1992: 63–75, 169–74). This strategy, which was largely unknown in the 1970s, is composed of three aspects. First, the repression of money laundering is supposed to make drug trafficking more risky and thereby a less rewarding business. Second, the strategy to 'follow the money trail' may help to identify drug criminals and those who support them. Third, some countries consider drug trafficking a major threat to the national and international economy. From their standpoint, the fight against criminal finance may help to protect the financial infrastructure. Taken together, these considerations have provided the rationale behind the crackdown on criminal finance since the late 1980s and led to the adoption of the 1988 UN convention against drug trafficking. In 1989, the Financial Action Task Force (FATF), today a technical body of the Organization for Economic Co-operation and Development, was established, which quickly became the cornerstone of an emerging regime on money laundering. Since then, the hegemonic practices have gained momentum by virtue of a long series of recommendations by the FATF. It provides for tight supervision of financial flows for even relatively minor sums and for substantial powers, e.g. for the confiscation of suspect money or the blocking of bank accounts for the participating states, and even touched upon the taboo of banking secrecy (Gilmore 2004). In addition to the UN and the FATF, the Council of Europe adopted the *Convention on Laundering, Search, Seizure and Confiscation of the Proceeds from Crime* in 1990, and only one year later the European Community agreed on a directive against money laundering, which was amended and modified several times and which forces Member States to transpose the norms into their national law and juridical practice (Council of Europe 1990; European Parliament and European Council 2005).

As a consequence, today's measures against criminal finance qualify as extraordinary measures since they cut deep into the penal code, financial sector regulation, and privacy laws of individual states (Savona 1997; Mitsilegas 2003a; Mascianduro 2004). These changes have also impacted domestic groups such as bankers and lawyers. At times these groups, often supported by constitutional principles, have prevented states from swiftly adopting the proposed measures. But resistance to the measures against money laundering has a very difficult stand. First, according to a survey on global financial relations, 'it is difficult to find examples of outright conflict among state actors on global financial matters in the postwar era' (Dombrowski 1998: 15). It is certainly true that states are very careful not to appear 'soft' on drug trafficking, since this would contradict their identification with the collective Self and undermine their participation in the political consensus of the drugs discourse. Of course there are the 'usual suspects' such as Switzerland and Luxembourg, Bermuda and Barbados, but a 'decent' state has to crack down on criminal finance.

Secondly, the tightness of the regime with regard to money laundering results from the fact that it provides an excuse to re-regulate the financial sector and, as a strongly desirable side effect, to make tax evasion more risky. Although this is usually not openly admitted by the decision makers involved, it is easy to see that the measures are conceived of as an antidote against some problematic aspects of globalization. As a consequence, they have been considerably expanded over the last fifteen years to include criminal transactions other than drug trafficking (see for instance Thomas 2003). For example, in Britain any kind of 'criminal conduct', from serious crime to petty credit card fraud, can be prosecuted under the anti-money laundering laws (United Kingdom 2002; United Kingdom Home Office 2002c; Whitehouse 2003: 143). French law is similar (Montebourg 2000: 625–58) and in Germany, the 1992 organized crime bill made money laundering a criminal offence. All serious crime, including drug-related offenses and organized crime, were brought under the remit of the law and the list was extended stepwise over the following years (Germany 1992; 2002). Around 2000 it seemed for a while that international measures against money laundering might even be extended to tax evasion; however, the US administration opposed the plans (Frankfurter Allgemeine Zeitung 2000; Süddeutsche Zeitung 2001a; 2001b).

From the outset, the idea was promoted to fight drug supply where it is produced, i.e. in the producer countries. In the 1960s and 1970s, operations on drug producing countries were discussed during the debates of the 1961 and 1971 conventions and the 1972 conference; for example, the 1961 Single Convention requested that producer states should not permit the production of drugs beyond the annual estimates (Articles 22 and 24). However, they were carried out on the bilateral level only, since at the international level there was considerable fear that these measures infringe upon national sovereignty (United Nations 1964b: 9, 11). Since the early 1990s, the operations on drug producing countries have been replaced by so-called crop eradication campaigns, which are part and parcel of the hegemonic regime's punitive approach. Violent crop eradication in producer countries is considered a legitimate means to reduce the availability of drugs, regardless whether the destruction of poppy fields and coca farms is counterproductive because of the harmful social consequences for the producers. Whereas the consumer countries are requested to provide for the necessary resources, the producer states are repeatedly called upon to do their duty and control drug production at the national level. For example, since the early years of the 'war on drugs', the US has managed to obtain a lot of support from other consumer countries as Britain and France are also fervent defenders of the crop eradication programs. The UK had provided logistical help to the US in Colombia as early as the 1990s and in late 2001, Prime Minister Tony Blair declared the war in Afghanistan as an opportunity to eradicate opium production. After the invasion, Britain took over the lead responsibility for counter-narcotic efforts in Afghanistan.[14] According to the rationale, the measures are also legitimate due to an intimate link between drug traffickers and terrorists: the latter are feed by the 'narco-dollars', via large-scale international money laundering or – as in Afghanistan – as a direct income to terrorist groups like the Taliban (International Narcotics Control Board 2009: 96).

The effects of these campaigns are harsh for the cultivators and their families. They are twice the victims of international anti-drug measure violence. On the one hand, their livelihood is dependent on the production of a prohibited substance, which they sell to local dealers for a ridiculous price compared to that on the world market. On the other hand, the eradication of the cultivator's crops by international means implies that their livelihood is destroyed – which makes them turn again to the drug buyers to secure their income and survival. Hence, crop eradication takes away farmers' means of subsistence, it fosters the development of subversive and criminal violence associated with drug trafficking. Furthermore, in coca-producing regions for example, coca consumption is a prime symbol of the identity of Andean and Amazonian people: this custom is practiced in communal work, by people carrying heavy loads or making long journeys on foot, and in traditional medicine or religious and pagan rituals (Transnational Institute 2005). The practice of eradication cuts deep into the traditions and identities of the indigenous population and leads to protests that are often quelled violently by government forces. Thus, the instable security conditions in many drug-producing countries, the poverty of the cultivators and their adherence to longstanding traditions increase the farmers' dependence on the production of drugs.

Of course, the problem of this double bind is well known to the international community. Its remedy consists in increasing developmental aid and targeting drug cultivators to help them to make their living from sources other than drugs. For instance, France is strongly involved in supporting drug-producing countries. In the last three years, the country has financed dozens of projects with various objectives, such as the formation of police officers or the build up of institutional capacities to combat drugs in Russia, Turkey, Uzbekistan, Niger or Burkina Faso (Chirac 2003; France 2003; Ministère des Affaires étrangères undated document-a; undated document-b). The same applies to Germany, which favours alternative development schemes (Friman 1996; Bundesministerium für wirtschaftliche Zusammenarbeit und Entwicklung and Gesellschaft für Technische Zusammenarbeit 2004). However, these actions have proven to be mostly inefficient. Eradication efforts in Afghanistan, as the INCB states in its latest annual report, are 'hampered by lack of security, poor planning and inadequate equipment and funding'. The measure has been largely inefficient: the initial target for eradication had been set at 50,000 hectares. However, as the Afghani government was unable to adequately carry out the eradication efforts only 5,480 hectares were eradicated. This inefficiency thwarts the 'increase in the number of provinces that have become opium poppy free' due to voluntary efforts by farmers (International Narcotics Control Board 2009: 96). In coca growing countries, the programs do not reduce the area under cultivation, since 'the increase or decrease of an area planted in coca is related more to the legal and/or illegal market for coca than to the "success" of interdiction and eradication policies' in these states (Transnational Institute 2005). The cultivators, as victim of measures, are unable to protest so it is also no secret that they sometimes destroy half of their harvest in order to obtain a better price for the other half, since scarce poppy increases prices (Hoegen 2005).

Despite these problems, one should not assume that these programs are not welcomed by the producer countries. On the contrary, they request the consumer states to assist them in their national fight against drugs. This assistance may take different forms: as regular developmental aid, as training of police officers (as in previous years US officers trained French and German police forces), educational seminars or logistical support.[15] However, requesting assistance has its price, since it brings about interdependence: consuming countries cannot deny assistance and producing ones cannot refrain from assistance – since they are all tied by the hegemonic regime calling for a fight against drugs.

When it comes down to *demand-side* measures, the question of controlled consumption of narcotics and substitution treatment stands out, as it is not only crucial for the stability of the regime but has also been discussed since the early 1960s without yet having been entirely settled. While during the early years, the question of drug addiction was considered to not be very much of a problem (for instance, large consumer countries like France have not acknowledged their national drug problem until the late 1960s – see Cusack 1974: 252). With rising drug-related death rates, the issue of addiction came back on the table and controlled consumption of narcotics or substitution treatment (read methadone) have been heavily debated.[16] Indeed, today, a number of demands have been raised considering controlled consumption of narcotics in drug-injection rooms as a useful way of minimizing the harm inflicted to drug users, especially when combined with substitution treatment. The UN convention of 1988 remains rather loose on this point by excessively using the verb 'may'· 'parties may provide [. . .] measures such as treatment, education, after-care, rehabilitation or social reintegration' and in cases of 'a minor nature may provide, as alternatives to conviction or punishment, measures such as education, rehabilitation or social reintegration, as well as, when the offender is a drug abuser, treatment and aftercare'.[17]

Furthermore, there is an increasing request by countries to regulate and handle the problem of drug addiction at the national level. For instance, the UK and Germany have been repeatedly criticized for establishing 'shooting galleries' and for testing the prescription of heroine to addicts. In pursuit of its harm reduction approach, the

UK has turned back to the practice of prescribing heroin, and not only methadone, to drug addicts. Whereas others consider this a violation of central provisions of the drug prohibition regime, Britain maintains that the prescription of heroin is formally legal (United Kingdom Home Office 2002d: 20; 2003; for current situation see Woolf 2007b). In 2000, the Federal German Government legalized drug injection rooms, which comes close to a defection from the UN regime (Friman 1996; Germany 2000; Drogenbeauftragte der Bundesregierung 2003: 27–43). These explanations very much remind of the request within the UN debates to respect national ways (*Sonderwege*). Considering heroin proscription and legalized drug injection rooms as effective national means to counter drug addiction shows how national sovereignty is appealed to restrict international control and underscores the early claim that 'the treatment of drug addicts [. . .] was primarily the responsibility of national authorities' (United Nations 1964b: 6).

Indeed, the regime's orthodox interpreters object that injection rooms and substitution treatment are in contravention to the drug prohibition regime, and that it is immoral for a state to foster the consumption of drugs, whether in injection rooms or in other localities, let alone to provide the drugs and utensils such as syringes and needles. For example, controlled consumption and drug injection rooms in France are an object of polemics and not at all seen as part of harm reduction. They are considered to pose a severe ethical problem and to be useless against infective diseases like aids (Mission interministérielle de la lutte contre la drogue et la toxicomanie 1999: 110–1).

However, the tide has changed since the 1998 special session of the UN General Assembly on drugs and an increasing call for a European approach to drug consumption is heard in the late 1990s. This reflects certain disagreement on whether and to what extent one must keep pursuing a repressive and punitive approach, or whether it would be better to rely more heavily on prevention and harm reduction. Due to an informal coalition between consumer countries in Europe and producer countries in the South, the so-called balanced approach has 'gained ground in relation to the American law enforcement approach that had been more traditional in UN circles hitherto' (Boekhaut van Solinge 2002: 15). As a matter of fact, most EU Member States are now promoting this balanced approach. The idea is to combine the international fight against the supply of drugs with appropriate measures of demand reduction at home.

What we can discern from this post 1988-development does not contradict my findings on the existence of a hegemonic regime in the international discourse on drugs in the period under scrutiny (1961–1988). On the contrary, it underscores the validity of the study's central argument with regard to the importance of the homogeneity of the Other construction. Hegemonic regimes are in need of a homogenous antagonistic Other and the current crisis of the drugs regime on the demand side is very much related to an increasingly heterogeneous Other constitution. As I have outlined, the drug addict has always represented a gash. This left the door ajar for alternative meanings, like considering an addict as a sick individual or a victim of circumstances and make a plea for the accordant demand-side measures to cure them – harm reduction or imprisonment.

It also left the door ajar for disassociating the drug addict from the antagonized chain of equivalence (as indicated by supplementary counter-hegemonic strategy *Underscoring particularity of subject*, which ultimately crosses the antagonistic frontier in order to weaken it). These meanings can be based on rates displaying the increase of drug deaths (and its stagnation on a high level). If one takes the number of drug-related deaths to be an indicator of the overall effectiveness of drugs policies, their number rose in Western Europe until the early 1990s and has stagnated since, with even a slight decrease since 2000 – showing the failure of the punitive approach of the regime.[18] Such numbers are reflected in the increasing demand of countries to regulate and handle the problem of drug addiction at the national level. Highlighting the resistibility of the regime, such demands refer back to the importance of a homogenous Other construction for the establishment *and* persistence of a hegemonic order.

Ultimately, the hegemonic order in the field of drug prohibition also depoliticizes political practices, since it withdraws certain policy options from political discourse. The prescription of heroine to addicts is not an option, alternative pain treatment is also difficult to defend and development-oriented measures that could be an alternative to violent opium or coca crop eradication have a hard standing, since they contradict elementary parameters of the hegemonic regime focusing on a 'war on drugs'. It is impossible to reconcile such options with the ultimate goal of a world free of drugs and the common vision shared among the discursive agents of the Self, since it would only allow the antagonistic drugs Other to maintain its presence in the midst of civilization.

The silence of heterogeneity in the international discourse on drugs

Having reconstructed a hegemonic regime and the institutionalization of specific hegemonic practices at the international level, the last section of chapter three contextualizes the results with a focus on the concept of heterogeneity in the international discourse on drugs. After reviewing the identified strategies, moments of dissent are analyzed. As the present study has made a case for a concept of identity ontologically flexible enough to allow the analysis of various mode of differentiation, a typology of different degrees of otherness is established in light of the results. They also show and support the overall homogeneity of the antagonistic drugs Other. Some reflections on the silence of heterogeneity intend to summarize in how far the drugs discourse deploys a whole host of values and morals manifesting a hegemonic regime of truths about drugs and their use.

The analysis identified 10.5 of the 15 discursive strategies. Table 3.3. lists all strategies located in the international discourse on drugs. The table displays the dominance of productive hegemonic strategies in the discourse on drugs (seven productive hegemonic vs. three and a half counter-hegemonic strategies).[19] Most importantly, while the analysis reconstructed the basic dimension of productive hegemonic strategies in its entirety, I was able to locate the basic counter-hegemonic strategies *Particularization* and *Weakening of the antagonistic frontier* only. On

Table 3.3 Reconstructed hegemonic strategies in the international discourse on drugs

Productive hegemonic strategies	Counter-hegemonic strategies
Basic dimension: • Universalization • Establishing an antagonistic frontier • Representation *Supplementary dimension:* • Extending the antagonizing chain of equivalence • Simultaneously emphasizing and downgrading the particularity of a subject of *chain A* • Crossing the antagonistic frontier in order to strengthen *chain A* • Enlarging the antagonized chain of equivalence	*Basic dimension:* • Particularization • Weakening of the antagonistic frontier *Supplementary dimension:* • Stressing the particularity of a subject of *chain A* explicitly at the expense of the general equivalent • Crossing the antagonistic frontier in order to weaken it: – Underscore particularity of a subject/element of *chain Z*

various occasions, I have outlined that for the establishment of a hegemonic order, the complete basic dimension of productive hegemonic strategies needs to operate; for the failure of such order, the entire basic dimension of counter-hegemonic strategies needs to be present. In consequence, the logic of equivalence dominates the discourse on drugs and this finding is supported by the majority of the strategies located.

Yet, speaking of an international hegemonic order at the current moment by no means implies to speak of *stable* meanings. As orders can only be partially fixed, we witness the momentary stabilization of a particular interpretation of what the Self (it aims a world free from drugs) and what the antagonistic Other(s) are about (they are threatening and blocking the identity of the Self). However, the Self, the Other and the hegemonic order have been re-inscribed over a number of years and the order's remit has been extended – extended with respect to the numbers of subjects in *chain A* but also with regard to the increased number of elements and subjects associated with the drugs Other. The order has been continuously rewritten in the sense of inscribing as to render permanent which is contingent and subject to failure. This explains the recurrent evocation of the general equivalent of an international drug control, the common and ultimate goals and interests, of cooperation as means to achieve these aims since their re-reading is necessary to sustain the hegemonic order at the international level.[20]

Moreover, this explains a major difference between the 1960s and the 1980s. We witness an increasing polarization in the discourse supported by a language full of confrontation and conflict. Not only the description of the antagonistic Other but also the depiction of the struggle against it and the action undertaken by the international community to counter drugs experiences an accentuation. During the deliberations of the 1961 convention, drugs were given a religious connotation by denoting them as 'evil' threatening the whole world whereas in the 1988 debates, drugs also became the 'enemy', the 'common enemy' that needs to be controlled. The 'contagious disease' drugs turned into a 'cancer' relying on networks 'immune' to uncoordinated international action (United Nations 1964a: 6, 109, 10; 1991: 9, 18). At the end of the 1980s, Self and Other, international community and drugs were much more explicitly juxtaposed. The opposition between both has turned into a frontal encounter using a language full of 'war-metaphors' to describe this encounter and the consequences for the Other. The debates in 1988 increased the polarization, the antagonistic divide. International 'control' of illicit substances turned from 'suppression', 'fight', 'combat' or 'crusade' (terms marking the heated and politicized atmosphere of the 1961 discussions) into 'battle' and 'war' which 'eliminate' or 'destroy' drugs as the war aims at the 'annihilation' of the Other. And international cooperation to control drugs was no longer simply cooperation or common action, but 'a fundamental', 'universal', 'powerful weapon', an 'arsenal' or a 'machinery' the international community disposes of to control drugs (United Nations 1964a: 43; 1991: 2, 3, 8, 11, 2, 28, 111, 8, 233). Religious and medical metaphors were replaced by war-metaphors, the crusade became a war and the evil was now the common enemy. At the level of the entire discourse, this reformulation of antagonism, its accentuation, deepening and widening invokes the respective supplementary productive hegemonic strategies *Crossing the antagonistic frontier in order to strengthen chain A* and *Extending the antagonizing chain of equivalence*. By constant articulation, description and reference to the antagonistic Other, the Self's identity is re-inscribed as the symbolization of the drug-free world. Going to the extremes, sharpening and deepening the divide between Self and Other increases the credibility of this symbolization. This process of enlarging the chain of equivalence also serves as a re-assurance of the Self: constructing the Other recurrently as the opposite of the Self re-assures the Self of its identity.

These reconstructions show that a hegemonic order profits from an ongoing radicalization of the Other. Especially since such radicalization allows going beyond the limits of routine political behaviour and installing the above-depicted extraordinary measures. The crop eradication programs are a case in point, since they not only provide for a legitimate explanation for the exertion of counter-violence, very much in line with the 'war on drugs'. They also thwart resistance to this practice within the society of those directly concerned by the measures and among the defenders of alternative measures. In particular, the latter can be subscribed as playing into the hands of the enemy, the international drug mafia.

In this sense, heterogeneity – defined as the differential remainder of subjects within a hegemonic project – threatens the development of the project into a 'full-fledged' hegemony at the international level, especially if it differentiates the homogenous construction of the Other. As the analysis has shown the discourse on drugs displays a number of varying degrees of otherness, which, however, have not impacted on the homogeneity of the Other construction in the period under scrutiny. Table 3.4. summarizes the antagonistic and non-antagonistic Other constructions from the early 1960s to the late 1980s.

While table 3.4. shows the presence of heterogeneity, it has not managed to be detrimental to the construction and persistence of a hegemonic order. The negative elements (the drug addict, the request for respecting national sovereignty or the demand to take the underlying causes of the drug problem into account) have

Table 3.4 Typology of different degrees of otherness in the international discourse on
drugs

Other	Degrees of otherness
Drugs • International drug 'mafia' • International drug trafficker • Individual drug dealer	Antagonistic Other and threatening
Individual drug addict	Antagonistic Other and criminal OR different and sick (but NOT alternative and tolerable way of life)
Drug cultivator	Different and poor, exploited

not obstructed the eventual construction of a hegemonic regime. This is all the more remarkable, since the differences rooted in the national identities, cultures or religious convictions of the various subjects gathered under the common banner of an international drug control. Ranging from the exclusion of alcohol from international drug control over the inclusion of indigenous or cultural use of drugs to the unsolved characterization of the drug addict either as 'criminal' or 'sick person', the differences reveal the difficulties for a number of subjects willing to participate in an international control of drugs. The suppression of these differences shows the power of the hegemonic regime considering specific substances (but not others) as illicit drugs and those who use them either as criminals or outsiders of the society, regardless whether their use is part of their cultural traditions or identities. Attempts to weaken the antagonistic frontier or to particularize a subject have damaged neither the credibility of the tendentially empty signifier 'international community' nor the general equivalent of ultimate and common goals and interest as well as the means. The symbolization of a drug-free world, of the globe as a healthy and peaceful place embodied by the international community, successfully suppressed the internal differences between the subjects. The general equivalent of an international drug control disposes of enough universalizing power to mitigate their damaging potential.

Overall, heterogeneity has remained largely silent while a hegemonic order at the international level has been constructed in the discourse on drugs, because everything voiced against international drug control was entirely *within* the parameters of the meaning constituted by the hegemonic order at the international level. The consensus on the international drug discourse – drugs are evil and threatening and their use deviant– is already highly sedimented and functions as a veritable 'gate-keeper'. It has led to the institutionalization of a number of practices in accordance with the punitive approach of the regime. The consensus keeps out any alternative meanings and practices that do not fit into the 'control-drugs vs. profit-from-drugs' scheme and stamps them as marginal, abnormal etc. This equally applies to attempts to include, for instance, alcohol in the remit of international drug control. They have remained unsaid, since the meaning of drugs as illicit excludes the drug alcohol, since it is defined as a licit drug – irrespective of what scientific studies or daily experience teaches about alcohol and its addictive potential.

In light of this, it goes without saying that the identified counter-hegemonic strategies validate the rules of the 'drug game' instituted by the hegemonic order at the international level. The pattern of inclusion/exclusion is taken for granted and reproduced in every single hegemonic strategy. The dominant meaning constructed thereby determines the Other in an act of power, of exclusion as an *antagonistic* Other. Earlier interpretations of drugs as an accepted or tolerated part of human life, or attempts to nuance the homogeneous antagonistic Other, are superseded by this dominant interpretation. And I argue that even the contentious meanings of the drug addict are in line with the hegemonic interpretation. For instance, states speaking of addicts as 'sick persons' portray themselves as working in the interest of health. Safely positioned on the 'health/control-drugs' side allows these subjects to operate without being suspected of questioning the established consensus or the ultimate goal of a drug-free world.

These parameters and constructions of antagonistic and non-antagonistic Others are neither innocent nor informative. A bulk of values and morals are deployed and the disagreement on the drug addict exemplarily shows how far today's discourse continues to operate under the mixed approach of medicine and moral incentives to strengthen the will of the addict. The discourse openly celebrates the moral superiority of the rational individual immune to the seductive sirens of drugs. Accordingly, the shift from 'evil' and 'fight' to 'common enemy' and 'war' legitimizes the sharpest control to protect exactly these individuals, the people with the will to refrain from consuming drugs. Was not there 'after all a binding obligation to protect young persons'? Weren't measures necessary 'designed to protect society against the scourge of addiction' (United Nations 1964a: 56; 1991: 48)? In the drug discourse, the range of the possible/impossible obviously constitutes a field of truths that operate in the parameters of the hegemonic order – since only this will lead to the desired goals.

Drugs are 'powerful', 'threatening' and we must 'fight' them: the constructions created leave no room for a permissive stance towards drugs. Isn't it ironic that we insist on giving drugs all the power, letting them play the central role, 'allowing [them] to hog the limelight, as it plays the demonic villain' when the primary aim is to 'rid the world of that scourge' (United Nations 1964a: 6; Driscoll 2000: 2)? All this questions a potential ethico-political context of hegemonic orders. In how far the constructions of antagonistic and non-antagonistic Others and the values and morals they invoke need to be considered in such context will be discussed in the conclusion.

4 Writing the 'war on terror'

The struggle of hegemonic projects

The following chapter is devoted to the analysis of the international discourse on terrorism since the attacks during the Olympic Games in Munich in September 1972. The central aim consists in analyzing whether and how a hegemonic order has been established. The preceding chapter already established the structure of the two empirical chapters: first, I reconstruct how terrorism has been construed as a threat to international peace and security. While equating terrorism with danger sounds consensual and justified to modern ears, throughout history terrorism has described entirely different things to different people. Emphasizing the historical contingency of the current interpretation of terrorism, the first part of chapter four outlines the development of the term terrorism from its first known appearance during the French Revolution to the attempts to find a universal definition of the phenomenon at the level of the UN starting in 1972. By identifying different hegemonic strategies in the discourse that share the common aim of constructing terrorism as the antagonistic Other, the analysis reveals the enormous difficulties of contemporary efforts to forge a global consensus on a definition of international terrorism.

The second part of chapter four starts by mapping out the hegemonic strategies aimed at the establishment of the Self, i.e. the entity opposed to terrorism as Other. While there is certain agreement among the discursive agents jointly confronting the global spread of terrorism that a world safe from terrorism should be achieved, the analysis identifies a far-ranging conflict regarding the question of *how* this vision can be accomplished. The third part questions how international measures are enacted and justified in light of the serious conflict on how to counter international terrorism. In contextualizing the findings of the discourse on terrorism, the last section addresses what it means to speak of the 'noisiness' of heterogeneity. In consequence, chapter four complements chapter three by offering a change of perspective on international efforts to deal with terrorism.

International terrorism as a threat to international peace and security

'Terreur' and 'terrorisme' – shifts of meaning

International terrorism has been considered as 'one of the most dangerous challenges to humanity' for a number of years and, indeed, 'it seemed impossible to speak of terrorism without speaking of war' (UN Sixth Committee 1972q: 246; 2000b: 5). Although today's perspective on international terrorism presents itself as the outcome of a recurrent theme in the history of mankind, perhaps the only recurrent element of terrorism is its negative reflection on those who are labelled terrorists.

According to the common reading, the word 'terrorism' dates back to the French Revolution, when it was given a distinct, political meaning. Walter Lacqueur argues that it was originally used in a positive sense by the Jacobins, a radical fraction under the lead of Maximilien Robbespierre in the French National Convention (Lacqueur 1987: 11). In 1793, their revolutionary government found itself threatened in a twofold manner: first, by aristocratic immigrants who conspired with foreign rulers to invade the country and, second, the suspicion of treason at home in support of this reactionary move. In light of this, the National Convention adopted a policy of terror, ordering mass executions of suspected traitors. These numerous executions spurred resistance, and in mid 1794, those who had originally supported the harsh measures proposed by Robbespiere began to fear for their own lives. To overthrow him, he could not be accused of *terreur* because the supporters themselves had declared terror to be a legitimate instrument of government. Indeed, Robbespiere was accused of *terrorisme*, a word that suggested illegal conduct; and with the end of his 'Reign of Terror', 'terrorism became a term of abuse that has since then been associated with thoroughly negative, criminal connotations' (Chalk 1996: 46; Schmid 1997: 12–3) and no longer with state behaviour.

By the late nineteenth century, the term *terrorist*, originally used for those who made unjust arrest in the name of the state, became strongly associated with its opposite, anti-state violence. This shift in meaning was mainly provoked by the anarchist movement, which first made deliberate use of terrorist means as a systematic policy. They killed political leaders such as Tsar Alexander of Russia, Empress Elizabeth of Austria, and King Umberto of Italy. Furthermore, it is often argued that World War I was unleashed by a terrorist incident and a wave of international terrorism swept over Europe in the 1920s and 1930s, when fascist Italy supported the murderers of the Yugoslav King Alexander I and French Foreign Minister Jean Louis Barthou (Dubin 1991; Gioia 2006: 3).

Notwithstanding the importance and effects of these movements, the Second World War set the scene for what is nowadays considered 'modern' or international terrorism. On the one hand, after the war the stance emerged that civilians could be legitimate targets of aggression and terror. On the other hand, the colonial struggles from the 1940s to the early-mid 1960s led West European governments to experience for the first time attacks inspired by programs of deliberative terrorism. Supported by prominent intellectuals like Jean-Paul Sartre and Frantz Fanon, these wars of national liberation threw up a variety of theories and justifications for the use of what is described as terror tactics within the context of a more general armed struggle. The success of three major struggles of decolonization (Palestine, Algeria and Cyprus) paved the way for a later formed 'nexus between terrorists and a colonial/domestic/global audience which effectively succeeded in systematically neutralizing the military capabilities of the colonial powers' (Chalk 1996: 51). Overall, the international terrorist campaigns that sprung up in the 1960s and 1970s are said to have learned a great deal from these earlier anti-colonial struggles (Crenshaw and Pimlott 1997: 128).

Thus, at the time when international terrorism was subsequently constructed as a problem with international dimensions, the phenomenon seems to have experienced a complete shift in meaning: from a label for those who make unjust use of force in the name of a state to designate those who carry out anti-state violence. Construed as a security threat, the early responses to international terrorism relied on the latter meaning; still, the question of what terrorism is about has since preoccupied the international agenda. From the very beginning and without a clear definition of the problem's scope and character, the legitimacy of a struggle against terrorism remained doubted. States shared the belief that a common understanding of the problem signalled by a common definition would justify the use of extraordinary measures as legitimate. The importance of such a universally acceptable definition of terrorism notwithstanding, reaching agreement on who is the terrorist and who is the liberator, who fights for a 'just' cause and who for an 'unjust' one, proved to be extremely difficult from the start.

Terrorism on the international agenda before and after Munich

Labours to define *international* terrorism do not reach as far back as those to prohibit drugs. There were attempts to deal with terrorism on a global basis as early as the 1930s, and among the most important are the very first (though inconclusive) efforts to draft a comprehensive convention of terrorism by the League of Nations, forerunner of the United Nations. As a reaction to the assassination of King Alexander I and French Foreign minister Barthou in 1934, the League drafted two conventions. One of them, the *Convention of 1937 for the Prevention and Punishment of Terrorism*, proscribed acts of terrorism which included attempts on the life of heads of state or their spouses, other government representatives and involving injury to persons or damage to property committed by citizens of one state against citizens of another. However, both conventions never came into effect and before the outbreak of the Second World War only 13 states had ratified them.[1]

The main reason for this failure was a lack of consensus over the legal definition of terrorism. Article 1 of the 1937 draft convention defines acts of terrorism as 'criminal acts directed against a State and intended or calculated to create a state of terror in the minds of particular persons, or a group of persons or the general public' (quoted in Wilkinson 1997: 672). States are said to have been reluctant to ratify the convention due to the considerable breadth of its definition, which would have subsumed state-sponsored political violence and political offences in general. The 'dead letter' of 1937 was the first and the last comprehensive convention against international terrorism up for ratification (Franck and Lockwood 1974: 69–70). Since then, all attempts on the international (read UN) level to settle on a legal definition of international terrorism have failed.

International terrorism in its modern form was constructed as a security threat when armed groups tried to internationalize the Middle East conflict in the late 1960s and early 1970s. With the terrorist attack on Israeli athletes at the 1972

Olympic Games in Munich, Western Europe became the main target of international terrorism. While the attack is usually considered as the hallmark event that triggered international cooperation against terrorism, the present analysis argues that we are dealing with an event of dislocation, as will be explained below. Shortly after the attack, UN-Secretary-General Kurt Waldheim added the topic of international terrorism to the agenda of the General Assembly, which passed it on to the UN Sixth Committee (Legal Committee). The most important issue was the necessity of finding an internationally approved definition of terrorism as part of a comprehensive convention on the same topic (United Nations 1972; Finger 1976: 329). Discussions began with a draft convention submitted by the United States by the end of September 1972 (UN General Assembly 1972). Limited to certain acts of international terrorism and without suggesting any legal definition of the phenomenon, the US declared that their draft did not present a comprehensive convention. This restriction, however, did not mitigate the opposition the draft faced and the discursive struggle for a hegemonic interpretation of what terrorism is about has since led to notorious confrontations between Western versus (the so-called non-aligned group of) African-Arabic states (supported by some European countries such as France). Whereas the former wanted to legitimize the fight against their most dangerous enemy, the latter suspected the West of proscribing their national liberation movements and of trying to re-introduce a modern type of colonial yoke through the backdoor (Friedrichs 2006: 72). The non-aligned countries perceived national liberation movements as less threatening and harmful compared to state terrorism (i.e. terrorism sponsored by states to undermine the political authority of another state), since they were mostly the offspring of such movements, thus, their designation as terrorist implies to outlaw integral elements of the national identity of these new states.

On instigation by Algeria and other non-aligned states, the GA established an Ad Hoc Committee on international terrorism which took up its work in 1973. Its main task was to find a common understanding of international terrorism leading to a definition, but from the outset the apparently innocent question of if and when concrete measures should be taken against terrorism provoked considerable disagreement. While non-aligned states requested to study first the causes of terrorism (as only their genuine understanding would separate the just from the unjust causes, would allow drafting effective measures and determine a common definition), the United States and other Western countries argued that in their national legislation they do not identify the underlying causes of a crime before enacting laws against criminals. During the course of 1973, it became apparent that the debates were likely to remain inconclusive; nevertheless, the Ad Hoc Committee on Terrorism debated until 1979, when it finally refrained from demanding the renewal of its mandate without any agreement reached on a universally acceptable definition of terrorism (UN Ad Hoc Committee on International Terrorism 1979d).

In the years to come, the UN followed what has been called the 'sectoral' or 'piecemeal approach' to terrorism. Up to this point, 13 UN conventions have convened to address such diverse features of international terrorism as aircraft hijacking, acts against diplomats or terrorist financing.[2] All of these conventions still apply, with minor variations and the common normative standard of prevention and punishment of the various acts they contemplate, is based, at least partly, on the model of the 1937 League of Nations' convention. More specifically, the punishment of these acts resides in the 'Parties obligation to establish them as offences in their national legislation, to establish their jurisdiction over such offences in specified cases, and to prosecute or extradite the alleged offender (on the basis of the well-known principle *aut dedere aut judicare*)' (Gioia 2006: 9, emphasis added). With the exception of the 1999 *Convention for the Suppression of the Financing of Terrorism,* none of these agreements attempt to define international terrorism. However, the 1999 definition does not remedy the need for a general definition, as it gives only an indirect definition: the convention determines a secondary offense (illegal financial activities), which are related to a primary offense (acts that are considered to be terrorist acts) without defining terrorism itself. According to critics, this has produced the paradoxical situation that the 'very existence of this definition makes the need to adopt a general definition of the "primary" offence even more evident' (Gioia 2006: 13).

Moreover, a good part of the agreements even shrink away from referring to 'terrorism' or 'terrorist acts' and the ones alluding to the terms confine themselves in defining the offenses to which they explicitly relate without giving any explanation of why these offenses are considered as manifestations of international terrorism. On the whole, the conventions confirm the assumption that some offenses are considered in themselves to be offenses of international concern, irrespective of any specific 'terrorist' intent or purpose (for instance, hijacking of aircrafts) (Gioia 2006: 8–13).

In 1999, a second round of debate was launched. Three years after the GA re-established the Ad Hoc Committee on Terrorism and provided it with the mandate to draft appropriate instruments against international terrorism, the Committee was requested to work once more on a comprehensive convention on international terrorism (UN Sixth Committee 2000d). Starting point was a new draft for a comprehensive convention by India – a draft very much mindful of the daunting attempts two decades earlier. This cautious handling did not prevent old disagreements from resurfacing. They are roughly the same, shared by the same Member States as in the 1970s and the main problem still lies in finding a legal definition of terrorism accepted by all members. Slight changes can be observed in the attitude of some states; the traditional view of the Arab states on the exclusion of state terrorism has now become negotiable under the condition that political violence by liberation movements also be exempted, and the classical request of the Western hemisphere to take concrete measures before studying the underlying causes of international terrorism has been somewhat watered down (Jachtenfuchs *et al.* 2008: 10).

After the attacks of 11 September 2001, the newly resumed attempts to reach a comprehensive convention once again failed, due to the opposition of new proposals by certain 'Third World' states, particularly by the Organization of the Islamic Conference, which still insisted on the exemption of national liberation movements. However, the current divides between the various sections of the GA not only separate the 'West' from the 'South' but also represent a division of a different nature, i.e. the increasing Western ideological and power struggles, notably between the USA and its 'Coalition of the Willing' versus the balancing stance of France and Germany (Wiesbrock 2002; Friedrichs 2006). The debates are currently still underway.

Yet, why has the quest for a universally acceptable definition of international terrorism failed at the UN? Why is agreement on the definition of such a major threat so difficult?[3] Despite their political importance (in particular with regard to their legitimating function), the bulk of current scholarly research does not deal with the UN debates but focuses on questions of international law or treats counter-terrorism measures in the context of the European Union (Gal-Or 1985; Schmid 1993; Chalk 1996; van Krieken 2002; Archick and Gallis 2003). Scholars who approach the topic from a more explicit IR perspective (and are less policy-oriented but theory driven) consider conflicting national interests and preferences as main explanatory factors. The argument says since the concept of what counts as terrorist offences is highly intermingled with the different interests of the nations, any concession to the other side is considered as a challenge to sovereignty. To give up the right to define terrorism according to one's own rationale, to define one's own public enemy, is interpreted as a direct attack to the core of the sovereign power. Hence, sectoral conventions restrict this right in only one point, but a universally accepted decision would delimit sovereign power considerably (Jenkins 1986; Friedrichs 2006; Gioia 2006; Jachtenfuchs *et al.* 2008).

Other scholars assert that the institutional context of the UN explains the inability of the UN to foster an agreement. The UN's powerlessness is not only related to it's lack of authority to command governments to agree on a definition and to avoid particular actions. It also refers to the ambivalence of the UN's treatment of the whole question of politically motivated violence. The *Declaration on the Principles of International Law concerning Friendly Relations and Co-operation among States in accordance with the Charter of the United Nations* spells out that all states have a the duty to realize the principle of self-determination 'in order to bring a speedy end to colonialism [. . .]' and that 'every state has the duty to refrain from any forcible action which deprives peoples [. . .] of their right of self-determination'. The declaration continues: '[i]n their actions against, and resistance to, such forcible action in pursuit of their right to self-determination, such peoples are entitled to seek and receive support' (UN General Assembly 1970: 123–4). Many take these clauses to mean that the UN legitimizes any struggle undertaken in the name of the principle of national liberation but also that it condones international support for such struggles. This ambiguity is said to be reflected in the UN attempt to define terrorism and severely hampers its role as a developer of a normative discourse and an encourager of cooperative action (Wilkinson 1997; van Krieken 2002; Osman 2003; Boulden and Weiss 2004; Frowein 2006).

In contrast, a growing body of literature analyzes terrorism from a discursive, critical perspective and the study ties in with the assumption of the constructed nature of the phenomenon and the critical investigation of the politicization of the issue for legitimizing far-reaching security measures.[4] Yet, the study adds a comparative perspective to the present body of works and argues that questioning in how far a hegemonic order has been constructed in the international discourse on terrorism provides a possible answer to the puzzle of the missing definition of terrorism and, thereby, offers a change of perspective on the topic of international terrorism. To ask whether and how a dominant pattern and a specific meaning of terrorism have spread in the field analyzes the quest for a definition as a quest for determining the antagonistic Other *and* the Self that is opposed to it.

Constructing the international terrorist threat – the imponderabilities of establishing an antagonistic frontier

The challenge of the present section consists in reconstructing the dynamics of the basic productive hegemonic strategy *Establishing an antagonistic frontier*. Thus, we aim to retrace in how far an Other is constructed as a threat to the subjects which equivalential articulations are trying to relate. In this respect, the UN did not deal with just any type of terrorism; the debates attempted to define *international* terrorism, which explicitly excluded any kind of national/domestic terrorism. 'International terrorism was international by definition' (UN Sixth Committee 1972k: 339) – and the global dimension only increased the threat emanating from terrorism. It is not surprising, then, that the Other terrorism is constructed in an unconcealed, antagonistic manner. Terrorists employ 'indiscriminate violence' since they are 'jeopardizing the lives of men, women and children' and this 'indiscriminate killing of innocent civilians could not be justified by any cause'. It would be 'morally untenable' to regard specific political motives as an excuse for terrorist acts – no cause can justify terrorist violence, neither in the 1970s nor in the twenty-first century, regardless of how serious the political considerations might be. Terrorism is terrorism and cannot be defended (UN Ad Hoc Committee on International Terrorism 2010: 11; UN Sixth Committee 1972c: 255; 1972f: 288; 2003a: 12). This denial is wrapped in a language of demonization of terrorism: it is an 'evil' that needs to be 'eradicated', a 'scourge', 'one of the most atrocious forms that violence could assume', it is 'barbarous, ignoble and heinous' (UN Sixth Committee 1972b: 246; UN Ad Hoc Committee on International Terrorism 1973c: 12; UN Sixth Committee 2005b: 8; 2008b: 6).

Most importantly, terrorism is constructed as a *threat to international peace and security*. It has 'assumed such proportions that it was currently threatening the very survival of the world community' (UN Sixth Committee 1972c: 256) and is now a problem which was threatening to destroy organized modern society and mankind itself (UN Sixth Committee 1972i: 326; 1997a: 3; UN Ad Hoc Committee on International Terrorism 1973b: 21). Despite 'the international community's efforts to combat terrorism, that scourge continued to claim countless human lives and cause incalculable damage to property, threatening the internal security of States and international peace and security' (UN Sixth Committee 2000c: 5). Indeed, terrorism poses a serious threat to peace and security and therefore endangers 'civilization, democracy, civil society and the rule of law. It also undermined human rights and fundamental freedoms, first and foremost the right to life' (UN Sixth Committee 2005b: 10). Hence, a phenomenon against which the civilized world has the right to wage war. As in the discourse on drugs, the Other is deemed responsible for the lack of the world, hindering the world to achieve the ultimate goal, i.e. to free itself from terrorism. By excluding all those who perpetrate terrorist acts, i.e. attack the world and its values, the notion 'international terrorism' is gradually emptied to the point where it can only be defined as barbaric and as a threat to the civilized world. Consequently, international terrorism prevents the world permanently from being what it originally should be: a peaceful place for every man, promoting universal values of liberty, freedom and equality. The civilized world cannot attain a full-fledged identity as long as international terrorism endangers it, it cannot overcome its lack – a clear blocking of identity: 'Terrorism would fail when global stability, based on prosperity, peace and a culture of human rights and tolerance for all, was established' (UN Sixth Committee 2004: 3).

Yet, this is only half of the story. The discourse is far from yielding a coherent picture of terrorism. Due to a number of restrictions and limitations, the construction of the Other becomes highly heterogeneous, whereby elements are constituted as terrorist and non-terrorist at the same time. Differential articulations criticize the unified picture of the Other and attempt to differentiate it. To nuance its image is based on the requests, first, to take the underlying causes of terrorism into account; second, to disassociate national liberation movements, the right of self-determination and wartime resistance from terrorism; and, third, subjects are accused of state terrorism.[5]

With regard to the underlying causes, it is striking to observe how the title of the GA agenda item concerning terrorism changed at the beginning of the debate. Late in 1972, the title altered from 'Measures to prevent terrorism and other forms of violence which endanger or take innocent human lives or jeopardize fundamental freedoms' to a lengthy formula explicitly stating potential reasons for terrorism:

> Measures to prevent international terrorism which endangers or takes innocent human lives or jeopardizes fundamental freedoms, and study of the underlying causes of those forms of terrorism and acts of violence which lie in misery, frustration, grievance and despair and which cause some people to sacrifice human lives, including their own, in an attempt to effect radical changes.
>
> (UN Sixth Committee 1972r: 1)

Since terrorism 'was not an isolated phenomenon' it 'should be viewed in the framework of several serious international problems for which, unfortunately, no solution had yet been found' (UN Sixth Committee 1972l: 345; 1972d: 259). The problem could not be resolved merely by the adoption of legal instruments because any measure needs to acknowledge the causes (see also UN General Assembly 1972: 11; UN Sixth Committee 1972c: 256). Yet, in the second round the title shifted back to 'Measures to eliminate international terrorism', which indicates that the request to study the underlying causes is watered down as outlined above (UN Sixth Committee 1997a; 2009: 5).

Contextualizing terrorism within its *causes* that are, first, somewhat innocent causes (who would not like to change her situation with every available means if poor, miserable and frustrated?) and, second, to consider the causes of terrorism also as the root of a number of other problems turns terrorism into one serious issue among others and deprives it from its outstanding role other articulations have tried to assign it. It also leaves the door ajar to legitimize violence: violence is justified if it is used to alter the unfortunate situation of an individual, and it is justified because terrorist violence is considered as the last resort for those who have no other options (see among other examples UN Sixth Committee 1972j: 333). Two forms of violence are created: the one that can be 'accepted' because it stems from 'just' causes versus a violence which cannot be 'accepted' because it is not rooted in the 'just' causes, misery, grievance and despair. According to the contenders of a study of the underlying causes, only the latter type of violence counts as international terrorism. More bluntly stated, if a specific type of violence is constructed as non-terrorist and justifiable because, in the end, its underlying causes are comprehensible (since they are all 'too human'), then it becomes impossible to associate it with the antagonistic Other, terrorism. This is the case when it is said that freedom fighters 'could not be regarded in the same light as international terrorists' (UN Sixth Committee 1972e: 272). Understanding the causes implies an Other with 'faults and quirks' but an Other that deserves certain empathy.

While the request for recognizing the causes attempts to produce a differentiated image of terrorism, it involves elements of power – and this is highlighted by what exactly the causes are about. In a supposedly neutral manner, the title of the agenda item speaks of misery, grievance and despair. In consequence, when 'foreign occupation and domination' deny 'the right for people to self-determination', then, the acts of 'peoples subjugated by imperialism and colonialism, neo-colonialism and racial discrimination' cannot be considered as terrorist acts since they are 'shaking off the yoke of exploitation and oppression' (UN Sixth Committee 1972d: 260; 1997c: 4; 2005b: 12; 2008b: 10). Terrorism as a reaction to exploitation and oppression excuses the terrorist's reaction at the expense of the causes. Consequently, subjects with a colonial past are constructed as being terrorists themselves, since their doings as colonial powers are considered to have laid the foundations of today's international terrorism.

In conjunction with this reasoning, articulations defame any attempts to disgrace the right to *self-determination* of particular subjects. Most importantly, it is demanded to free the national liberation movements and the right of self-determination from any association with terrorism. For those subjects – in particular a great number of African states – who consider themselves as the offspring of these movements and, therefore, justify the violence of the movements with reference to the right of self-determination of the peoples, this disassociation becomes a critical issue. 'The fight of peoples to self-determination did not come within the scope of international terrorism' since the movements are 'the struggle of peoples for their national identity' and, therefore, those subjects can only comply with a 'definition of international terrorism [that] would not include the just struggles of liberation movements' (UN Sixth Committee 1972o: 459; UN Ad Hoc Committee on International Terrorism 1973a: 13; UN Sixth Committee 2001: 4; 2008a: 10). To designate the struggle of national liberation movements as terrorism disqualifies and discredits those who are a product of theses struggles and doubt their quality as sovereign identities.[6]

Conversely, the same is requested for the association of terrorism with *wartime resistance movements* and the wars Western states fought in the years thereafter.

> In that connexion, the equating of transnational terrorism with resistance movements during the Second World War was unacceptable. [. . .] They had never practiced indiscriminate terrorism, operated against neutral territory or taken hostage. The difference between wartime resistance and transnational terrorism was thus enormous.
>
> (UN Sixth Committee, 1972h: 313)

Again, two forms of violence are created: one that is justifiable because of its legitimate motives (resistance) while the other is non-justifiable since it is not based on legitimate motives and is indiscriminate (terrorism). Thus, the legitimacy of the motives of freedom fighters is doubted by the defenders of the wartime movements, since they could claim to have fought out of legitimate motives, whereas the others are terrorists without just causes. Yet, there are also some rare moderate voices aligning resistance movements with the struggle for national liberation. 'The French Maquisards, the Algerians who had fought for their independence and freedom-fighters struggling to recover their basic rights in Southern Africa [. . .] could not be regarded in the same light as international terrorists' (UN Sixth Committee, 1972h: 313). From this alternative view, the motives of both movements are equally legitimate, thus, they are both different from international terrorism. However, these voices are sidelined very early in the debate, since they do not match the general, already established parameters of the discourse.

Thirdly, *state terrorism* is considered as a manifestation of terrorism because it violated the right of peoples to self-determination (see among many others UN Sixth Committee 1972e: 271; 1972h: 313; UN Ad Hoc Committee on International Terrorism 1979c: 5). In this respect, state terrorism may take two forms. First, 'state action to enforce domestic policies by terror might endanger the maintenance of international peace and security, and might thus become international terrorism' (UN Sixth Committee 1972l: 355). Second, 'terrorists included not only those who committed terrorist acts but also those who harboured terrorists' and, therefore, '[s]tates must ensure that their territories were not used for terrorist installations or training camps or for the preparation or organization of terrorist acts to be committed against other States or their citizens' (UN Sixth Committee 2002a: 3; 2005c: 13). The accusation of state terrorism does not only associate the suspected subjects with international terrorism but also considers them as terrorist. Those targeted by state terrorism consider it a danger to their sovereignty and therefore suspect especially Western states of making use of state terrorism. Ultimately, these powers (read the West) are responsible for the spread of terrorism and, now, as terrorism has 'gotten out of hand' they misuse the UN for their own interests. The world will only be able to fill its lack (i.e. to get rid of terrorism) when 'those powers [that are accused of state terrorism] ceased to resort to expedients and to act in accordance with their special interests' (UN Sixth Committee 1972b: 246). In this mélange, the UN is frequently accused of a 'double standard', i.e. of promoting a Western interpretation of terrorism only. The rationale of these accusations resides in determining the antagonistic Other by associating specific subjects with terrorism and declaring them responsible for the lack the world and humanity are experiencing. Hence, antagonistic frontiers are drawn between those subjects that are accused of supporting terrorism and those that are 'genuinely' interested in freeing the world from the evil terrorism.

While the issue of state terrorism and national liberation movements has receded, the content of the underlying causes has shifted since the end of the 1990s and at the beginning of the twenty-first century. It is now fiercely repudiated the causes of terrorism lie in specific cultures or religions, i.e. any relation between Islam, Arabs and terrorism is strongly rejected. Terrorism as indiscriminate violence 'should not be associated with any specific race, religion or culture' (UN Sixth Committee 1998: 4). Moreover, 'terrorism was antithetical to the teachings of Islam, which advocated peace, tolerance, non-violence and harmony' and 'it had nothing to do with the truth of any religion' (UN Sixth Committee 2003b: 7; 2008a: 14). Therefore, measures 'should not target the followers of one religion or another, as that would be to fall into the trap set by extremists who hoped to sow division and provoke a clash of civilizations'. And 'the international community should be more involved in countering defamatory campaigns against Islam' (UN Sixth Committee 2005b: 3, 5). To reject any association of terrorism with specific elements or forces is an attempt to 'shorten' the chain of equivalence representing the antagonistic Other and increases the heterogeneity of the latter's construction. These rejections account for the supplementary counter-hegemonic strategy *Attempts to disarticulate floating elements of chain Z*. As with the national liberation movements, we again witness an 'identity-struggle': for subjects that conceive themselves as Arabic or Islamic nations, the association of region and religion with terrorism discredits integral elements of their national identity. Therefore, any association of these elements with terrorism needs to be repudiated.

Overall, these various associations or their refutations signal two further counter-hegemonic strategies. To request the study of the underlying causes goes not only hand in hand with crossing a (presumed) antagonistic frontier but also with attempts to weaken the latter by replacing it. In addition, to accuse other subjects of being terrorists (as with state terrorism) is also an attempt to displace an antagonistic frontier. This movement of crossing the antagonistic frontier is embraced by the supplementary counter-hegemonic strategy *Underscore particularity of a subject/ element of chain Z*. Further, to request the exclusion of resistance movements, of national liberation movements, and the full respect of the right of self-determination accounts for the preservation of the particularity of a subject that is articulated as part of the antagonizing chain of equivalence, a dynamic which is addressed by the supplementary counter-hegemonic strategy *Protect particularity of a subject by articulating its particularity as part of chain Z*. Both movements equally indicate the operation of counter-hegemonic strategy *Weakening of antagonistic frontier* of the basic dimension.[7]

The identified counter-hegemonic strategies are highly interwoven. As chapter two has outlined, the basic counter-hegemonic strategy implies the weakening of the frontier and the two above mentioned supplementing strategies specify the 'how' of this weakening. Yet, they do not strive to displace the antagonistic frontiers to the margins of the discourse but to re-draw it at another place. This is a clear signal for the struggle of at least two hegemonic projects attempting to install their particular meaning of terrorism as universal understanding. They aspire to install a particular world organization by drawing the frontier of terrorism in a specific manner, claiming that this particular meaning will heal the lack of the world; thus, both projects claim for universality while each denies the validity of the other.

This struggle explains well the overall weakness of productive hegemonic strategies in the discourse on terrorism. The larger number of counter-hegemonic strategies producing a highly heterogeneous picture of the Other let us conclude that the construction of a stable antagonistic frontier and homogenous Other has failed. In contrast, the delineation from the Other turns into a 'battlefield' of different hegemonic projects, since to describe a discursive movement as counter-hegemonic always involves a productive part. For instance, to cross the antagonistic frontier by refusing the association of national liberation movements with terrorism and simultaneously associate colonialism with terrorism comes as counter-hegemonic strategy. The productive part, then, resides in the attempt to establish an antagonistic frontier – though in a different place.

The analysis reveals the difficulties of constructing an unambiguous antagonistic Other in the discourse on terrorism. Too many different meanings of terrorism impede *one* homogeneous antagonistic Other represented by an antagonized chain of equivalence. At minimum, the discourse is marked by two contradicting meanings of what terrorism is about. A highly heterogeneous discourse appears as different and contradicting understandings of terrorism are struggling to become hegemonic. Both retraced meanings exclude certain possibilities from the political space (for instance, terrorists as civilized persons) but each of them makes other things possible: on the one hand, subjects with a colonial past are associated with terrorism and national liberation movements are disassociated from terrorism; on the other hand, national liberation movements are related to terrorism and subjects with a colonial past are disconnected from terrorism. As both meanings are essentially contradictory and the discourse is abundant with counter-hegemonic strategies, it is impossible to construct an antagonistic frontier.

Attempts to construct the 'good' Self

Attempting to forge a consensus on how to fight international terrorism

In 1972, the taking of Israeli hostages by Palestinians represented an event of an unknown scale, disrupting the entire discourse on terrorism to date. To say it in UN-Secretary General Waldheim's words, the event showed that the scope of terrorist activity as well as its underlying causes have increasingly become international [. . .] because modern technology has added a formidable new dimension to that ancient problem [. . .]. Such a development would inevitably also endanger international relations and make even more difficult the efforts of the United Nations and the Governments to achieve peaceful solutions of serious problems.

(UN General Assembly 1972: 11)

What is at stake here can best be circumscribed by the notion of dislocation, which I introduced in chapter one. The moment of dislocation is a rupture, a breach of the discursive structure by an event that cannot be represented within the discourse. Thereby, dislocation reveals to the subject the contingency of this very structure. Facing the destruction of signifiers it formerly identified with, the subject now needs to reconstitute itself and therefore relocates its identity(ies) by identifying with a different signifier in a renewed or different discourse. Exactly such a moment of dislocation can be reconstructed in the discourse on terrorism. The brief historical outline has already mentioned that the taking of hostages during the Olympic Games in 1972 is considered as the triggering moment for international cooperation against terrorism, as it threw an issue – though with a different meaning – back on the international agenda. It is this event which, as I argue, provides for a dislocation of the discourse on terrorism of that time. Obviously, there existed a discourse on terrorism before 1972, not only because of the earlier attempts to forge a comprehensive convention by the League of Nations but also due to the adoption of the three UN-conventions against specific types of terrorist offenses.[8] However, exactly this discourse is dislocated by the attacks.[9] The taking of hostages was an event that could not have been represented or integrated in the terrorism discourse of that time, since this event indicated an unknown sort of phenomenon: international terrorism carried out everywhere, by perpetrators and victims without binds to the place of the attacks.

Keeping this in mind, it is no surprise that in the discussion in the UN Sixth Committee delegations strenuously outlined the 'importance and urgency of the problem posed by international terrorism' of which 'all delegations were aware' (UN Sixth Committee 1972s: 11). 'Terrorism was above all a condemnation of international society and of the unjust order prevailing therein', moreover, 'it was the symptom of the ills of the contemporary world, which must be sought and cured before a world equilibrium free from fear and violence could be established' (UN Sixth Committee 1972j: 333). It is the world's task to confront the new challenges in a 'concerted effort', since without such an effort 'a more just and safer world' would be difficult to build (UN Sixth Committee 1997a: 5). Hence, the discourse aims at 'a world free of terrorism' because without terrorism the world would be 'a safer place' (UN Sixth Committee 2005c: 8; 2005d: 3). From 1972 on, the world is constructed as experiencing a *lack* of freedom and peace because terrorism prevails: as long as terrorists are able to carry out their attacks, humanity is not safe and the achievements of civilization endangered by the 'barbarians'.

However, subjects in the terrorism discourse are voicing quite different demands on how to fill and remedy this lack. They express a number of *goals* (ultimate and common), attempt to establish a consensus and point out the *means* to achieve consensus and goals. The lack also encompasses the *ultimate goal*, i.e. the goal represents the flip side of the lack: since the world suffers from terrorism, it cannot be a safe and just place. To free the world from terrorism and 'maintain international peace' is constructed as the ultimate goal of any debate attempting to define and, thereby, counter terrorism (UN Sixth Committee 1972f: 289). This is even more important, as every country in the world is not spared by terrorism – to free the world from terrorism needs to be a *universal concern*. Terrorist acts are perpetrated in circumstances involving 'international relations' and therefore 'become the concern' of the 'international community' which 'must confront the challenge of terrorism, which could strike any state in the world' (UN Sixth Committee 1972e: 271, 3; UN Ad Hoc Committee on International Terrorism 1973a: 24). In the twenty-first century, terrorism is even more an 'international phenomenon affecting the entire world' and it was 'one of the serious problems facing the international community, because of the threat it posed and the fact that no State, small or large, could escape its consequences'. Moreover, terrorism is a highly 'contagious disease' that has demonstrated its power since 'no people or region was immune to horrors of terrorist violence' (UN Sixth Committee 2000c: 2, 12; 2005d: 10). Without a doubt, the reference constructing a universal concern represents an ideal type of equivalential articulations because they attempt to even out any differences between the various subjects: inasmuch as no country in the world remains untouched by terrorism, every country needs to be concerned by it.

But what can free the world from terrorism? The lack of the world can be filled only by identifying with the *fight against terrorism* and forging an agreement on a universally acceptable definition of and a comprehensive convention against terrorism as common goals. All 'measures designed to eliminate terrorism' need to be carried out and the 'United Nations should take action against terrorism as a matter of urgency' (UN Ad Hoc Committee on International Terrorism 1973a: 24). The 'increasing concern of the international community at the acts of terrorism' (UN Sixth Committee 1997b: 6) implies to redouble the efforts 'to combat terrorism in all its forms and manifestations' as 'terrorism must be fought and all terrorist acts condemned' (see also UN Sixth Committee 1972m: 371; 2005b: 9; 2008b: 9; UN Ad Hoc Committee on International Terrorism 1999: 15).[10] Since all subjects participating in the discourse agree on the necessity to fight terrorism, we can consider the fight as the general equivalent, i.e. as 'the something underlying' all subjects need to share in order to forge a chain of equivalence. This wide-spread agreement on the fight against terrorism is forcefully underscored by the high number of frequencies and co-occurrences in both rounds of the debates.[11]

A universally acceptable *definition of terrorism* is presented as the essential step in the fight, since the 'expression "international terrorism" lent itself to subjective interpretations and must be defined before such terrorism could be condemned' (UN Sixth Committee 1972a: 249). Moreover, 'for the sake of legal clarity and in order to ensure that possible future developments in terrorist activities were provided

Table 4.1 Frequencies and co-occurrences of 'fight against international terrorism'

	Hits
Overall frequency of the fight against terrorism	3574
Occurrences with all codes (overall 279 codes)	2427
Occurrences with Other codes	913
Occurrences with Self codes[1]	422
Occurrences with cooperation codes[2]	607

1 Self codes are all codes related to the international community, particular countries or organizations and their respective self-descriptions, based on national identities or their engagement in the fight against terrorism.
2 Cooperation codes are: 'Call for cooperation', 'willingness to cooperate', 'disposition to cooperate', 'fight via international cooperation'.

for' subjectivity needs to be avoided in the evaluation of terrorist acts (UN Sixth Committee 2007: 4). Indeed, the

> [t]ime had come to arrive at consensus on a clear and universally accepted definition of terrorism, for without it, all efforts to do battle with a common enemy would be in vain. Such a definition would make it possible to agree on the requisite legal characterization of terrorist acts and to determine the procedure for prosecuting and punishing them.
>
> (UN Sixth Committee 2005d: 4)

The definition should be part of a broader convention on terrorism since 'there was now a need for a broader convention that would fill the gaps' earlier instruments against international terrorism had left and a considerable number of countries 'supported the idea of a general convention on terrorism' (UN Sixth Committee 1972i: 321–6). This common goal was re-inscribed over the years: from 1972 to the beginning of the present century, delegates still support 'the *goal* of concluding a comprehensive convention on international terrorism' as it will 'effectively supplement the existing conventions and deny safe havens to terrorists anywhere in the world' and 'would unambiguously demonstrate a global political commitment to criminalize all terrorist acts' (UN Ad Hoc Committee on International Terrorism 2010: 6; UN Sixth Committee 2000a: 2; 2005d: 14, emphasis added; 2008a: 4). In order to achieve these common goals the engagement of every country in the struggle against terrorism is needed. In turn, this demand is embedded in the call for *international cooperation* against terrorism and the call for a consensus that should unite the countries countering terrorism. The entire skeleton of goals and concern are substantiated with reference to these means (thought to achieve the goals). In this respect, particularly revealing are the high frequencies of cooperation in the international discourse on terrorism: overall, cooperation scored 1,131 times in the entire discourse with 145 hits in the first round of debates (1972–1979) and 986 hits in the years from 1997 to 2010.

Pointing out that every country of the world needs to be engaged in the struggle against terrorism addresses predominantly the status of adherence to existing international conventions, since 'states should take all necessary measures within their domestic jurisdiction to prevent acts of international terrorism' (UN Sixth Committee 1972c: 257; see also 1972e: 274). While this element has played an important role in the first round of the debates, its relevance decreases in the second round because the individual engagement of every country is mostly referred to by itself, i.e. by pointing out the efforts one has undertaken to confront terrorism on the national level (see UN Sixth Committee 2000a: 6; 2005b: 6). The more every nation's participation in the struggle against terrorism is requested, the louder and more drastic the call for international cooperation as a means to counter terrorism is. To be precise: the call for international cooperation is more forcefully heard in the second round. Besides the sheer number of frequencies, the links between general equivalent, ultimate and common goals is the same in both situations of analysis. Compare, for instance, the following examples:

> [. . .] to develop international co-operation with a view to protecting the international community against acts of international terrorism which threatened basic values and the very fabric of international legal order.
>
> (UN Sixth Committee 1972c: 258)

> The international community must muster the same firm resolve to confront terrorism whatever the mask that it sought to hide behind. In so doing, it was important to remember not only what was being fought against but what was being fought for, namely the most fundamental principles cherished by individuals and society at large: the right to life, the most basic freedoms and the rule of law. Those were the values that the terrorists sought to destroy and they were the values that Member States must commit themselves to defend.
>
> (UN Sixth Committee 2005d: 14)

Such statements are accompanied recurrently by the appeal to a consensus indispensable to counter terrorism, since 'a collective approach to the problem required consensus' or 'in order to ensure co-operation in the taking of joint measures, it was necessary to achieve a closer identity of views' (UN Sixth Committee 1972c: 252; 2000c: 8). The central position of cooperation as means to achieve the goals is supported by the above-mentioned overall number of 1,131 hits in all documents of the terrorism discourse.

Yet, the fight against terrorism is embedded in a mesh of reservations and limitations implying a fight subject to numerous restrictions. Such restrictions are determined by specific conditions deemed relevant or essential to particular subjects. Most importantly, these reservations arise on *how to* fight terrorism: while it is undisputed *that* terrorism has to be fought, the 'how to' is highly contentious. Reservations range from the call to bear in mind 'the over-all context in which the phenomenon had its roots' (a clear reference to the above-discussed underlying causes) or the assertion that one is in favour of an 'all-out campaign against terrorism, provided it was aimed at terrorism as a whole, i.e. both its causes and effects' to the advice that 'the best way of coping with the complexity of the question, would be to delimit the scope of the convention by excluding certain categories or acts rather than by devising an abstract definition' (UN Sixth Committee 1972e: 271; 1972c: 277; 1972g: 302). Raising such reservations tends to 'culminate' in the assertion that a delegation could only accept a particular type of definition; assertions which are more often than not the opposite of each other, as the following quotes illustrate:

> His delegation did not deny the value and necessity of defining international terrorism and studying its underlying causes, provided that did not hinder the adoption of urgent and concrete measures to combat terrorist acts.
>
> (UN Sixth Committee 1972k: 337)

> His delegation welcomed any international regulations designed to prevent and eradicate terrorism. But there was a need to formulate an adequate and acceptable definition of that phenomenon while duly reserving the principle of self-determination and the legitimacy of national struggles against colonialism and foreign domination.
>
> (UN Sixth Committee 1972j: 328)

As I have outlined on the construction of the terrorist Other, the underlying causes of terrorism represent the stumbling stone for a consensus. Either the demand is voiced to study these causes before measures are devised: '[b]efore any remedial steps were taken, a study must be carried out and a deeper understanding of the problem achieved' (UN Sixth Committee 1972m: 369). Or concrete measures are called for without analyzing the causes since this represents a too lengthy endeavour: 'A knowledge of the underlying causes did not necessarily bring a solution nearer' (UN Sixth Committee 1972h: 312; 2001: 5; see also 2006: 10). Or – as third option – 'measures to prevent international terrorism and the study of its underlying causes' should 'be pursued simultaneously' (UN Ad Hoc Committee on International Terrorism 1973a: 9).

Reaching a consensus is further complicated by an increasing climate of mistrust which dominates the debates. Delegations start to raise *accusations of hypocrisy* and *to doubt the engagement* of other delegations. They suspect each other of lacking 'a genuine desire for cooperation' or of '[m]aking false and unfounded allegations against others' and both are 'not conducive to the collective struggle against terrorism' (UN Ad Hoc Committee on International Terrorism 1979b: 4; UN Sixth Committee 2000c: 4). Especially in the first round, representatives do not hesitate to single out particular countries and to accuse them. 'The Portuguese delegation [. . .] had also expressed condemnation of international terrorism; but the sincerity of a condemnation that came from the representatives of colonial oppressors of the peoples of Angola, Guinea (Bissau) and Mozambique was highly dubious'. (UN Sixth

Committee 1972g: 295) Accordingly, it must be assumed that 'in the minds of certain people terrorism was only that which was directed against them. The terrorism which they themselves perpetrated was not supposed to be terrorism' (UN Sixth Committee 1972f: 288). Here, not only single delegations but also the UN are guilty of applying double standards by accepting 'violence and terror as the natural lot of the poor, the weak and the oppressed' and now being 'scandalized to see the rich and the powerful made the victims of those evils' (UN Sixth Committee 1972e: 271). In the 1970s, these differential articulations culminated in the denial of the general equivalent, i.e. it was claimed that the world has other, more pressing problems than to fight international terrorism (UN Sixth Committee 1972i: 318). The fight is refused and repudiated by referring to poverty; hunger etc., problems the world needs to solve first. Therefore, the general equivalent – *that* terrorism has to be fought – comes under serious pressure. As these issues are most often raised by those subjects calling for the study of underlying causes of terrorism before devising measures, the construction of terrorism as an outcome of 'misery, grievance and despair' is again stressed. Yet, in the second round, terrorism as *the* most pressing worldwide problem is no longer doubted.

Although the tone attenuated somewhat in the debates in the twenty-first century, accusing others and doubting their engagement still involves a strong moment of differentiation, even more as these accusations frequently construct other subjects in a negative manner. Working in an admittedly simple manner *à la* 'I accuse you of not supporting the fight against terrorism while saying I do support it', the negative singling out of a subject serves to differentiate another subject in a positive way. Subjects re-emphasize their differential character and deliver a number of self-descriptions (being in favour of an international fight against terrorism, calling for cooperation in this fight, considering terrorism as enemy etc.) by the accusations of others – this is exactly what the basic counter-hegemonic strategy *Particularization* of subjects is about.

Against these accusations, delegations defend themselves by referring to their status as a sovereign member of the international community. Their *sovereignty* is invoked in the context of the right of non-interference in the domestic affairs of a state proclaimed by the UN Charter (Article 2(7)) and a comprehensive convention on terrorism (including a definition of it) should respect the principle of national sovereignty. This implies that 'a terrorist act in which the actor and the victims were nationals of the same State and which took place within that State was purely an internal matter and should be settled in accordance with national criminal law'. In brief, international terrorism was perpetrated only when 'foreign elements [. . .] associated themselves with acts unrelated to the exercise of the right of self-determination' (UN Sixth Committee 1972g: 299; see also 1972i: 321; 2005a: 7). Sovereignty serves not only to differentiate a subject from others but also emphasizes the particularity of a subject at the expense of the – already instable – general equivalent, a movement which signals the supplementary counter-hegemonic strategy *Stressing the particularity of a subject of chain A explicitly at the expense of the general equivalent*. Having said that the general equivalent consists above all of the agreement that terrorism has to be fought without agreement on *how to* fight, the request to respect national sovereignty also limits the scope of this fight. By reiterating that the fight is directed against international terrorism only, domestic terrorism is relegated to the sole authority of the state concerned. Constructing a subject as sovereign and therefore able to decide on appropriate measures on how to treat domestic terrorism, differentiates the subjects from each other.

As in the drugs discourse, differentiation springs less from a specific interpretation of sovereignty by each Self. It is much more the general idea of what sovereign nations look like that drives acts of differentiation against attempts to forge equivalential bonds between subjects. Sovereignty implicitly calls upon elements of national identity, culture and traditions, all the more, since the issues of extradition and asylum are raised in its context. While there should be no place for terrorists in the world, the national traditions in these issues should not be altered by the international fight against it. How to deal with asylum seekers and how to handle extradition is constructed as firmly rooted in a specific understanding of law, which are in their turn part of the identity of a state (UN Sixth Committee 1972i: 315; 2000a: 4).

Subjects in the process of universalization

So far, the international community has been repeatedly referred to, as well as the states and other actors forming this community. This leads us to question what kind of subjects are present in the discourse on terrorism. Most importantly, we encounter states as subjects which are frequently characterized with regard to their position towards terrorism, for example, Turkey which considered itself as 'a country which had long suffered from terrorism, therefore called on the international community to take effective action against [. . .] terrorism' (UN Sixth Committee 2000a: 7). Therefore, a country's experience with terrorism not only portrays the nation but also draws a line between those '[g]overnments which were more in touch with the factual situations' and 'victims of continuing aggression' by terrorism and countries 'less' touched by the phenomenon (UN Sixth Committee 1972k: 341; 1972m: 369). A more aggressive distinction is drawn between those countries who are the offspring of national liberation movements and the 'colonial and imperialist regimes': while the former 'should be given no excuse for suppressing the legitimate struggle of national liberation movements' the 'colonial regimes' do not explicitly reject the accusation (UN Sixth Committee 1972n: 454–76). However, this distinction fades in the renewed discussions from 1999 onwards.[12]

Individuals affected by terrorism emerge as objects rather than subjects in the discourse. These individuals 'are not parties to that conflict' as they are constructed as 'innocent victims' of terrorism (UN Sixth Committee 1972n: 453; UN Ad Hoc Committee on International Terrorism 1973a: 19). Victims are 'men, women and children', 'anyone who happened to cross his [the terrorist's] path' or 'vulnerable populations' in need of protection from terrorism – a duty that should be undertaken by the international community (UN Sixth Committee 1972c: 253; 2005a: 9; 2005d: 3; see also 2008a: 9).

It is worth underlining that the identified subjects – albeit to a different degree – acknowledge the ultimate goal and the general equivalent of a fight against international terrorism. Yet, I have also outlined that subscribing to both as common goals is embedded in a web of restrictions and limitations, which alters the meaning of the general equivalent considerably and is captured by the disagreement on the *how to* of the fight against terrorism. The ambiguous quality of the general equivalent impedes a coherent universalization of the differential subjects as requested to identify the basic productive hegemonic strategy *Universalization*. This is particularly the case in the 1970s. Here, 'the something that underlies them all' is obscured by the reservations uttered along with the fight against terrorism; therefore, universalization is perturbed and the equivalential bonds stressing that all subjects want to fight terrorism is too often restricted and limited to specific areas, cases, acts etc. In the course of the second round, the picture becomes clearer, with the fight against terrorism less implanted in various, even contradictory restrictions. The character of equivalential articulations stressing the commonalities of particular subjects is much more palpable than in the first round.

Consequently, the reconstruction of basic productive hegemonic strategy *Universalization* produces a mixed picture in the discourse on terrorism. Too many restrictions are raised in direct relation to the general equivalent, damaging its capability to universalize the subjects present in the discourse and work as their common reference point. While the ultimate goal of a world free from terrorism is not doubted, the question of the substance of the general equivalent remains disputed. Now, on the one hand, one may argue that a general agreement on an ultimate goal is sufficient as long as the other strategies of the basic dimension can be unambiguously reconstructed. On the other hand, one may claim that just an agreement on the fight against terrorism is not enough to adopt a common stance on how to counter the phenomenon. Or that universalization can only proceed with an entirely undisputed general equivalent, since this only forges a chain of equivalence. Without deciding upon this question now, it can be concluded that a *Universalization* of subjects (as encompassed by the first basic productive hegemonic strategy) has only been partially reconstructed.

Representing the Self – the difficulties of constructing the international community as tendentially empty signifier

The reconstruction of basic productive hegemonic strategy *Representation* would typically conclude whether a hegemonic order has been successfully constituted in the field of terrorism. Keeping in mind that the attempts to reconstruct an antagonistic frontier (which would have indicated basic productive hegemonic strategy *Establishing an antagonistic frontier*) has yielded a highly ambiguous picture and that a linking of subjects in a chain of equivalence (basic productive hegemonic strategy *Universalization*) has only partially occurred, the question of whether one particular signifier is able to take over the task to represent a chain of equivalence – which we have not been able to reconstruct – seems obsolete. Especially since the incomplete and failed reconstruction of the two other basic productive hegemonic strategies forcefully sustains my central argument stating that hegemonic regimes are in need of a homogenous, clear-cut interpretation of the antagonistic Other. Just as much as they are in need of an unambiguous vision and a political consensus shared among subjects jointly opposing the Other – the Self. However, it is necessary to allow for a complete comparison of both discourses to try to identify the moment of representation in the discourse on terrorism.

This implies to locate a particular signifier that can represent the absent fullness of a chain of equivalence while being already part of this very chain. In accomplishing this function, the signifier is largely emptied from its particular content and turns into a *tendentially empty signifier*. As in the discourse on drugs, the best method to search for tendentially empty signifiers consists on the one hand in locating nodal points and on the other hand in reconstructing the two theoretical conditions of availability and credibility the signifier needs to meet to count as a tendentially empty one. Nodal points offer the additional advantage that they function as a site of discursive concentration and represent a tendentially empty signifier at the same time. The procedure of identifying nodal points in the material followed each step outlined in chapter three.

After the coding procedure only two terms have been identified that could function as nodal points of the discourse on terrorism, 'international community', and 'international terrorism'.[13] As in the drugs discourse, the high score of 'international terrorism' first indicates the topic or theme of the discourse. Second, and more importantly, 'international terrorism' represents a nodal point, since it represents the antagonistic Other that must be fought. The score of 3,888 hits is supported by the co-occurrences of 'international terrorism' with the remainder of the codes: in 188 documents, it co-occurred 2,364 times with all other codes (overall 279 codes) in the discourse. Relevant to the analysis are its co-occurrences with Self codes: here, 'international terrorism' appeared 594 times in conjunction with all Self codes. Obviously, on the level of numbers, Other and Self are not often juxtaposed.

Table 4.2 Frequency of potential nodal points in the international discourse on terrorism

Terms	Hits
International community	1889[1]
International terrorism	3888

1   419 hits in the first round (1972–1979) and 1287 hits in the second round (1997–2010).

Table 4.3 Co-occurrences of 'international terrorism' in the international discourse on terrorism

	Hits
Occurrences with all codes	2364
Occurrences with Self codes	594
Occurrences with cooperation codes	396
Occurrences with fight international terrorism (general equivalent)	682

Table 4.4 Co-occurrences of 'international community' in the international discourse on terrorism

	Hits
Occurrences with all codes	1575
Occurrences with Other codes[1]	594
Occurrences with fight international terrorism (general equivalent)	365
Occurrences with cooperation codes	329

1 Others codes are formulations describing and characterizing the antagonistic Other terrorism, for instance by considering it as a threat to international peace and security, as a global phenomenon or the common enemy.

The score of 'international community' (1,889 hits) indicates that it is the only signifier occurring recurrently enough to function as a nodal point and tendentially empty signifier representing a potential chain of subjects. However, its co-occurrences with the remainder of the codes present it as not consistently rooted in the discourse and the low co-occurrences with the general equivalent 'fight international terrorism' allows doubting its credibility as a tendentially empty signifier (see Table 4.4).

Thus, in contrast to the discourse on drugs, with the help of frequencies we do not dispose of a relatively clear idea, which terms might work as a tendentially empty signifier. It is necessary to reconstruct the two theoretical conditions in order to identify whether there is indeed the possibility that 'international community' serves as tendentially empty signifier. Starting with *availability*, we have the problem that the international community was apparently not immediately present when the debates began, as the increase of references to it imply. In the first five documents directly after the attacks, the international community is mentioned only nine times, compared to 297 hits from November to December 1972 (22 documents).

With regard to the potential *credibility* of the international community as a tendentially empty signifier, one needs to, first, search for acts of identification of the subjects with the signifier 'international community' and second, for identification acts with the general equivalent (fight international terrorism). Concerning acts of identification with the international community it becomes apparent that it is often referred to in relation to 'humanity'. The community is constructed with reference to its past; it is ascribed to dispose of very precise wishes, wills, rights and obligations that should be expressed by the United Nations. In the face of terrorism, the international community needs to act and fight terrorism collectively; it owes to future generations the adoption of a comprehensive convention on terrorism; it is resolved to counter terrorism etc. (see UN Sixth Committee 1972c: 254; 1972b: 245; 2000a: 4, 8; 2005a: 2; UN Ad Hoc Committee on International Terrorism 1979a: 4). Humanity comes into play when the international community is called upon to overcome the split in mankind, since '[t]errorism threatened the very ideals of humanity and peaceful coexistence' and 'mankind was governed by a common destiny, and [. . .] all were potential victims' (UN Sixth Committee 1972l: 350; 2005b: 12).

Though increasing, the references to the international community are highly enmeshed in other discursive elements. The increase allows for two conclusions. On the one hand, various subjects identify with the signifier 'international community' from the very beginning. Indeed, identifying with the international community goes hand in hand with considering oneself part of this community. This is the case, for example, when a member state's interest in the fight against international terrorism is equated with the interest of the international community in this fight. Particularly, the construction of a universal concern bespeaks of an ongoing identification when a state

> urged the international community to redouble its efforts to conclude the negotiations on the draft comprehensive convention on international terrorism [. . .] which would [. . .] send a powerful message that the international community was determined to deal with the threat of terrorism effectively.
>
> (UN Sixth Committee 2000c: 12)

Thus, 'no state [. . .] could escape its [terrorism] consequences' and the international community is called upon to counter the phenomenon in a concerted effort (UN Sixth Committee 2002b: 4). On the other hand, the increase highlights that subjects *start* to identify with the signifier international community during the debates of the 1970s, whereas in the 1990s it is an introduced signifier; hence, the references to the community are more or less evenly distributed over the course of the second round of the debates.

However, the increase of references in the 1970s does not come without a cost. The credibility of the international community to 'truly' represent *all* subjects constructing terrorism as their antagonistic Other is doubted, when the principles of the international community are invoked to call for coordinated action in the fight against terrorism and not as a means for the 'subjection of the weak to the strong' (UN Sixth Committee 1972d: 260; 1972f: 280). The same applies when speakers urge others to acknowledge the changing character of the international community; therefore, 'the same attitude [towards terrorism] could not be expected from the international community of the present day, which was practically universal and consisted of so many different civilizations' (UN Sixth Committee 1972f: 280). These are acts of identification and differentiation at the same time – identification with a specific interpretation of the community but instant differentiation from former meanings of the community and particular members of it. Thus, the references as such might bespeak of a growing discursive presence of the signifier 'international community' but its credibility as a tendentially empty signifier, as representing a Self opposing terrorism as antagonistic Other, is severely hampered by the restrictions and limitations that accompany these references.

Secondly, the credibility of the international community needs to be investigated with regard to the general equivalent. In light of the co-occurrences, the relation between the general equivalent and the international community is not very strong (only 365 hits). This is a rather meagre result, in light of its overall appearance in the discourse (1,889). This picture is sustained by a closer look at each round: in the first round (1972–1979), the co-occurrences between both signifiers mount up to 169 hits, in the second round (1997–2010), 196 hits can be recorded. As the relation to the ultimate and common goals is perturbed, the credibility of the international community is further damaged (the above-mentioned quotes have highlighted how strongly the goals are embedded in a mesh of reservations and limitations). Especially in the 1970s, and despite terrorism being constructed as an international problem threatening humanity at large, the international community is neither considered as the ideal locus to fight international terrorism nor as symbolizing the imagined, perfect community. The observation that the ultimate and common goals are embedded in so many restrictions and limitations hints at the various interpretations of the fight against terrorism.

Moreover, since no clear-cut antagonistic frontier has been established and the picture of the terrorist Other is particularly heterogeneous, the ultimate goal of a world without terrorism struggles with the different interpretations of the *how to* fight terrorism. If the general equivalent is interpreted differently – and therefore, as has been outlined, its quality as a general equivalent is spoiled – the international community can hardly symbolize and embody in a credible and equivalential manner the lack of the discourse, the absent, perfect community within which humankind is not threatened by terrorism. The different interpretations and constructions of the terrorist Other and the general equivalent have impeded that neither the signifier of the international community nor any other particular signifier takes over the task of representation. While this conclusion holds especially for the debates in the 1970s, in the second round, the international community slowly develops as the central addressee of the fight against international terrorism. Fewer limitations and restrictions in connection with the ultimate goal and the general equivalent are voiced and the community is more and more perceived as an entity that assembles different subjects, despite the meaning they attach to terrorism.

Ultimately, the basic productive hegemonic strategy *Representation* cannot be reconstructed, since no signifier can be identified exemplifying the quality of a tendentially empty signifier. The international community does not dispose of the necessary credibility for representing a potential chain of equivalence. Despite a certain increase in its credibility in the course of the second round, this yields the rather different assertion that the international community provides in theory for a floating rather than for a tendentially empty signifier. The former experiences a loosening from the relational systems that constitute it, it becomes entirely ambiguous and, therefore, can be partially fixed in different discourses but it is not empty. In contrast to the tendentially empty signifier, the floating signifier is unable to take over the task of representation (Laclau 2004: 322).

Be that as it may, we can conclude that without being able to reconstruct the basic productive hegemonic strategies *Establishing an antagonistic frontier* and *Representation* and despite a partial reconstruction of productive hegemonic strategy *Universalization*, no hegemonic order at the international level has been established in the discourse on terrorism. Subjects have not been universalized to form an equivalential chain and no antagonistic frontier has been established; in consequence, no signifier was able to take over the task of representation. The agreement *that* terrorism has to be fought is neither sufficient to construct a homogeneous antagonistic Other nor an unambiguous vision shared by subjects jointly opposing the Other – the international community is not able to represent this Self.

We are left with the insight that the terrorism discourse is crisscrossed by numerous lines of conflicts and exclusions within which the demarcation to international terrorism is only one among others. Hence, despite locating an ultimate goal – the imaginary of a world free from terrorism – we are only able to identify different hegemonic projects. Most problematically, interpretations of Other and Self put forward by these projects often link potential cooperation partners with international terrorism: for example, when delegations accuse others of being a source of terrorism or consider national liberation movements as terrorist endeavours. And as these linkages frequently draw on elements of national identity, culture or religion of the concerned subjects, the discourse becomes more and more heterogeneous. Overall, the terrorism discourse is a discourse marked by the imponderability of constructing antagonistic frontiers. The flip side of this finding is that a 'war on terror' appears difficult to justify without significant political consensus on *how to* fight terrorism. Indeed, in how far the discourse's heterogeneity impedes the legitimization of international measures of the 'war on terror' will be discussed in the next section.

Institutionalizing hegemonic projects? Justifying international measures against terrorism

I have argued that the stronger the authority of the hegemonic discourse and the tighter the ties between the subjects identifying with the collective Self, the more likely the institutionalization of specific practices in accordance with the order. A hegemonic regime of practices emerges and excludes alternative meanings and frameworks of behaviour, since they are considered as irrational, illegitimate and amoral. In this respect, the main problem of examining the institutionalization of international counter-terrorism measures consists in the failure to reconstruct a hegemonic regime in the international discourse on terrorism. One may raise the question of what kind of measures can be agreed upon when there is neither such thing as a comprehensive convention on terrorism nor a definition of the phenomenon. Yet, what kinds of practices claim to have universal appeal (i.e. hegemonic practices) if there is no hegemonic order temporarily stabilizing the constructions of collective Self and antagonistic Other? What kinds of alternative meanings are excluded and considered illegitimate? And what does it imply to speak of the 'war on terror' in the absence of an *international* hegemonic regime – is this formula a unilateral attempt to justify extraordinary measures, hinder resistance and present these measures as the single promising avenue to reach the ultimate goal, the imaginary of a world free of terrorism?

The analysis of the international discourse on terrorism has thus far shown a very complex and heterogeneous construction of the terrorist Other. While terrorists have been described either as frustrated (religious) fanatics or associated with wartime resistance movements, the label 'terrorist' as such serves to denounce a threat and to demonize an Other. Now, the questions to address are, first, in how far these heterogeneous constructions are still able to generate political support and institutionalize practices that would normally be opposed; and, second, in how far this heterogeneity is not appreciated by powerful actors. For both questions, representing terrorism as an existential threat, i.e. to securitize the issue of international terrorism proves to be crucial. As in the discourse on drugs, a climate of fear and moral panic makes it a lot easier to justify why the civilized world needs to be united against terrorism – since without such unanimous support the terrorists will triumph. Thus, it is essential to radicalize the Other by demonizing and de-humanizing terrorism and every individual or organization that can be associated with it. The 'war on terror' is impossible without such identity construction, as only identities that are threatened in their existence – even if they consider themselves civilized – can legitimately use large-scale violence to counter the threat. And as the latter is constructed as existential and violent, regular law-enforcement measures that are appropriate in times of peace are untenable here and need to be replaced by violent counter-measures promising to free the world from terrorism.

Due to the heterogeneous Other construction and the lack of a political consensus on how to fight terrorism, the effects of the discourse on public contestation are sweeping. Most importantly, as a clear definition of terrorism is lacking, no one knows precisely which actions could already be considered terrorist acts. This leaves ample room of manoeuvre for specific subjects to justify extraordinary measures, such as in the case of the US-led intervention in Iraq or agreeing on a rather broad and encompassing definition of terrorism in the European Union. Moreover, these measures are presented as achieving the ultimate goal of a world free of terrorism and it becomes highly difficult to formulate plausible arguments why fighting terrorism with all available means, including large-scale violence, has severe consequences on both sides, for terrorists and non-terrorists alike.

One major consequence of the discourse on international terrorism for the international community and its members resides in the entrenchment of a particular approach to terrorism. The language of radicalization makes countering terrorism largely inflexible, not only as it precludes reflections on other, more effective measures but also since it is the language of failure. 'Once the enemy has been so thoroughly demonized and dehumanized, there is little possibility of anything but annihilation' (Jackson 2005: 91). And the best and logical way to eradicate an evil enemy is to wage war. Any measures not following this rationale are stigmatized as illegitimate, amoral and irrational. In this context, alternative meanings and policy-options have a very hard standing, as they are suppressed or defamed regardless of whether they question the legitimacy of the extraordinary measures or favour a different construction of the antagonistic Other.

What kind of international measures can we observe at the global level against international terrorism, although a hegemonic definition of terrorism is lacking? It is interesting to see that a number of measures against international terrorism have been agreed upon. As I have outlined, a number of sectoral conventions on terrorism exist. Between 1963 and 2005, 13 universal legal instruments relating to the prevention and suppression of terrorism were negotiated, establishing an important framework for international anti-terrorist cooperation. In general, these conventions and protocols define a particular type of terrorist violence as an offense under the convention (such as seizure of an aircraft in flight by threat or violence). They require parties to penalize that activity in their domestic law; they identify bases upon which the parties responsible are required to establish jurisdiction over the defined offense (such as registration, territoriality or nationality). They further create an obligation of the state in which a suspect is found to establish jurisdiction over the offense and to refer the offense for prosecution if the party does not extradite. This latter is commonly known as the principle of 'no safe haven for terrorists', which has been stressed by Security Council Resolution 1373 of September 2001 as an essential obligation of Member States in the fight against terrorism (UN Security Council 2001).[14] So far, these instruments have not significantly led to a closer, shared understanding of the problem since the word 'terrorism' is rarely used, let alone defined, in these instruments.

In addition to these conventions, an array of resolutions by UN institutions exists. New bodies like the Counter-Terrorism Committee (CTC) have been created which monitor the implementation of Resolution 1373 and increase the capability of states to fight terrorism, including bringing Member States to an acceptable level of compliance with the terrorism-related conventions and protocols. The CTC, established by the UN Security Council, has since become the United Nations' leading body to promote collective action against international terrorism.[15] In September 2006, the General Assembly launched a *Global Counter-Terrorism Strategy*, which represents the first agreement on a common strategic and operational approach to fight terrorism (UN General Assembly 2006). The strategy

> gathers all the various counter-terrorism activities of the United Nations system into a common strategic framework and builds on the consistent, unequivocal condemnation of terrorism by Member States. It seeks to strengthen the individual and collective capacity of countries and the United Nations to prevent and combat terrorism all while ensuring the protection of human rights and upholding the rule of law.[16]

Next to the UN, the EU has introduced a number of anti-terrorism measures and a number of other regional organizations such as the South Asian Association for Regional Cooperation (SAARC) and the Organization of African Unity (OAU) have also introduced a number of anti-terrorism measures.[17] Still, in comparison to the measures outlined by the hegemonic regime in the field of drugs, the measures against terrorism remain at best a patchwork at the international level, since they are either directed towards specific features of the phenomenon terrorism without defining it (like the UN conventions) or adopted by an individual state, a 'coalition of the willing' or a regional organization. Hence, we cannot speak of measures that are globally accepted *and* globally enacted.

If we cannot speak of an institutionalization of a hegemonic regime of practices against terrorism, we nevertheless can address how different practices have become installed and routinized to a certain degree. This implies that the following examples are meant as illustrations of how a particular construction of the terrorist Other and an accordant vision of a Self – by an individual state for instance – led to the enactment of specific measures. I will focus on the recent measures of the UN list of international terrorist suspects, the Europol-US agreements on the exchange of data and the EU-US agreements on judicial cooperation in the 'war on terror'. These illustrations will also indicate how the complex problem of international terrorism defies easy answers, and how fiercely measures are resisted and their legitimacy contested, since they are not based on an international political consensus.

The UN list on terrorist suspects

The freezing of funds belonging to persons and entities suspected of having links with terrorism is one of the cornerstones of the counter-terrorism measures at the UN level. Central to this measure is the creation of lists of organizations and persons who are suspected of having terrorist links, resulting in the freeze of the assets of the respective organizations and persons. Such listings started as a reaction to the terrorist bombings on US-American embassies in Nairobi, Kenya and Dar es Salaam, Tanzania in the late 1990s. As both attacks were attributed to the Al-Qaida network, the Security Council ordered the freezing of Taliban funds in particular, since with resolution 1267 the Council attempted to coerce the Taliban regime to extradite Usama bin Laden and to ensure that the Afghan territory was no longer 'a safe haven' for terrorists (UN Security Council 1999). However, the Taliban regime did not react to the resolution and in December 2000, the Security Council adopted Resolution 1333, which meant to tighten the measures of 1999 by specifically ordering the additional freezing of all funds and financial assets of Usama bin Laden and of individuals and entities associated with him, including those in the Al-Qaida organization (UN Security Council 2000). Furthermore, Committee 1267 (created by Resolution 1267) was given the task of drawing up a list of the above-mentioned persons and entities and to update this list regularly. As the sanctions of the committee are binding under international law, Member States are obliged to freeze all accounts and assets of the listed individuals and bar them from leaving the country (Stoll, Mißling and Juretko 2004: 23).

The way the UN list has been established and its consequences for the targeted individuals have led to a number of controversies. Most importantly, the procedure raised concerns of human rights compliance. In view of framing the international anti-terrorism policies as means to protect innocent citizens from future terrorist acts (on the politics of protection see Walker 2006), 'bring those to justice' who have perpetrated such acts in the past as well as locate those who are about to commit a terrorist act, the question remains what is implied for those individuals who are suspected of being terrorists. How does the state go about identifying these individuals and what are the consequences of being labelled a terrorist? Of course, these questions address the criteria on which the selection of organizations and individuals are based. The listing of a particular person or organization occurs on demand by a Member State, and most probably relies on intelligence information of the requesting state. Other UN Member States can object the inclusion within 48 hours. Yet, the Security Council resolutions do not contain any substantive criteria to which the 1267 Committee can refer in its decisions on whom to include on the list. Furthermore, when updating the listing on the basis of the information provided by Member States and/or regional organizations such as the EU, the Committee meets behind closed doors (Vennemann 2004: 243). Of course, the use of confidential information may be necessary where national security is at stake. But that does not mean that authorities are free from any review by national or international courts simply because they state that the case concerns national or international security (Guild 2008: 188)? And in absence of a common definition of terrorism and terrorists, it does not seem farfetched to conclude that the listing follows the preferences of Member States (Stoll, Mißling and Juretko 2004: 23) and that objections to an inclusion from other states is unlikely to happen.[18]

However, missing or unclear criteria are not the only concern that needs to be raised. Most importantly, the listing is bound to have severe effects on the lives of listed individuals. By now, a number of cases have shown the intolerable individual consequences, since the measures are by their nature coercive and aimed at punishing the individual for engaging in terrorism. Consider, for instance, the case of Mr Arar,

> the Canadian national who because he was on a list which was available to the US authorities was stopped when transiting through New York and rendered to Syria where he was tortured for more than a year. When he was finally able to return to Canada, the Government opened a Commission of Inquiry which found him completely innocent of any allegations of terrorism, and the Canadian Government complicit in his torture through the passing of his name to the US authorities. The Canadian Government settled 10.5 million Canadian dollars in compensation, including legal costs, on Mr. Arar for the damage he suffered.
>
> (Arar Commission 2006, quoted in Guild 2008)[19]

Those persons and organizations concerned by the listing are confronted with the absence of any protection of their elementary rights. The Committee 1267 neither hears the cases of the persons and entities concerned nor informs them of the fact that their inclusion on the list is being discussed or has been decided upon. Once on the list, they have no judicial procedure for requesting a review of the decision, arguing for example that they do not have links with the targeted groups or that they have been put on the list as a result of a mix-up (Vennemann 2004: 243).

It was only in November 2002, that a possibility to reach a de-listing was introduced in reaction to international criticism. A person concerned can hand in a petition at her government of residence and/or citizenship who will eventually bring a de-listing request to the attention of the Committee. The latter decides by consensus and if a consensual decision is impossible, the matter may be submitted to the Security Council.[20] These peculiarities of the listing procedure can hardly be regarded as conform to human rights. Meanwhile (and due to many objections), the procedure is not only subject to regular examination and deepened monitoring by a group of experts who are advised to consider the humanitarian and personal effects of the measure as well as to allow for exceptional cases. Also, in December 2009, the Security Council has adopted Resolution 1904

> to fine-tune its decade-old sanctions regime imposed on Al-Qaida, Usama bin Laden and the Taliban, including through the establishment of an ombudsperson who could mediate requests from individuals, organizations and companies to be taken off the sanctions list [and the] Council authorized the establishment of an Office of the Ombudsperson for an initial period of 18 months to assist the Sanctions Committee in its consideration of delisting requests.[21]

While the members of the Security Council have agreed on the new position of an Ombudsperson to bring fairness and transparency to its anti-terrorism measures as outlined in the resolution, the decision must also be seen in the context of repeated criticism raised against the listing. From now on, persons and organizations listed have the possibility to file a request to be removed from the sanctions list which the ombudsperson will have to review. Furthermore, states are emphatically requested to inform concerned individuals and organizations of discussions on their inclusion on the list and their later listing (Stoll, Mißling and Juretko 2004: 39). However, these improvements are by no means sufficient to silence the grave humanitarian concerns implied by the UN list: it

> not only violates fundamental rights, by doing flagrant injustice to many persons against whom there is no proof of any wrong doing. It also discredits the whole of the international fight against terrorism, which is badly needed and ought to be able to rely on the widest possible support from the international community and public opinion.
>
> (Marty 2007: 4)[22]

Of course, clear criteria on whom to include on the UN list do not imply that such resistance will cease. But legitimacy of the listing would greatly increase by making transparent why and how one is listed. Especially since this would foster clear possibilities on how individuals and organizations concerned can achieve their delisting after having proven their innocence. Elspeth Guild rightly points out that

> [t]his rather unsavoury approach to protection of the individual [. . .] appears to be having a consequence rather more extreme than [. . .] one might have intended or expected. The fact that individuals are clearly being affected in a highly prejudicial manner without any recourse against the state which is inflicting the treatment appears to be creating strong pressure to exert judicial supervision.
>
> (Guild 2008: 191)

The Europol-US agreements and the EU-US agreements on judicial cooperation

The agreements between Europol and the United States on the exchange of data and the ones between the EU and the United States on judicial cooperation in criminal matters are cases in point within the framework of the present book. By scrutinizing these agreements, the study's finding of a failed hegemonic regime against terrorism at the global UN-level is brought into the regional and national context of the EU and the United States as it highlights how particular practices were installed in a smaller geographical space as means in the 'war on terror' – while lacking a universal definition of the terrorist Other as well as a common definition between EU and USA. Still, agreements have been concluded which enable the exchange of information about and the extradition of individuals (not only, but above all) suspected of terrorist links – thus, we are dealing with agreements in need of some sort of understanding what terrorism is about in order to become effective.

As international terrorists act beyond territorial boundaries, information exchange is not only key in the fight against terrorism but also represents the backbone of the EU's counter-terrorism policies; hence, it equally bolsters judicial cooperation in criminal matters (Balzacq 2008: 77). The Europol-US agreements are among the most prominent reactions of the EU to 11 September 2001. After the Justice and Home Affairs Council of 20 September 2002 called for the adoption of a wide range of anti-terrorist measures (among those the European Arrest Warrant and the European definition of terrorism)[23] and requested to improve cooperation between the EU and the USA in the 'war on terror', the Council invited the Director of Europol to negotiate an agreement on the transmission of personal data with the US. Within a short period of time, two accords were signed: the first on 6 December 2002, the second – the *supplementary agreement* – on 20 December 2002.[24]

This swift course of action is particularly worrisome since the development of the agreements was marked by a significant extension of the range of data to be transferred to US authorities by Europol. Whereas the initial agreement allowed the transmission of strategic and technical information only (information will be transmitted for purposes including 'the prevention, detection, suppression, investigation and prosecution of any specific criminal offences, and for any specific analytical purposes' (Article 5(1)), the supplementary agreement allows exchanging a wide range of personal data, i.e. 'any information relating to an identified or identifiable natural person'. According to Articles 2 and 6 this includes 'race, political opinions, or religious or other beliefs, or concerning health and sexual life' (Europol 2002). Thus, although the agreements have been concluded as a means in the 'war on terror', the exchange of data is not limited to information related to this 'war' but embraces 'any offence'.

Hence, notwithstanding the unwary urgency with which the agreement has been pushed through, hampering a thorough scrutiny of national parliaments and the discrimination of EU Member States vis-à-vis local US authorities as recipients of data, the main issue of concern is the broad scope of information exchange (Dubois 2002: 331). First, the nature of the offences in Article 5(1) is not specified and the scope of information exchange 'is interpreted in the most extensive manner, to include information on immigration proceedings (which are not necessarily criminal) and confiscation, regardless of the existence of a criminal conviction' (Mitsilegas 2003b: 522). Second, this leads also to an extension of antagonistic Others without establishing an intimate link to the 'war on terror': new subjects and elements are turned into threats by considering 'a natural attribute (race), social creed (political opinions or religious beliefs), intimate behaviour (sexual life) and an accidental state (health), as significant sources of threat' (Balzacq 2008: 91). Obviously, this reminds of supplementary productive hegemonic strategy *Enlarging the antagonized chain of equivalence* by adding new elements, here the attributes of individuals. The result of this vague language and extension is a loss of control for both Europol and the EU Member States to overview US authorities in their use of the data transferred in the 'war on terror' (Lavranos 2003: 268; Wagner 2006: 106).[25]

As the US expressed their interest in judicial cooperation with the EU in criminal matters (which was welcomed by the EU), negotiations began in summer 2002 with the mandate for an agreement covering above all 'extradition, including the temporary surrender for trials and mutual legal assistance including the exchange of data, the setting up of joint investigation teams, the giving of evidence (via video conference) and the establishment of single contact points' (Council of the European Union 2002a: 13). The EU-US agreements on mutual legal assistance and extradition were both signed in June 2003 (Council of the European Union 2003a; 2003b) and entered into force in February 2010.

The EU-US agreements raise a similar set of problems as the Europol-US agreements do. For instance, parliaments were equally not provided with a sufficient amount of time to scrutinize the accords (for a full assessment of the agreements and the negotiations see Mitsilegas 2007: 471–7).[26] Again, we witness formulations bypassing a concrete clarification of what is meant by terrorism: Article 4 considers something

> an extraditable offence if it is punishable under the laws of the requesting and requested States by deprivation of liberty for a maximum period of more than one year or by a more severe penalty. An offence shall also be an extraditable offence if it consists of an attempt or conspiracy to commit, or participation in the commission of, an extraditable offence. Where the request is for enforcement of the sentence of a person convicted of an extraditable offence, the deprivation of liberty remaining to be served must be at least four months.
> (Council of the European Union 2003a)

It should be noted that unambiguous language and legal clarity are decisive in instances which touch upon fundamental human rights and freedom issues. This is even more important if the area of freedom, security and justice aims to succeed in building and fostering a transparent international legal order (Alegre, Bigo and Jeandesboz 2009: 15).

Furthermore, guarantees to respect and protect fundamental rights were not as strongly emphasized as hoped for in the agreements. For instance, as regards the death penalty, the text of the agreement 'allows extradition on the basis that the death penalty would not be carried out if it were imposed'. Now, '[g]iven the lack of explicit specialty provisions, the risk of an extradite being subsequently moved to Guantanamo Bay to face trial before Military Commission was not addressed' (Alegre, Bigo and Jeandesboz 2009: 16). This problematique is aggravated as Article 17(2) of the extradition agreement only enables 'consultations' between the parties concerned 'where the constitutional principles of, or final judicial decisions binding upon, the requested State may pose an impediment to fulfilment of its obligation to extradite' (Mitsilegas 2003b: 528). Eventually, this implies that the agreement is void of explicit provisions on how to handle cases in which human rights bar extradition. Since EU Member States are bound by the decisions of the European Court of Justice and the European Court of Human Rights (Mitsilegas 2007: 471), this is clearly a disquieting development undermining the rule of law. As the agreements have not been ratified for nearly seven years, some already hoped that they do not represent an effective blueprint for future cooperation. However, in February 2010, both agreements have been finally ratified and the concern that they are 'a worrying precedent for future agreements between the EU and third countries in this field' (Alegre, Bigo and Jeandesboz 2009: 16) regains in actuality.

Ultimately, the depicted agreements have far-reaching humanitarian implications for the EU's ability to speak with 'one voice' in matters of human rights and fundamental liberties affected by the 'war on terror'. The way the agreements have been pushed through while sidelining national parliaments may have serious implications for the legitimacy of the EU when it aims to negotiate further agreements of such sensitivity and constitutional importance. Moreover, the EU missed the opportunity to include specific European data protection standards and human right provisions in the agreements. 'One would expect the EU as a global actor in matters as sensitive as judicial cooperation in criminal matters to safeguard and promote the human rights values upon which the Union is founded and which form part of its identity' (Mitsilegas 2003b: 535).

In conclusion, the controversial surroundings of the UN listing, the Europol-USA agreements on data exchange and the EU-US judicial cooperation in criminal matters illustrate how the lack of a homogeneous Other construction lent itself to secrecy from the official side and public contestation. Yet, measures making it easier for police and other law enforcement authorities to exchange information about individuals suspected of terrorist links should not be demonized immediately. But they need to be based on evidence justifying coercive action. They must be monitored to ensure that the individual, against whom there is nothing more but suspicion, and her rights are not violated. This only creates further victims, in addition to those who are the direct victims of a terrorist attack. Those who are targets of coercive action because someone somewhere suspects them of some involvement with terrorism are equally victims – victims of policies, which are initially meant to protect. This is somewhat of a 'second victory' of terrorism, since it succeeds in creating new victims by the UN listing or by extending the scope of data exchange to attributes and qualities of individuals, creating new sources of threat as in the case of the Europol-US agreements. As has been invoked, it would give the fight against terrorism a lot more legitimacy than it currently experiences if evidence and not suspicion was the yardstick against which law enforcement agencies decided upon coercive action.

The noisiness of heterogeneity in the international discourse on terrorism

While it has not been possible to reconstruct a hegemonic regime, the last section of chapter four contextualizes the above results with a focus on the concept of heterogeneity in the discourse on terrorism by reviewing, first, the discursive strategies identified in the discourse. Second, as the present study argues that the homogeneity of the antagonistic Other is essential for hegemonic orders to emerge, a typology of different degrees of otherness is established in light of the results. Third, some reflections on the noisiness of heterogeneity intend to question in how far the discourse produces values, morals, and truths about the nature of terrorism.

Beginning with the reconstructed hegemonic strategies, we have identified six of fifteen discursive strategies in the international discourse on terrorism – though it should be noted that one strategy has only been partially reconstructed. The table shows the dominance of counter-hegemonic strategies in the discourse on terrorism (five counter-hegemonic strategies vs. one productive hegemonic strategy). However, this dominance is a feeble one, as only the basic counter-hegemonic strategies *Particularization* and *Weakening of the antagonistic frontier* have been reconstructed. I have, on various occasions, outlined that the basic dimension needs to be identified in its entirety in order for both logics to dominate: for the logic of equivalence to prevail, all three productive hegemonic strategies (*Universalization, Establishing an antagonistic frontier* and *Representation*) of the basic dimension need to operate; for the logic of difference, the three basic counter-hegemonic strategies (*Particularization, Breaking off the chain* and *Weakening of the antagonistic frontier*) must be located.

Table 4.5 Reconstructed hegemonic strategies in the international discourse on terrorism

Productive hegemonic strategies	*Counter-hegemonic strategies*
Basic dimension: • Universalization (partially)	*Basic dimension:* • Particularization • Weakening of the antagonistic frontier *Supplementary dimension:* • Stressing the particularity of a subject of *chain A* explicitly at the expense of the general equivalent • Crossing the antagonistic frontier in order to weaken it: – Protect particularity of a subject by articulating its particularity as part of *chain Z* – Underscore particularity of a subject/element of *chain Z* • Attempts to disarticulate floating elements of *chain Z*

The picture to emerge is a picture of struggle between different hegemonic projects aspiring to dominate the discursive field. Most palpable in the 1970s, but still rumouring in the current debates on a comprehensive convention on terrorism, different projects struggle to establish a particular construction and meaning of the antagonistic Other and thereby, a specific understanding of the Self. Supported by the majority of the reconstructed strategies, this allows concluding that attempts have fallen short to construct a hegemonic order in the field of terrorism at the international level.

However, identifying different projects by no means implies that we can speak of stable meanings. What we witness is a partial fixation, a momentary stabilization of a particular interpretation of how a collective Self that aspires to a peaceful and safer world free from terrorism should look like, how the fight against terrorism should be carried out, and how the antagonistic Other has to be constructed. These meanings are rearticulated and specific, contingent constructions of Self and Other are re-inscribed in the discourse to render more permanent that which is originally subject to flux. This explains the recurrent evocation of the ultimate goal (a world free of terrorism) and the resumption of the debates on a comprehensive convention while lacking an agreement on how to construct the antagonistic Other and how to counter it. In their constant reiteration, the different hegemonic projects are re-inscribed in the discourse on terrorism. Indeed, as any repetition is never completely the same, this rewriting further explains a previously mentioned development of the terrorism discourse: the recurrent invocation of terrorism as antagonistic Other, the slow emergence of an antagonized chain of equivalence (due to mitigated disagreement on the issues of state terrorism and underlying causes) and the slowly accepted constitution of terrorism as a threat permits to envisage that a more homogenous Other is in the making. This is accompanied by an international community with which the subjects increasingly identify while they construct terrorism as their antagonistic Other and aim at a world free of terrorism.

However, this way towards a more unified picture of the antagonistic Other – terrorism as the 'common enemy' – is paved by an ongoing demonization of terrorism. Especially the 'war on terror' but also the overall increase of a war-like language bespeak of this sharpened divide. Albeit in a different manner, this confirms one result of the drugs discourse, namely, that a hegemonic order as well as a hegemonic project can only profit from an increasing radicalization of the Other construction. Since this also implies homogenization, extremes are bound to offer less nuanced pictures and the dynamics towards a more unified picture of the antagonistic Other are highlighted.

With regard to heterogeneity, it is above all detrimental to the emergence of a hegemonic order at the international level if a seemingly homogenous constitution of the Other is differentiated by associating subjects with the antagonistic Other (state terrorism has been a case in point). In the case of the terrorism discourse, this detrimental effect of heterogeneity bursts out in the struggle of the different hegemonic projects and the different meaning they confer to terrorism. This makes it impossible to construct a collective Self. From the refusal to include national liberation or resistance movements in a definition of terrorism to the rejection of amalgams between specific religions or cultures (read Islam) and terrorism, the reconstructed differences denigrate elements of the subjects' national identity, culture, and traditions that also consider international terrorism as their antagonistic Other, and numerous frontiers are drawn between these. Thus, in contrast to the discourse on drugs, the international discourse on terrorism reveals a much more complicated picture. While the analysis has reconstructed a number of different Other constructions, tables 4.6. and 4.7. present the constructions of antagonistic and non-antagonistic Others of two hegemonic projects among the potentially indefinite number of projects.

As both tables show, heterogeneity has made itself forcefully heard and deployed a wealth of different meanings of the antagonistic Other. While all subjects present in the international discourse on terrorism agree in one way or another that terrorism represents the antagonistic Other, the field is crisscrossed with antagonisms, since disagreement reigns on what terrorism is exactly about. Hence, attempts to hegemonize the discursive field and, thereby, establish the parameters of the discourse are countered by other hegemonic articulations with the same intentions.

Overall, the signifier terrorism is very much emptied of its particular content and, therefore, lends itself to these various interpretations. However, regardless of what terrorism means to you exactly, you have to condemn terrorism before you determine what you understand by terrorism. To doubt the necessity of condemning terrorism is *outside* the established parameters of the discourse. Still, to condemn terrorism is not enough to bring about an agreement on one meaning, i.e. to hege-

Table 4.6 Typology 1 of different degrees of otherness in the international discourse on terrorism

Other	Degrees of otherness
Terrorism as a threat to international peace and security	Antagonistic Other and threatening
National liberation movements and religious networks	Antagonistic Other and threatening
Individual terrorist as frustrated fanatic	Antagonistic Other and threatening

Table 4.7 Typology 2 of different degrees of otherness in the international discourse on terrorism

Other	Degrees of otherness
Terrorism as a threat to international peace and security	Antagonistic Other and threatening
Resistance movements and States supporting terrorism and non-religious networks	Antagonistic Other and threatening
Poor, exploited or socially privileged but frustrated individual resorting to violence	Different and in need of assistance

monize it. It is also not enough to establish the concrete rules of the game at the international level.

As such, the discourse on terrorism deploys a range of values, judgments and truths which make it impossible to consider the constructions of otherness and difference as innocent representations of antagonistic and non-antagonistic Others. Especially if one keeps in mind a main result of the analysis of the terrorism discourse: the protection of a subject works at the expense of other subjects by associating them with the antagonistic Other. Here, the pledge for morality becomes one-sided. Since the meaning of the Other is so highly disputed, anyone can be associated with terrorism and become part of the antagonistic Other the moment a specific meaning is attached to the phenomenon. And due to its purely negative meaning, calling someone a terrorist disqualifies, devaluates and delegitimizes one's counterpart. To label someone a terrorist implies not only a moral judgment but also the instant legitimization of one's own means and actions. As such, terrorism is a sort of 'universal secret weapon' in the struggle for legitimacy and conceals and justifies one's own use of violence. The power inherent in the term 'terrorism' is its amorphous character. It is a weapon with an ever-extended remit: from vagueness over threat to international peace – terrorism is globalized. Accordingly, it justifies and necessitates a global 'war on terror' to eliminate the force of this weapon.

In light of this, the 'use' of terrorism as a provider of legitimacy, as a *passepartout* is lost the moment it is defined. On the other hand, smashing the Gordian knot with a definition of terrorism that relies on the subjective nature of the act – as, for instance, the EU has done (Council of the European Union 2002b) – works only in a framework of smaller, regional arenas. To install and legitimize practices at the international level, a global meeting of minds is necessary which does not wear out in simply condemning terrorism without agreeing on a common understanding of the Other or justify far-reaching measures which heavily impact on the freedom and rights of individuals, as witnessed in the case of the UN listing, the Europol-US agreements and the EU-US agreements on judicial cooperation in criminal matters. Especially since a globally and legally binding definition of terrorism could work as an insurance against the tendency of single subjects to define the Other unilaterally (Friedrichs 2006). This might avoid that subjects use the label 'terrorism' as a permanently available authorization and legitimization to attack their own occasional enemies as it currently is very much the case.

5 Comparing the 'war on drugs' and the 'war on terror'

The present chapter pulls together the findings from the two case studies and reflects on the theoretical and methodological approach applied. In support of the central argument of the book, the chapter emphasizes that the overall result of the analysis lies not only in the importance of a clearly defined antagonistic Other for an hegemonic order to emerge. But also the creation of an unambiguous vision of a Self is needed, which is shared by the various discursive agents joining to counter the spread of either phenomenon. Comparing both discourses brings about the central insight that a hegemonic order has been established in the international drug discourse at the international level, whereas the international discourse on terrorism is devoid of such a regime.

In order to explain this difference, the chapter carries out a detailed comparison of the analyses of the two discourses. The comparison entails four conceptual steps: First, a comparative overview on both discourses is given. The chapter then focuses on the hegemonic strategies and the language of war aimed at the construction of an antagonistic Other, and analyzes the web of less threatening Others in which the former is embedded. By comparing both discourses, this step stresses the centrality of a homogenously constructed Other for the establishment of hegemonic orders. Third, the parallels and dissimilarities between both discourses are investigated with regard to the dynamics of building a political consensus upon which a broader collective Self could be based. This is followed, fourth, by an analysis of the consequences of the presence or absence of a hegemonic order for the justification of counter-measures. Since the study is meant to address the current lack of systematic and methodologically coherent poststructuralist research of the politics of hegemony in the security field, the chapter closes with some general methodological reflections on broader evaluation criteria from qualitative methodology in the social sciences.

Comparative overview

At a general level, we witness two main parallels and one important difference between both discourses. Starting with the parallels, both articulated a *lack*: due to drugs, the world is an unsafe and unhealthy place; due to terrorism, the world is an insecure and violent place. Both articulated *ultimate* and *common goals* to fill and overcome this lack. The discourse on drugs aimed ultimately at creating a drug-free world; therefore, an international drug control is necessary. The terrorism discourse aspired at a world free of terrorism, a non-violent, civilized world, safe for states, peoples and individuals. Fighting terrorism was the only way to achieve this ultimate goal and a comprehensive convention including a definition of terrorism would support this. While in the drugs discourse, the international drug control represented the *general equivalent*, i.e. the something all subjects share that consider drugs as their antagonistic Other, it consisted of the fight against terrorism in the second discourse. Furthermore, in both discourses cooperation is considered as the best *means* to control drugs and fight terrorism. They experienced the same lack and, therefore, they shared the same *imaginary* – a world, a community, a civilization, a society that is free from the lack that haunts it. This congruency represents an interesting result: while, in general, discourses attempt to overcome their lack (that constitutes them at the same time), in the two under scrutiny the *eradication* of the lack is the ultimate goal and not any kind of incorporation or merging.

While this observation holds for any discourse with antagonistic frontiers, it seems to be particularly pertinent to security discourses: security helps a political community to define 'who it is' and where the enemy can be found. Threats and insecurity are not just potential dangers to identities but simultaneously constitute them. This is particularly true when we are dealing with 'national security'. IR poststructuralism understands this traditional concept in its own historical context and semantic specificity, and as a particular form of identity construction, i.e. one connected to the nation state because 'the meaning of security is tied to historically specific forms of political community' (Walker 1990: 5). Consequently, the international and national are constructed as different spheres but mutually constituting oppositions (Ashley 1987: 416–7; Walker 1993: 159–61): 'the state only knows who he is and what it is through the juxtaposition against the antagonistic threatening Other' (Hansen 1997: 375). Furthermore, security discourses not only attempt to define identity, they also legitimize the exercise of power against the enemy, as we have seen with regard to the international anti-terrorist and anti-drug measures.

Concerning general equivalent and means, however, the discourses part company. Whereas the drug discourse rarely revealed ruptures or breaches, the terrorism discourse disclosed a mesh of reservations and limitations restricting the remit of the general equivalent and the means. While agreement existed that terrorism has to be fought, the *how to* of this fight remained entirely disputed. Despite this incongruence, however, the main difference of both discourses resides in the role of the international community.

In the drugs discourse, the latter represented the equivalential chain that has been forged by the universalization of particular subjects and by drawing an antagonistic frontier that juxtaposed a collective Self – the international community – with the drugs Other. In the drug case, this has led to the constitution of a hegemonic order at the international level. In the discourse on terrorism, things are not as clear. Lacking an unambiguous general equivalent and a chain of equivalential subjects, no particular signifier was able to represent the collective Self and the vision of a terrorism-free world. This is related to the observation that the terrorism discourse does not reveal a homogeneous Other construction. On the contrary, different hegemonic projects have been reconstructed promoting different meanings of terrorism and of what a Self that should fight terrorism is about. This has led to the conclusion that no hegemonic order at the international level can be reconstructed in the discourse on terrorism.

The reconstruction is supported by contrasting the co-occurrences of the collective Self (read the international community) and antagonistic Other (read terrorism or drugs) in the two international discourses as Table 5.1 shows. The most striking difference resides in the general occurrences of Self and Other codes. While the terrorist Other is highly referred to (3,888 hits overall), it rarely coincides with references to the Self (594 hits overall) and vice versa. These spurious co-occurrences sustain the general conclusion on the terrorism discourse: there are Other and Self constructions; still both do not match in the sense of being two sides of the same coin. Indeed, one may conclude that the identified Selfs and Others may all be somewhat related to each other and while establishing relationships of radical difference necessary for identity construction, more than one radical difference is created producing a discursive field crisscrossed by numerous identities. In its entirety, the discourse on terrorism experiences considerable dispute of all facets of the phenomenon and the 'attitude' a collective Self should adopt towards it. Contrary the drug-discourse: constructions of the Other co-occur with visions of the Self and vice versa (1,548 hits overall). These occurrences conclude that a recurrent juxtaposition of Self and Other (while not always a direct one!) has been achieved, giving the drug discourse a homogeneous outlook.

Table 5.1 Co-occurrences of Self codes in international discourses on drugs and terrorism

	Drugs	*Terrorism*
General occurrence of Self codes	902	1889
Occurrence with all codes	4330	1575
Occurrence with Other codes	1548	594

Table 5.2 Co-occurrences of Other codes in international discourses on drugs and terrorism

	Drugs	*Terrorism*
General occurrence of Other codes	2904	3888
Occurrence with all codes	3649	2364
Occurrence with Self codes	1548	594

Hegemonic strategies, the construction of the antagonistic Other and the language of war

While there are a number of important and relevant results that pertain to one of the discourses only, the subsequent analysis focuses on those that permit comparison. Accordingly, the focus of this section is on the hegemonic strategies aiming at the construction of an antagonistic Other and the web of non-antagonistic Others the former is embedded in. Furthermore, comparing the typologies of different Other constructions and different degrees of otherness, it asks for similarities or dissimilarities in constituting antagonistic and non-antagonistic Others. For instance, in how far have the constructions changed over time, i.e. what kind of attempts have been undertaken to stabilize the antagonistic frontier? While the section emphasizes the relevance of a clearly defined antagonistic Other for an international hegemonic order, it investigates parallels and differences in the relationship between Self and Other in both discourses. This equally allows questioning in how far heterogeneity has impeded an unambiguous Other construction as well as a clear consensus and vision creating a Self and in how far the language of war has helped to establish and sustain these constructions. Table 5.3. summarizes the results on the reconstructed strategies and their repartition on the two discourses.

Overall, 12 of all 15 strategies have been located; 10.5 strategies in the drugs discourse compared to six strategies in the discourse on terrorism. Unsurprisingly, productive hegemonic strategies dominate the drugs and counter-hegemonic strategies the terrorism discourse, an observation directly in line with the study's main result. Reviewing the picture of the reconstructed strategies with regard to the basic and supplementary dimensions, shows that three strategies have been located most often: basic productive hegemonic strategy *Universalization* of subjects to form a chain of equivalence, basic counter-hegemonic strategy on the *Particularization* of subjects and basic counter-hegemonic strategy *Weakening of the antagonistic frontier*. Their frequent reconstruction underlines what has been said on the relevance of the basic dimension, in comparison to the supplementary: only the presence of all three basic strategies bespeaks of the emergence or failure of hegemonic orders and signals whether the logic of equivalence or difference is at play. The simultaneous presence of the basic strategies in both discourses highlights the mutual subversion and constitution of the logics that has been outlined in chapter two. Where the logic of equivalence universalizes subjects (productive hegemonic strategy *Universalization*), the logic of difference attempts to particularize the subjects of a discourse (counter-hegemonic strategy *Particularization*) and to deteriorate the frontier (counter-hegemonic strategy *Weakening of the antagonistic frontier*). In this respect, the frequent interplay between these basic strategies shows how much both logics are in need of each other, since a certain degree of difference is conditional to establish equivalential chains which are necessary to make the particularization of subjects possible.

Within the supplementary dimension, two counter-hegemonic strategies have been most recurrently reconstructed.[1] First, counter-hegemonic strategy *Crossing the antagonistic frontier in order to weaken it* on the one hand centres around the

Table 5.3 Repartition of reconstructed strategies in international discourses on drugs and terrorism

	International discourse on drugs	International discourse on terrorism
Productive hegemonic strategies	*Basic dimension:* • Universalization • Establishing an antagonistic frontier • Representation *Supplementary dimension:* • Extending the antagonizing chain of equivalence • Simultaneously emphasizing and downgrading the particularity of a subject of *chain A* • Crossing the antagonistic frontier in order to strengthen *chain A* • Enlarging the antagonized chain of equivalence	*Basic dimension:* • Universalization (partially)

Counter-hegemonic strategies	*Basic dimension:*
	• Particularization
	• Weakening of the antagonistic frontier
	Supplementary dimension:
	• Stressing the particularity of a subject of *chain A* explicitly at the expense of the general equivalent
		Basic dimension:
		• Particularization
		• Weakening of the antagonistic frontier
		Supplementary dimension:
		• Stressing the particularity of a subject of *chain A* explicitly at the expense of the general equivalent
		• Crossing the antagonistic frontier in order to weaken it
		  – Protect particularity of a subject by articulating its particularity as part of *chain Z*
		  – Underscore particularity of a subject/element of *chain Z*
		• Attempts to disarticulate floating elements of *chain Z*

attempts to safeguard the particularity of a subject that is considered to be part of the antagonistic Other (sub-strategy *Protect particularity of a subject by articulating its particularity as part of chain Z*). This worked, for example, by accusing other countries of supporting terrorists, and the request to exclude the national liberation or wartime resistance movements from a definition of terrorism. On the other hand, the second sub-strategy *Underscore particularity of a subject/element of chain Z* of the same counter-hegemonic strategy stresses the differential remainder of a subject that is also treated as an element of the antagonistic Other. Here, the underlying causes of the drug problem and terrorism are a case in point. Second, counter-hegemonic strategy *Stressing the particularity of a subject of chain A explicitly at the expense of the general equivalent* encompasses the demand to preserve national sovereignty frequently requested in both discourses.

With regard to the constructions of the antagonistic Other in both discourses, one main similarity can be discerned: in both cases, the Other is constituted as the denial of the ultimate goals and as the source of the lack. The world is an unhealthy, insecure, barbaric and violent place because of drugs and terrorism, and both are deemed responsible for this lack and, therefore, block the world's 'full-fledged' identity. This explains why terrorism and drugs are constructed as antagonistic Others in the first place. Despite this general similarity, we find blatant differences in the construction of the respective antagonistic Other. The dissimilarities centre on two main aspects: first, whether a recurrent and frequently direct juxtaposition of Self and Other can be reconstructed and, second, whether the same articulations produce different effects. With regard to the juxtaposition, the discourse on drugs reveals a clear picture. While the antagonistic Other 'drugs' represented not only a denial of the ultimate goal, the discourse equally constructed drugs and their universe as the explicit opposite of the collective Self, the international community and of all subjects it represents. The typology of different degrees of otherness has demonstrated the juxtaposition between community and drugs that worked toward the creation of an antagonizing chain of equivalence on the side of the international community and an antagonized chain headed by the excluded common reference point drugs.

The antagonistic terrorist Other was neither construed as one single chain of equivalence, nor was an antagonizing chain of equivalence established headed by the international community. As the typologies of different degrees of otherness reflect (and most obviously the need for more than one!), the construction of terrorism was entirely heterogeneous and the target of different hegemonic projects aspiring to install one specific meaning of the phenomenon as hegemonic (but failed). The terrorist Other is particularly heterogeneous since the meanings conferred to it involved elements of subjects struggling against their articulation as part of the Other. The antagonistic frontier established by one hegemonic project was crossed by another when linkages between potential cooperation partners and terrorism were invoked (as supplementary counter-hegemonic strategy *Autonomization of subject of chain A* indicated). Because of the various antagonistic frontiers that crisscrossed the discourse of terrorism, no juxtaposition occurred.

Second, some of the articulations that have been reconstructed in both discourses produced – despite their similarity – different effects. Especially, the various accusations are of interest for the comparison, since the accusation of being the source of drugs or terrorism took a different path in the two discourses. In the drugs case, it served to stabilize the antagonistic frontier in the place where it was already drawn and strengthened the hegemonic regime instead of obstructing its emergence. But compared to the terrorism discourse – and this is the main reason for the difference – the accusation in the discourse on drugs did not involve any defamation of elements of the national identity, culture, and traditions of the subjects that are accused. It is not about *producing* drugs; the problem evolves from the *ab*use and their diversion to illicit channels – that is what threatens the Self. Accusing others of being the source of terrorism nearly always implied defamation of other subjects' national identity. For example, those with a colonial past were responsible for terrorism since their colonialism produced the violence they now label terrorism. Hence, the accusations in the drug discourse were less problematic than in the terrorism discourse, since by calling someone a terrorist or a source of terrorism, the identities of subjects were always discredited, disqualified and devaluated. The result that a hegemonic regime emerged in the field of drugs *also because* of a homogeneous construction of the Other and failed in the area of terrorism *also because* of a heterogeneous Other strongly points at the importance of a homogeneous construction of the antagonistic Other. Still, an antagonistic frontier can only be drawn if it is not crossed by associating elements of subjects' national identity, culture, and traditions with the antagonistic Others that are originally meant to be cooperation partners. To stabilize (in principle instable) frontiers turns into a litmus test for hegemonic orders at the international level.

As a second main conclusion, I have outlined that the antagonistic Other is embedded in a web of multiple non-antagonistic Others, and the typologies of different degrees of otherness have corroborated this reasoning. In both discourses, the threatening character of the antagonistic Other was not only formed, enlarged and deepened with the help of further subjects and discursive elements assigned to it. Also, by outlining which subjects and elements *do not* belong to the Other, the contours of the latter have been strengthened (drugs) or blurred (terrorism). To not consider the cultivators of drugs as part of the antagonized Other but as a group of individuals to be protected from the harm of the drug-business, and the producer countries as different and in need of assistance, shows that being a source of drugs does not automatically mean becoming associated with the antagonistic Other.

Such nuancing has failed and is virtually absent in the terrorism discourse, since the construction of non-antagonistic Other only worked at the expense of the rigidity of the antagonistic Other. However, the reconstruction of non-antagonistic Others has enriched the analysis, given the study's call that the mesh of subjects, identities and elements an antagonistic Other is separated from or associated with needs to be considered to develop an ontologically flexible concept of collective identity construction. It has also paved the way for the result that an unambiguous Other is essential for collective identity construction at the international level. Or, to put it differently, non-antagonistic Others bring to mind that antagonistic Other constructions are always historically contingent. They show how much antagonistic Others are the contingent product of specific powerful strategies aiming at exclusion to hegemonize a discourse.

Have the constructions of the antagonistic Others changed over time? From a poststructuralist stance this question is misleading, if change is meant to designate an overhaul of a stable and given construction. If change is considered in light of its interplay with continuity, i.e. as discontinuity, it is possible to investigate it in the present context. The most prominent discontinuity appears with regard to the description of the encounter of the Self with its Other and the increasing resort to the language of war. According to both discourses, we live in a *state of war*: war against terrorism and war against drugs. I contend that this is the major change between the 1970s and early 1990s, up until today, a change that is manifest in an increase in formulations of demonization and damnation in both discourses. Indeed, when international terrorism turns from the last resort of poor people into the common enemy; when international drug control turns from suppression into battle meant to eliminate drugs, and cooperation is no longer a mode of coordination but a powerful weapon against the enemy, we know that we are in a state of war. And while the problematic consequences of such language cannot be overseen, the perfidy of hegemonic orders resides in the fact that they are feeding the state of war because they are in need of the homogenizing effect of the martial language.

To sum up: hegemonic orders at the international level are in need of a homogeneously constructed antagonistic Other, and this is possible, at best, if the constitution of the Other does not involve any elements of national identity, culture, or religion (encompassed by the concept of heterogeneity) of the subjects present in the respective discourse. Moreover, the need for an ontologically flexible concept of collective identity construction offered by the present study is strongly underlined by identification of the web of non-antagonistic Others in which the antagonistic one is embedded. The comparison of the discourses on terrorism and drugs at the international level has corroborated this conclusion.

The dynamics of building a political consensus – constructing the Self

As I have argued that the construction of hegemonic orders is a dual process, the creation of the Self needs to be addressed, i.e. the establishment of an unambiguously shared vision and a political consensus. This implies to compare the discourses with regard to three central elements indicating the success of hegemonic projects: the rebuttal of heterogeneity, the extension of antagonizing chains of equivalence and the moment of representation.

Beginning with the two latter points means to investigate whether the chain has been extended by recruiting further subjects and whether one particularity was able to represent an equivalential chain in its entirety. In the discourse on drugs, a hegemonic regime has been located in a recurrent *extension* of the chain with an increasing number of subjects subscribing to the general equivalent of an international drug control. This is best visible in the constantly increasing number of parties to the three conventions with near universal adherence by today. The analysis of the discourse on drugs further revealed that a 'drug-free world' is the unambiguous vision shared among the discursive agents jointly opposing the global spread of drugs. Therefore, the international community is construed as the agent responsible for confronting the Other and able to create a 'drug-free world'. The community is unequivocally imagined as the locus of concerted action, and as a realm of ethical 'goodness': the values it holds (among these human rights, freedom, and worldwide peace) accord legitimacy to cooperation and any agreement against drugs – the community *represents* the chain of subjects sharing the consensus of fighting drugs. In contrast, in the struggle against terrorism, we have neither been able to reconstruct the moment of representation nor a single chain of equivalence. Crisscrossed by antagonisms, various hegemonic projects have not merged into a unique equivalential, hegemonic pattern. The international community does not act as the main agent responsible for confronting the terrorist Other and enabling accordant concerted action. More bluntly stated: while the drug discourse appears as a veritable 'success story', the discourse on terrorism appears as an 'accumulation of failures'.

Next to representation, the third aspect to indicate success, consists in the *suppression of heterogeneity*, and here above all in the suppression of the differential remainder that hampers the formation of a chain of equivalence. Now, comparing the elements inducing a strong presence of heterogeneity in both discourses, we witness that the same elements have different effects. In both discourses, these elements are: first, the request to respect national sovereignty and specific national ways (*Sonderwege*) or principles and the differential articulations of, second, 'doubts of engagement' and, third, 'accusation of hypocrisy'. While sovereignty has produced rather similar results, the latter two triggered dissimilar outcomes. Finally, retracing how the subjects joining forces to fight drugs and terrorism conceive of each other allows not only pinning down different degrees of otherness but also indicates whether the presence of heterogeneity has been successfully suppressed. In this respect, it proves to be particularly rewarding to investigate the moment of cooperation, since the way subjects imagine and present their cooperation partners has effects on the equivalential bonds within a chain of equivalence.

First, *sovereignty* stressed the differential character of a specific subject, since it indicates its status as a state (with legitimate access to the discourse) and it is considered an integral element of the subject's national identity. As I have outlined in chapter three, to describe a subject as sovereign differentiates it from other subjects. In particular, states (which are the main actors in the analyzed debates) ground their sovereignty in the idea of representing the will of a nation and in their monopoly of the legitimate use of force (Connolly 1991: 64–6; Walker 1993; Doty 1996: 122). Exactly this general meaning of sovereignty puts into motion the process of particularization, which is based on self-descriptions of what determines sovereign nations.

In the drugs discourse, an international drug control was requested that respects sovereignty and the national ways of dealing with the drug problem, while the need of an international control was not at all doubted but embedded in this demand.

This is exactly what productive hegemonic strategy *Simultaneously emphasizing and downgrading the particularity of a subject of chain A* is about. In the discourse on terrorism, appeals to sovereignty stressed the particularity of a subject at the expense of the already instable general equivalent 'fight against international terrorism' (what accounts for supplementary counter-hegemonic strategy *Stressing the particularity of a subject of chain A explicitly at the expense of the general equivalent*). The fight was not only weakened because an agreement on *how to* counter terrorism was missing, but also since sovereignty implicitly calls upon elements of national identity with the issues of extradition and asylum raised in its context. How to deal with asylum and extradition was constructed as dependent on a specific understanding of law and legislation – clearly an element of national identity of the subjects present in the discourse. Hence, specific national traditions should remain unaltered despite an agreement on the international fight against international terrorism.

Second, subjects have been particularized by *doubting their engagement* or, third, by *accusing each other of hypocrisy*. In the drugs discourse, accusations and doubts have led to assurances of fully subscribing to the ultimate goal. Therefore, the need for an international drug control (the general equivalent) was forcefully rearticulated and reiterated in the discourse. In the terrorism discourse, doubts of engagement and accusation of hypocrisy decreased the strength of the (already instable) general equivalent. Especially in the 1970s, the articulations led to an explicit denial of the equivalent, since the fight against terrorism was considered less important than, for instance, the eradication of poverty, hunger and the like. Most importantly, both articulations involved a strong moment of differentiation: by accusations and doubts – in other words, by 'pointing the finger at others' – subjects constructed themselves as being in favour of an international fight, calling for cooperation in this fight or referring to their own experience with terrorism. Hence, self-descriptions are used to acquit oneself of the (potential and false!) charge of not being 'really' engaged in the fight against terrorism.

Sovereignty, doubts of engagement and accusation of hypocrisy – the same differential articulations produced dissimilar results in the two discourses under scrutiny. In the drug discourse, the differential articulations led to a rewriting of the consensus shared by all subjects and rendered the need for an international drug control an essential element of the drugs discourse. This was only possible because none of these internal differences mounted to an explicit denial neither of the general equivalent nor of the international community as tendentially empty signifier. Heterogeneity was present but successfully suppressed and its silence signalled the successful construction of a hegemonic regime at the international level. The terrorism discourse showed that in the absence of a hegemonic order, heterogeneity has been present, above all as differences that impede the constitution of such order. Highly detrimental to the emergence of a consensus on how to fight terrorism, these differences were, first, intimately linked to elements of national identity, culture, and traditions of the subjects in the discourse, which were in turn connected to the terrorist Other provoking, second, a diffuse construction of the antagonistic Other.

Finally, what role did *cooperation* play with regard to the suppression of heterogeneity? In the discourse on drugs, cooperation is the common means that tightens equivalential bonds and sustains the construction of a hegemonic order. Cooperation partners are conceived of as non-antagonistic Others, they are *different* but all are responsible for international drug control: either responsible for assisting in a successful implementation of the control or in need of such assistance. This difference stems from their role as consuming or producing state and both characteristics go together with their status as developed (consumer) and developing (producer) state.[2] Regardless at which end of the chain of drug production and trade a country positions itself, all states share the responsibility of actively supporting international drug control. The consuming countries are responsible for assisting the producing countries in developing the necessary features to successfully implement the control of illicit substances, whereas the producer countries are in need of this assistance. Inversely, consumer countries cannot deny assistance and producer states do not dispose of the possibility to refrain from assistance. Still, this differentiation is not about antagonistic otherness. Conceived of as non-antagonistic Others, they are constructed not as equal (giving vs. receiving assistance) but valued equally. Of course, the value judgements placed on each other are positive, since knowledge about each other's identities is shared through self-descriptions. These include constructing oneself as willing to cooperate or as disposing of an experience in fighting drugs, or by the subscription to the antagonistic construction of drugs. Hence, the knowledge – regardless whether false or correct, complete or incomplete – about the identity of one's cooperation partners allowed imposing a positive value judgement on the respective non-antagonistic Other (Todorov 1992: 185).

However, in the discourse on drugs, cooperation could only play such positive role because there was a strong agreement on the necessity and the determinants of international drug control (the general equivalent) and cooperation was the means to carry out this control. Cooperation is the transmission belt between the subjects in the chain of equivalence, since it ensures their equivalential bonds. It cannot induce a non-antagonistic Other construction on its own but is *dependent* on their non-antagonistic constitution beforehand by the universalization of the particular subjects.

In the discourse on terrorism, cooperation was not able to play this role. Since the 1970s, a general agreement on the necessity of cooperation as means to fight terrorism can be reconstructed, and it is reaffirmed in the current discourse on terrorism which increasingly considers it as the only means to fight terrorism. Nevertheless, the problem of associating potential cooperation partners with the antagonistic Other has impeded that cooperation works as a transmission belt between subjects in a chain of equivalence. In particular, the differentiations between former colonial powers and ex-colonies and between wartime resistance and national liberation movements point to these problematic linkages.

Yet, these differentiations not only serve to de-legitimize potential cooperation partners but also legitimize a particular understanding of terrorism. On the one hand, a meaning which excludes national liberation movements from the remit of a definition and sustains the right of self-determination; on the other, a definition of terrorism which excludes the resistance movements during the Second World War. This problematique has not been surmounted entirely: while today, those subjects are constructed as cooperation-partners that had been associated with the antagonistic Other in the 1970s, novel linkages with the Other are made: for instance, associations between Islam or Islamic countries and terrorism are drawn. Indeed, cooperation as a means was invoked at a very early stage, but as long as the struggle between different hegemonic projects promoting different meanings of the antagonistic Other persists, it cannot intensify a non-antagonistic construction of cooperation partners.

Cooperation played its role in the middle of a hegemonic order as a means that tightens the equivalential bonds between the subjects forming a collective Self, thus, *after* they have been constituted as non-antagonistic. It is a supportive element if no linkages between potential cooperation partners and the antagonistic Other have been made. In sum, heterogeneity has been reconstructed in both discourses albeit with different results or to different degrees. It was less present in the process of forging a Self when the differential remainder of subjects led to a rearticulation of the ultimate or common goals, if elements of national identity, culture traditions etc. of subjects have not been associated with the antagonistic Other. In this process, the invocation of cooperation has been particularly rewarding for the suppression of heterogeneity, since it ensures equivalential bonds between subjects and promotes the perception of cooperation-partners as non-antagonistic. Conversely, heterogeneity developed to full presence when different hegemonic projects struggled with each other associating diverse elements (of, most frequently, national identity) with the antagonistic Other and, this, in turn, led to a diffuse constitution of the Other. Again, this presence bespeaks of the interplay between the logic of difference and equivalence: any subversion of the logic of equivalence by the logic of difference (and, therefore, the emergence of a hegemonic pattern) only works in the presence of differences. Both discourses have allowed reconstructing this mutual subversion – but, to pinpoint down the results: in the discourse on drugs, the logic of equivalence is dominant whereas in the terrorism discourse the logic of difference is prevailing.

Justifying counter-measures in presence and absence of hegemonic orders

What follows from this result for the justification of counter-measures and their legitimacy? Of course, if a hegemonic order has been installed and partially fixed, measures can be justified and legitimized by referring to the regime's parameters. Over time, specific measures become institutionalized and routinized and are rarely questioned. However, it is crucial that these measures are considered to comply with the regime, i.e. if they deviate from the regimes remit, they are not immediately regarded as illegitimate; but they are in need of substantial effort of justification. It remains central to their status as legitimate measures that they are congruent with and based on the political consensus shared among the discursive agents identifying with, supporting and aiming at the expansion of the regime. Since we do not speak about stable orders but about orders that are contingent and subject to change, the substance of acceptable measures and the range of legitimate justifications vary over time.

In contrast, in the absence of a hegemonic order legitimate measures are always only legitimate from particular points of views, since their universal aspiration is opposed by different interpretations of how to counter a threat. The universal reference point for legitimacy is lacking (as neither a homogeneous Other construction exists nor a common vision or a political consensus); thus, subjects aiming at fighting an existential threat tend to refer back to their national (or regional) interpretations of legitimacy and justice. Of course, a national understanding can be shared within a wider community such as the EU but they are only partial interpretations that are transferred to the wider, global level, since, first, subjects are very much aware of the necessity to justify security measures impacting on the lives of their own nationals and on those of foreign citizens; and, second, the transferral always holds the promise that one's own antagonistic Other construction and vision could become the yardstick of the global interpretation of Self and Other and the ensuing international measures.

With respect to the discourse on drugs, the presence of a hegemonic regime has led to the institutionalization and routinization of a number of measures against drug abuse, and opposition has difficulty to assert itself. Thus, though resistance to the current interpretation of drugs as evil Other exist, as, for example, the discussions surrounding the drug addict have demonstrated, any justification of alternative visions of the drug addict always need to be embedded in a particular argumentative pattern. Those struggling for a different handling of drug addicts or for the de-penalization of cannabis cannot simply demonstrate the 'uselessness' of the therapy. Neither can they refer to scientific evidence on the much higher addictive potential of alcohol or tobacco in contrast to cannabis, outlining that the harm to society done by alcohol and tobacco is much higher than by cannabis (see Nutt *et al.* 2007).

Overall, current oppositional demands follow a specific pattern, since they argue that their demands are still *within* the remit of the drugs regime. For instance, in 2002, the British government decided to reclassify cannabis and *de facto* to decriminalize its personal consumption. The government persistently maintained that such action is not tantamount to formal legalization and therefore *de jure* in conformity with international law. However, this did not prevent the International Narcotics Control Board from criticizing the UK for this measure. In an open letter to the INCB, a British official responded that it would do 'great damage to the credibility of the messages we give to young people about the dangers of drug misuse if we try to pretend that cannabis is as harmful as drugs such as heroin and crack cocaine'. He rejected the Board's 'selective and inaccurate use of statistics' and its 'failure to refer to the scientific basis on which the UK Government's decision was based' (United Kingdom Home Office 2002a; 2002b; International Drug Policy Consortium 2008: 12). However, this permissive stance has been abandoned partially in February 2009, when cannabis was reclassified from a 'Class C' to a 'Class B' drug. Interestingly, the reasons given rearticulate – albeit in a different manner – the still oppositional stance of the British Government: the reclassification of cannabis was not the result of any kind of final compliance with the UN drug prohibition regime but reflected 'the fact that skunk, a much stronger version of the drug, now dominates in the UK. Skunk has swept many less potent forms of cannabis off the market, and now accounts for more than 80% of cannabis available on our streets, compared to just 30% in 2002'.[3]

Furthermore, in pursuit of its harm reduction approach, the UK has turned back to the practice of prescribing heroin, and not only methadone, to drug addicts. This, together with the practice of supervising the consumption of drugs, is seen by many as another breach of the drug prohibition regime (Woolf 2007a; 2007b). More important, though, is *how* these measures are justified: Britain maintains that the prescription of heroin is for 'medical use' and therefore formally legal (United Kingdom Home Office 2002b: 20; 2003). Since the medical use of drugs is not proscribed by the regime, it is crucial for the oppositional demands' success to demonstrate their compliance with the order. This is precisely what has been circumscribed by the supplementary productive hegemonic strategy *Simultaneously emphasizing and downgrading the particularity of a subject of chain A*. Subjects *simultaneously* embed their particularity (heroin for 'medical use only') into their subordination to the general equivalent, i.e. to internationally control drugs, which is – so claimed – not violated by the subject's differential movements.

In the terrorism discourse, the absence of a hegemonic regime makes such global justifications impossible. Since a consensus does not exist upon which globally accepted measures could be built, Other constructions are amenable to particular demands of specific subjects who tend to define the Other according to their own imaginations and needs. The measure of the UN list has exemplified this problematique: the inclusion of suspected individuals is not the outcome of a common antagonistic Other construction but entities and persons are selected on the basis of particular preferences of Member States, which are unlikely to be disputed. The same logic can be reconstructed at the regional level in the Europol-US agreements and the EU-US agreements on judicial cooperation in criminal matters within which it has been avoided to determine the terrorist Other although the agreements have specifically been created as means in the 'war on terror'. This logic further applies to the national level when the US Government claims for itself the discretion to define the terrorist Other on an ad hoc basis. Other states are left with the choice of either joining the 'Coalition of the Willing' and fighting the enemies as defined by the US, or being sidelined and running the risk of being associated with the enemies (Friedrichs 2006). Indeed, the Iraq intervention has forcefully demonstrated that the United States is in the position to define who the terrorist is on a case-by-case basis. It therefore comes as no surprise that the United States is not actively participating in the debates of the Ad Hoc Committee and the Working Group, since a comprehensive convention on international terrorism stating who is a terrorist and who is not would limit US-freedom of action too much. Still, the justifications of these national 'anti-terrorist' measures in the absence of a hegemonic regime are based on a particular, non-universal argumentation which is considered as legitimate, since the idea of 'condemning terrorism' is shared world-wide – while blatantly ignoring the dissent on the *how to* of the fight against terrorism.

To conclude, it is obvious that in the absence of a homogenous construction of the Other and of a political consensus on how to counter the Other, international counter-measures are difficult to sustain and can neither claim universal acceptance nor coerce other subjects to comply with these measures. Thus, the institutionalizations and the justifications of practices are dependent on the establishment or presence of a hegemonic regime.

The benefit of 'bringing methodology back in'

Before turning to the conclusion of this study, it is necessary to scrutinize the analysis under the headings of reflexivity, validity, reliability and generalizability. Such a procedure allows us to assess whether the presented discourse analytical method has been suitable to investigate hegemony and collective identities from a poststructuralist perspective. Moreover, the critical appraisal of the study's method rounds off one of its central aims to address the clear need for methodological rigor in IR poststructuralism.

Chapter two has especially insisted on the necessity of an analysis, first, tightly interwoven with theory and, second, open and flexible enough to investigate the construction of hegemonic orders. This included *inter alia* a code system not set in stone, a deductive-inductive generation of hegemonic strategies stipulating the enactment of theoretical concepts in analyzing the discourses. The interconnectedness of theory and material has become apparent at various occasions; to advance theory, chapters one and two needed to anticipate particular aspects of the analysis and chapters three, four and the comparison of the present chapter referred back to the theoretical parts. Accordingly, discourse theory and analysis are highly integrated: while discourse theory allows a certain generalizability of particular aspects or operations in the discourses, discourse analysis questions and verifies this generalizability which opens up avenues for further theorization. But not only the issue of generalizability can be raised in the present context, the entire methodological *modus operandi* provokes the question of credibility of research, i.e. whether the common evaluation criteria reliability and validity are applicable at all and if yes, whether they are satisfied.

It might seem surprising that a poststructuralist confronts herself with these general criteria to evaluate qualitative research but I fully share the observation by Jacob Torfing that 'we need to reflect, openly and critically upon many methodological choices that we make in the analysis of specific discursive formations. That will [. . .] help us to improve the quality of our discourse analysis [. . .]' (Torfing 2005: 25). In my understanding this calls for a confrontation with some general criteria of qualitative research, though slightly adjusted to the exigencies of a poststructuralist approach. Thus, first, in how far can the re-current transformation and adaptation of theoretical concepts and codes according to the cases at hand allow for statements of a wider range (i.e. generalizability)? How can be ensured, secondly, that the above-depicted results are credible, relevant for and consistent with the aims and research question of the study (i.e. reliability and validity)?

First, I argue that neither poststructuralism nor discourse analysis categorically exclude the possibility of the generalizability of statements or concepts. Obviously, this understanding should not be equated with the positivist understanding of generalizability as a universal or general subsumption of phenomena to causal laws and mechanisms. Rather, one may speak of a generalizability of specific statements and concepts implying that only specific types of discourses (political, medical etc.) in specific historical and social contexts can step up to the standard of generalizability. The dynamic nature of discourses and the ensuing impossibility of a complete portrayal of the developments and functioning of one single discourse notwithstanding, it is possible to reconstruct selected parts of the discourse allowing for generalizable statements about these very parts (Howarth 2000: 142; Nonhoff 2006: 243). In this regard, the present analysis represents a 'photo, film or video still' exposing exemplarily the reconstruction of a specific part of two discourses at a given moment in time and space. Some generalizable statements that can be deduced are, most importantly, the abstract logic of hegemonic operations (the logic of equivalence) which offers ample space for such statements. As one of the main ways to relate discursive elements, attempts to reconstruct it can be made in other discourses, as well.

Applying these general reflections on generalizability to the findings, the role of the homogenously constructed Other and the differential articulations 'doubts of engagement', 'accusation of hypocrisy' and 'sovereignty' should be highlighted. From the presence of a homogeneously constructed Other and the ensuing successful constitution of a hegemonic regime in the drugs discourse versus the lack of such an Other and the failure of hegemonic projects to transform into a hegemony in the terrorism discourse, the general statement is possible that for a dominant pattern to emerge, an antagonistic Other or frontier *as such* is not sufficient. Both need to be constructed in a clear-cut and homogeneous manner. While to some this may sound trivial, both discourses have indicated that the constitution of a homogeneous antagonistic Other is a difficult task. Especially if discourses deal with phenomena imagined as existential threats and if different subjects with different interpretations of what this Other is about populate the discourse. Yet, the nature of the discourses under scrutiny delimits the generalizability, as we are only dealing with security discourses.

The analysis has outlined that among the internal differences *sovereignty* is raised most prominently in both discourses. In combination with the understanding of national sovereignty by IR poststructuralism as a moment of frontier-building, its quality as differential element in the midst of the process of forging a Self can be extended to other security discourses. Furthermore, among the differential articulations, *doubts of engagement* and *accusation of hypocrisy* have been most often reconstructed. Their potential as generalizable statements lies, first, in their quality as discrediting strategies void of any particular content. Being available as a general strategy of discrediting and unfair reasoning, they can be deployed in discourses within which a hegemonic pattern and meaning can be reconstructed (Schreier 1997).

Yet, the comparative method proves to be highly rewarding with regard to generalizability. While it is not about constructing 'generally applicable laws of social and political behaviour', the 'point of comparison is to further our understanding and explanation of different logics of identity formation and hegemonic practice in different historical conjunctures'. Especially since the functioning of a discourse of each particular case 'can be "tested" in different contexts' (Howarth 2000: 138–9). Nevertheless, comparisons prove only fruitful if the cases to be compared are described, analyzed and reconstructed independently and afterwards compared. The present study responded to the latter challenge by investigating each discourse separately (chapters three and four). Contrasting the two discourses in the earlier sections allowed for further discovery of the social contingency of the discursive praxis, but also revealed a number of similarities that permit for larger claims on the process of hegemonies and collective identity construction, which can be explored in further research.

With regard to reliability and validity, one has to pay attention to their interconnectedness.[4] In the qualitative analysis of texts, reliability can be made possible by defining codes and concepts more abstractly, at best beforehand. For discourse analysts, such a procedure holds no advantages, as their interest in strategies and patterns makes it impossible to allow a precise and invariable definition of codes and concepts before the analysis – it is not only impossible but also contradicts the aim of a flexible and open research strategy. Hence, to attempt an increase in reliability inevitably seems to decrease the validity of the analysis. In the present context, the problem is remedied with the help of intra-rater reliability. The entire material has been recoded after it has been worked through completely. This allows searching for inconsistencies in the coding process and ensuring their coherence. And, in a certain sense, the reader functions as a 'second coder': with the help of extensive quotes from the debates, she is able to judge the study upon the plausibility and validity of its analysis, procedure and findings.

Ultimately, the validity of the results is also increased by the awareness of the unavoidable reflexivity of poststructuralist discourse analysis. The strong social constructivist epistemology that forms its foundation applies not only to the discourses of politicians but to the work of academic researchers as well. The academic discourse also constitutes a particular reality, and researchers are continuously challenged to retain sensitivity to their role in the constitution of categories and frames that produce a reality of a particular sort. In turn, the study's reconstructions deliver further 'truths' on drugs and terrorism. I fully subscribe to the basic assumption of the discourse analytical perspective that 'the discourse theorist is always situated in a particular discursive formation and within a specific tradition, in which he or she has been constituted as a subject just like any other subject' (Howarth 2000: 124). Hence, as discourse analysts we are 'part of the game' and need to be aware of the socially constructed nature of the research categories themselves.

Boundaries and capabilities of the book's approach

As this study began with a call for an explicit discussion of methodological choices, decisions and their consequences and implications within a poststructuralist framework, it is necessary to discuss the capabilities and boundaries of the book's approach. The first caveat concerns the 'origin' and the 'completeness' of the discourses and hegemonies under scrutiny. The reconstruction of the international discourses on drugs and terrorism has always been the reconstruction of a specific interpretation of both phenomena – terrorism and drugs as antagonistic Other. Although they have been embedded in their respective historical context, this should not be misunderstood as a reconstruction of the discourse from their acclaimed 'beginning' nor of their moment of 'birth'. As has been outlined, the present analysis is a photo or video still, the reconstruction of a discourse in a specific moment in time and space. Especially, since the contingency and temporality of the discursive practice makes it impossible to reconstruct, trace or 'discover' any moment of origin. When 'terrorism' was 'invented' it was already a derivative of 'terreur'. The moment the understanding of drugs as illicit and their use as deviant surfaced in the discourse, their interpretation as a tolerable facet of human life already existed. Additionally, hegemonic struggles are much too complex, ambivalent and diverse to be analyzed in one single study. Even a focus on two discourses cannot claim to capture the entire hegemonic struggles in a field, let alone encompass the 'complete' discourses on terrorism and drugs – which has not been the endeavour here.

Secondly, the study is not about 'why collective identities matter' usually asked in the IR literature but on 'how they are constructed'. It does not attempt to explain why an international drug prohibition regime has evolved and why this has not been the case with terrorism by referring to national interests, state's preferences, institutional constraints or external factors. Even if it attempted to do so, it would not be satisfied to take recourse solely to interests, preferences, constraints or external factors. These are one part of a much broader discursive complex and the perspective on hegemonic orders and collective identity construction broadens the view for the conditions under which the latter aspects operate.

Finally, it is not only modesty but also honesty to admit that the present study does not aim at giving concrete policy advice on how to deal with drugs and terrorism (efficiently). However, the reconstruction of collective identity constitutions, of Self and Other are an inherently critical enterprise. While acknowledging that any advice to handle both phenomena can only be voiced from one particular discursive position, dealing with terrorism and drugs from a critical perspective adds important insights to the very much needed informed assessment of the two threats. This is an important endeavour as it paves the way to think differently about terrorism and drugs than currently done. Reconstructing and questioning the links between Self and Other, between 'good' and 'bad' is a crucial step in the participation of a lively debate on the normative assumptions these constructions rest on, instead of hiding behind seemingly technical and organizational questions as policy advice usually does.

However, I claim that the study offers a number of advantages and the 'added value' of a discourse analytical approach, as well as the subsequent methodological benefits, deserves attention. By accepting the question of the 'added value' of a poststructuralist discourse analytical approach, a first response consists in the different kinds of questions the study posed in comparison to those addressed by institutionalist, rationalist or moderate constructivist approaches in IR analyzing security issues. Above all, the study's different question – *how and why* are hegemonic orders constructed – aimed at a *change of perspective*. The study took us one step back: reconstructing how drugs have been constructed as illicit and their use as deviant and how it was possible to constitute terrorism as an existential threat, the study reviewed the conditions for the establishment of a drug regime and for the failure of such a regime against terrorism. Apparently the discrepancy in the international handling of terrorism and drugs is a discrepancy essentially linked to attempts to construe a homogeneous Other according to different imaginations of Selves. Furthermore, terrorism and drugs can only serve as antagonistic Others if their constitution permits each subject present in the discourse to distinguish it as its clear opposite – as everything a subject is not. Other constructions incorporating elements of subject(s) – as this was the case in the terrorism discourse – do not lead to a dominant pattern and meaning but to a discursive field crisscrossed by various antagonisms, marked by different hegemonic projects aspiring to represent a universal imaginary fullness that is only a particular one.

Second, the study's interest in hegemony and collective identity construction addressed the driving forces behind the formation of an international drug control and the failure of a definition of terrorism. The analysis claimed that the formation of collective identities at the international level is the main response to dislocations. Collective identities are not only often held together by particular self-descriptions and by the exclusion of Others but also by their totalizing, imaginary dimension, 'as they brandish the promise of a fully achieved identity in a land of idle happiness' (Torfing 2005: 24).

Bringing hegemony and identity together in the framework of one analysis allowed, thirdly, investigating power struggles in terms of acts of inclusion and exclusion that shape social meanings and identities, that condition the construction of antagonisms and political frontiers. Accordingly, the study refrained from analyzing power 'as a resource or capacity one can possess, store or retrieve or as a relation of domination' (Torfing 2005: 23). Conceiving of terrorism and drugs as discursive phenomena and not as facts permitted the consideration of these discourse as acts of inclusion/exclusion of identities and subjects – power and discourse are inextricably intertwined.

Indeed, and fourth, with its emphasis on the contingent nature of identity and social phenomena in general, the poststructuralist discourse approach proves to be ideally suited to investigate such diffuse threats of terrorism and drugs. Without taking pre-given subjective interests or institutional constraints as sole starting points for analysis but acknowledging that it is the contingency of political processes leading to the process of how terrorism and drugs are constructed as threats and why hegemonic orders are in need of consensus and shared vision, the study has also delivered an idea of the overall landscape in which these acts of inclusion/exclusion take place. Exactly this stance allowed comparing the changes in the discourses on drugs and terrorism as the interplay of continuity and discontinuity.

Finally, the main advantage of the present approach resides in its attempt to bring methodological rigor to IR poststructuralism not only by clearly developing the concepts employed but also by ensuring above all their flexibility and openness through modulation and adjustment to the present context (the combination of subject and strategy is a case in point). Furthermore, the book's procedure guaranteed an intimate connection between theory and concrete material by modifying and adapting the theoretical concepts in light of the material (the development of hegemonic strategies is a case in point). And, perhaps most importantly, by making the analytical decisions and steps transparent, comprehensible and outlining their consequences, methodological thoroughness can be achieved.

As the procedure has been developed precisely in light of the call for 'bringing methodology back to' IR poststructuralism, I am confident that it might guide other studies or serve as their 'stone pit' or resource. Combining IR poststructuralist concepts with those of poststructuralist discourse theory and supplementing this merger with a qualitative method (inductive coding) can stipulate further methodological advance in IR poststructuralism. Furthermore, the concept of heterogeneity can be adjusted and adapted to other contexts. Although the present study has suggested that the particularity of equivalential demands comprises above all elements of the national identity, culture and traditions of differential subjects, this particular content can be scrutinized more thoroughly. Further research could specify these elements and investigate what kind of myths, national narratives, traditions etc. are relevant and which of them are particularly detrimental or conducive to the establishment of chains of equivalence.

The abstract character of the catalogue of hegemonic strategies would equally allow such a transfer. Although the complex was developed in intimate connection with the discourses under scrutiny, its rooting in the theoretical concepts permits an application in different contexts. And as it was never meant to be exhaustive, other fields, such as the internal struggles of institutions or international organizations, could be researched with its help. Taken together, transferring the catalogue of strategies to other areas would also permit investigation into whether some of the main insights of the present study hold outside the terrorism and drugs discourse. Here, for instance, the importance of a homogeneously constructed Other or the recurrent articulation of elements of national identity to differentiate a subject in the midst of hegemonic struggles might be relevant. Eventually, procedure and catalogue might be transferred to other security issues within which collective identity construction seems likely or imaginable (for instance, migration, trafficking in women and children or less diffuse threats such as military interventions or nuclear proliferation).

To conclude, the comparison of both discourses has demonstrated that without a consensus on a common vision as well as a homogenous construction of an Other, a hegemonic regime cannot be installed and sustained or generate support for counter-measures. Overall, chapter five has highlighted that comparative and systematic studies are needed to gain insights into the production, persistence and transformation of hegemonic forms of international order, whether in the field of security or elsewhere.

Conclusion
Rethinking hegemonic orders

The central question of this study has been to inquire about the production and transformation of hegemonic orders, the identities constructed thereby and the practices legitimized by these orders and identities. More precisely, I asked how and why specific interpretations of international terrorism and drug abuse have become hegemonic at the global level. My analysis of the efforts to counter both security issues relied on a distinct theoretical and methodological approach shaped by crucial insights of IR poststructuralism and poststructuralist discourse theory.

The ontological starting point of the present study was the conceptualization of hegemonies as dichotomizing the discursive space by establishing a frontier separating two entities. Yet, the drawing of a frontier also implies conferring a particular meaning to these entities, which brought about the study's understanding of an intimate relationship between the establishment of hegemonic orders and the construction of identities. Thereby, identities have been perceived as always failing identities, since there is an insurmountable lack at the root of every subject which means that subjects need to efface this lack in order to acquire a 'full-fledged' identity. They project their lack onto something external, i.e. onto the Other. Whether this Other is considered as an impediment to achieve the desired identity involves a moment of force and repression inherent in hegemonic orders. Thus, the identities created by hegemonies deduce from their lack that they are blocked by an external force negating them. It is this force which is constructed as an enemy, as antagonistic Other. Such negation does not come without a cost: exclusion works only by homogenization of inner differences.

Hence, subjects with a common antagonistic Other undergo a process of universalization, i.e. they are made equivalent with regard to 'something that underlies them all', and identify with one particular signifier (the tendentially empty signifier) representing their unambiguously shared vision (the unachievable 'full-fledged' identity of, for instance, a drug-free world) of the collective Self. Crucial for the successful establishment of a hegemonic order remains the participation in a consensus between the subjects identifying with the Self, since the consensus is necessary to legitimize internationally accepted counter-measures like a 'war on drugs and terror'.

However, not all hegemonic operations are successful. Especially the moment of an unmitigated particularity of the subjects meant to be universalized plays a decisive role. The concept of heterogeneity encompassed this particularity, the differential remainder of every subject that escaped the inner homogenization of the collective Self. In order to analyze the production and transformation of hegemonic orders, it became essential to trace in how far the presence of the differential remainder is conducive or detrimental to the construction of such orders. In light of these conceptualizations I was able to fully develop my *central argument*. I claimed that the establishment of hegemonic orders is a dual process: first, they rely essentially on the interpretation of an unequivocal, radically different, and homogeneous Other. Second, an accordant unambiguous vision shared among the discursive agents jointly opposing the Other and forming the collective Self needs to be based upon a political consensus between these agents to enact internationally accepted measures countering the Other.

In the following, the question arose how one could practically reconstruct the emergence and re-inscription of hegemonic orders in the two discourses under scrutiny. Therefore, I introduced the notion of *discursive hegemonic strategies*, conceptualizing them as modes of dislocation and suture on the one hand, but also as specific arrangement of discursive elements and subjects based on power calculations (i.e. antagonism) and structured around specific objectives, intentions and aims on the other hand. Such strategies can be distinguished according to their effect within hegemonic struggles: productive hegemonic strategies are conducive to the establishment and persistence of hegemonic orders, whereas counter-hegemonic strategies are detrimental to this process.

The analysis of the international discourse on drugs and terrorism has highlighted the importance of a homogenously constructed Other as well as the necessity of an unambiguously shared vision and consensus among those subjects represented by a collective Self to justify international counter-measures, i.e. to wage a 'war against terror and drugs'. While the drug discourse conveyed a homogenous picture and the erection of a hegemonic order considering drugs as illicit and their use as deviant, the discourse on terrorism has been marked by a long-lasting struggle of different hegemonic projects assigning different meanings to terrorism and those fighting it. This main result of the present analysis does not conceal that heterogeneity has been present in the discourse on drugs and that there are moments of homogenization in the terrorism discourse. Yet, in the drugs case, the presence of heterogeneity has not been detrimental to the hegemonic regime on drug prohibition (remember the treatment of the drug addict) whereas the rare moments of homogenization in the discourse on terrorism (the condemnation of terrorism regardless of the meaning attached to it is a case in point) have not induced an agreement on the 'how to' of this fight.

Notwithstanding, this main result and the further insights gained leave us with a number of questions. Beginning with the outcome that both discourses are abundant of a war-like metaphoric, a language meant to draw boundaries, we need to address more fully the function of this language in light of hegemonic orders. Second, I have argued that hegemonic orders rely on constructions of collective identities via exclusion and radical difference. Such hegemonic orders leave no room for non-antagonistic Others or a nuancing of the picture of the antagonistic

Other, let alone offer different ways of encountering an existentially threatening Other. Still, by making extraordinary counter-measures possible, acceptable and 'normal', such as a UN list of terrorist suspects, or agreements between Europol, the EU and the United States on data exchange and judicial cooperation in criminal matters, despite the human rights problems they raise, one needs to probe into the implications for the communities created by hegemonic orders. What does it imply for their stability when unity is imposed and dissent demonized? And what does it imply for the subjects gathered under the banner but also bound by the ultimate goal? This questions, finally, whether one can imagine different types of hegemonic orders, i.e. orders able to pave the way for policies which do not simply amount to the exertion of greater counter-violence but advance the search for long-lasting solutions to the phenomena of international drug abuse and terrorism.

Stabilizing hegemonic orders – the language of war

While the 1960s started with 'crusades' against drug abusers, in the 1980s people went to 'war against drugs'. While in the 1970s it was a 'fight' against terrorism, people now go to 'war against terrorism'. And the 'evil' of the 1960s and 1970s now needs to be 'annihilated' because 'they are trying to destroy us'. The main effects of this language of war are well known: first, it draws not only a dividing line between those who are defending themselves against those who are attacking. Second, it also produces a permanent state of threat, a condition of perpetual war and presents terrorism and drugs as existential threats.

The power of the first effect resides in the homogenizing dynamics of the language of war. As the analysis of the international drug discourse has shown in particular, hegemonic orders are in need of clear-cut constructions of Self and Other, which leave no doubt about who belongs to which entity. It is the language of war that facilitates and deploys such homogeneous images through an ongoing radicalization and accentuation which has deepened the trench between Self and Other over the years. Indeed, this language exemplarily bespeaks of the study's conceptualization of subject and strategy: whenever discursive agents employ metaphors of war, describe the fight against terrorism and drugs as a 'battle', a 'combat', they have, of course, intentions in mind. Constantly restaging the encounter with terrorism and drugs as a battle between good and evil, between the civilized and the barbarians, between humanity and non-humans allows re-inscribing the two security problems as attacks on humanity and civilization sui generis. For instance, when the Colombian delegate speaks of the 'drug holocaust' which is threatening humanity, drugs are no longer a danger only to Columbia or the international community but to humankind as such (United Nations 1991: 9). Of course, this juxtaposition of humanity vs. non-human beings aims at gaining support and acceptance for extraordinary measures such as campaigns of large-scale counter-violence (see the crop eradication programs) against drug traffickers, cultivators and addicts within a country.

Still, the effects of such strategies – in this context, they accounted for strategies deepening and enlarging the consensus on the constructions of Self and Other[1] – will depend on much more than an individual's or a state's intention, since strategy is never simply a function of intention. The price of such radicalizations resides in the limited room of manoeuvre the language offers to the subjects. And in line with my central argument, this radicalization also comes at the expense of an ever scantier agreement of what all subjects fighting terrorism or drugs share – it hampers the establishment or persistence of hegemonic orders in the long run. Thus, the constant extension of the chain of equivalence by considering the enemy as evil and the opposite of civilization, i.e. constructing terrorists and drug abusers as 'barbarians' or 'non-humans' against whom a war has to be fought, increases the number of subjects in the chain and, inevitably, 'the something underlying all subjects' becomes thinner and thinner. Only civilization or humanity as such remains to be juxtaposed to the Other, the barbarians, the non-humans.

Seeing the leeway vanish makes any attempt to nuance the picture of the antagonistic Other impossible: to consider drug consumption as an alternative and tolerable way of life or to discuss the underlying causes of terrorism becomes increasingly difficult, since such positioning plays into the hands of the 'barbarians'. Especially since in the case of terrorism, 'it is no longer their cause that makes them evil. They just are evil, and that is why it is right for us to fight them' (Bittner 2005: 210). Or, to put it differently, one could also consider the invocation of barbarism as bespeaking of the failure to reach agreement. The analysis has shown that any convergence of understanding amounted to a condemnation of terrorism; however, this has not led to the necessary consensus for a hegemonic regime to come into being. This is, of course, a further downside of the language of war: it makes agreement increasingly impossible even on the least common denominator.

But in the end, what does it mean to present terrorists and drug traffickers and addicts as 'non-humans', as 'barbarians'? In principle, a barbarian could be considered whoever believes that a population or an individual does not completely belong to humanity and can be treated in a manner that he would indignantly refuse to tolerate (Todorov 2008: 30–40). While charges of terrorism and drugs have often included the topos of 'barbarism' committed by those who 'paid no attention to country, religion or flag' and aimed to 'provoke a clash of civilizations' (United Nations 1991: 28; UN Sixth Committee 2005b: 12), these constructions preclude any understanding of the Other, of the way in which the antagonistic construction was presented as an authoritative one, and how other views have been suppressed (Emcke 2005: 235). Resistance turns into a delicate matter when calling the fight against terrorism and drugs a war of the civilized against the uncivilized. How can other nations hesitate to join the fight, to declare themselves as allies, i.e. as civilized, human nations – since the other option would imply to be uncivilized, to be barbarians? This 'either/or' logic impedes not only any attempt to differentiate the picture of the antagonistic Other or to account efficiently for the web of non-antagonistic Others it is embedded in. It also limits the options of the Self, since the latter is forced to enact measures corresponding to the 'war on terror' and the 'war on drugs' it might initially not have wished to subscribe to.

As we have seen, these representations allow a number of extraordinary measures (counting as the second main effect of the language of war), which qualify as emergency measures, since they are beyond the normal political routines and do not necessarily take human right aspects into account or suspend civil rights. For instance, the refusal of harm reduction programs involving controlled consumption of illicit drugs fits into the rationale of the hegemonic vision of a drug-free world. Public contestation and resistance are increasingly difficult under the international hegemonic regime on drugs, since any objection against the rescue of civilization and humanity in the face of an existential threat can be discarded as subversive, irrational and alien. Indeed, for those carrying out the respective measures, the hegemonic order on drugs represents a solid justification for their actions. Hence, the language of war and the radicalization it entails are stabilizing factors for the identities created by hegemonic orders because they sharpen the edges of these identities and ensure coherence among the group-members. As we have seen, coherence is predominantly guaranteed by constructing a homogeneous antagonistic Other *and* by building on a vision (of a drug-free world) and a political consensus (drugs have to be fought) shared by the subjects identifying with the collective Self. Moral distinctions between 'good' and 'evil' help to stabilize the home front.

However, and most interestingly, while this language is able to stabilize a hegemonic order as in the drugs case, it is not sufficient to establish agreement on the nature and quality of the antagonistic Other, let alone of the Self in the discourse on terrorism. Despite the recurrent tendency in the international realm to use the label 'terrorism' as an instant legitimization for one's counter-violence against one's own enemies, the discourse on international terrorism has demonstrated that the Self remains equally diffuse and a hegemonic order cannot emerge as long as there is no clear understanding of what the terrorist Other is about.

Moreover, the language of war hampers the search for non-violent solutions more than it facilitates it. While alarmingly poor in its variety, the language conceals and obfuscates alternative ways to handle terrorism and drug abuse. What measures other than extraordinary means are appropriate in light of existential threats? In a state of war, one can hardly think about different measures other than the annihilation of the enemy, since the matter is life and death. Thus, the language of war makes it enormously difficult to step behind this stage of exception, to de-securitize an issue by shifting it out of the emergency mode and into the normal bargaining processes of the political sphere (Buzan, Wæver and de Wilde 1998: 4). For instance, to deal with terrorism and drugs not in terms of a war would be a considerable step towards bringing both phenomena back into the realm of the normal political routine. Therein obviously resides the danger of the recourse to such language, since it leaves no doors ajar for a different encounter. The language is indiscriminate: whether beneficiary or objector to the language of war and the effects it entails, the huge difficulties of returning to a state of peace, of non-war count for both. Or to paraphrase Pierre Verginaud: as the revolution, the 'war on drugs' and the 'war on terror' are also able to successively devour all their children.

Hegemonic regimes and their consequences for Self and Other

Having reconstructed a hegemonic order in the discourse on drugs, the collective Self was forged by promising to seal the lack of the world, to achieve a 'full-fledged' identity of a world without drugs. While this might appear as illusion, pious hope or nightmare, the promise yields consequences for those subjects identifying with and sharing this vision and the political consensus it encompasses. They are no longer free in their respective decision on what to consider their goals, they are universalized, restricted in their political subjectivity and even if particularities have been raised they have not damaged the hegemonic regime. The latter represents a regime of truths, it is a normative power of inclusion and exclusion, it constructs a universe of morals and values, constituted as capable of devising a universe of 'evil' versus the universe of 'goodness'. To object that a single subject is not forced to comply with such a regime – just don't sign or abide by the UN drug treaties! – is to miss the point. We have already seen the difficulties in stepping out of the universal, totalized parameters established by the hegemonic regime and advocating a different meaning of drugs and the accordant appropriate measures. Hence, an international hegemonic order is a straitjacket or a fundament, a prison or a home – its acts of inclusion deploy as much power as its acts of exclusion silence alternative meanings of drugs, drug addicts and drug dealers.

While the hegemonic regime in the field of drugs exerted power by acts of exclusion *and* inclusion, the subjects in the discourse on terrorism (within which the construction of a hegemonic order has failed) experience power by exclusion only. No one wants to be called a terrorist. Despite denouncing others as terrorists, the danger to be associated with the antagonistic Other is always present, as the identification of the various counter-hegemonic strategies aiming at a weakening of the antagonistic frontier in its current place has demonstrated.[2] To avoid any association with terrorism forces subjects to re-inscribe permanently the evil terrorism, its immorality, its cruelty etc. and through this constant re-writing, it turns into an indefinite danger to civilization, a never-ending threat. Again, it is outside the parameters of the discourse – no, not to consider terrorists as freedom fighters (and vice versa) – but to not condemn terrorism regardless of what one understands thereby. And it is perfectly within the parameter of the discourse to designate others as terrorist when it is about justifying one's violent, and potentially illegitimate actions. To legitimize violence by pointing to others as terrorists is like an old pair of shoes, too comfortable to refrain from slipping into. That is the perfidy of the terrorism discourse: even without a totalized promise of a fully achieved identity in a 'place without terrorism', antagonistic othering achieves a foundational status – not by absenting the Other – but by eliminating its consideration in the civilized world altogether.

Yet, what does this imply for the identities created by hegemonic orders if the antagonistic Other is successively and successfully pushed into the realm of barbarism? And what does it mean for the stability of the collective Self? 'It is the fear of the barbarians that threatens to turn us into barbarians. And the disaster we create will be greater than the cause of our fear' (Todorov 2008: 18). It turns out to be a mimetic relation: the threat for the Self not only resides in the danger represented by the antagonistic Other, it also resides in itself. As the analysis of both discourses has shown, it is the moral hazard of becoming like terrorist and drug abusers when fighting them, for example, by ignoring requirements of human and civil rights when defining individuals and organizations as terrorist without agreeing on common, transparent criteria or allowing for large crop eradication programs without taking the needs of drug cultivators fully into account. While being outside all law, i.e. not following the rules of civilization circumscribes exactly the verdict on the 'barbarians' (drug traffickers and terrorists alike), this verdict comes back like a boomerang. The consequences of such actions are very different from routine law-enforcement operations and, in particular, with regard to the 'war on terror', they seem to occur in an empty space within the domain of the law (Žižek 2006). Especially since holding the moral high ground also provides for potential escapes of the demands of law, regardless whether international or domestic. Once our enemy is 'evil plain and simple, we seem to have an argument for no longer obeying laws' (Bittner 2005: 210).

Thus, the hegemonic order in the drugs discourse and the language of war in both cases create the illusion that only breaking the rules of civilization will lead to the 'final' destruction of drugs and terrorism – and not following these rules. And in turn, this logic encourages terrorism and drug abuse and increases the risk for the vulnerable populations the 'war on terror and drugs' intended to protect in the first place.[3] One cannot help feel one is stating the obvious, since it seems all too myopic to wage a 'war on terror and drugs' without at least reflecting *beforehand* on the 'collateral damage' for the societies both wars are fought against. This not to argue that the effects for the subjects of the collective Self could have been foreseen; however, the histories of terrorism and drugs provide at least one lesson each which merits to be taken into account. On the one hand, the shift in meaning of the notion of terrorism from acts perpetrated by the state against society to actions carried out by actors from within society against the state should alert states of the dangers inherent in using the term terrorism. On the other hand, it was only 150 years ago that today's illicit drugs were consumed by the inner circles of society and while substances like tobacco or alcohol have always been excluded from the list of drugs, it is well-known that in particular the latter is very much 'implicated in issues of addiction, violence and loss of self-reliance offered as the paradigmatic reasons for a *war* on drugs' (Connolly 1997: §18, original emphasis).

What does all this imply for the stability of the identities forged by a hegemonic regime? With regard to the discourse on terrorism, we can retain that a 'war on terror' and the unilateralism on the part of different nations it entails weakens international institutions and tests the relationships between long-standing allies. This weakening will, in turn, only deteriorate the ability of the international community to discourage terrorism in the future and to agree on a consensus on the *how to* of the fight against terrorism.

Conversely, the central danger to the stability of the international hegemonic regime in the field of drugs resides in the violent suppression of heterogeneity, of the differential remainder. The analysis has shown how dissenting voices are demonized and unity has been imposed. Whether calls to decriminalize cannabis or to allow for a more humane conceptualization of the drug addict, the practices of the drug regime have led to the de-legitimization of these alternative understandings, or at least placed them in a difficult position. Of course, from the point of view of the persistence of the regime obedience, conformity and compliance are as necessary as the bifurcation of international life, since hegemonic regimes are born out of a clear-cut, homogeneous construction of an Other as much as of an unambiguously shared vision and political consensus on which the collective Self is based. However, as has been outlined, the stability of the drugs regime is on the decline, in particular with regard to the demand side. Due to the recent differentiations of the antagonistic drugs Other – movements which bespeak of counter-hegemonic strategies aiming at the particularization of subjects tied by a chain of equivalence[4] – the edges of the Other are constantly blurring. Not without leaving traces on the Self: for instance, when states justify controlled consumption of heroine as being in line with the regime or when British and German governments consider drug injection rooms as a viable instrument to counter drug addiction.

Suppressing dissent over a longer period of time for the greater good of a drug-free and terrorism-free world inevitability leads to delegitimizing alternative voices and practices and, most importantly, narrows the discursive space for political debate. In particular, for democratic states this suppression proves to be deteriorating for loyal, agonistic opposition to hegemonic meanings and truths (Jackson 2005: 184). To call for the decriminalization and de-penalization of cannabis, as various citizens groups do (among them an increasing number of people using cannabis as a pain therapy) tends to turn into a subversive endeavour when former minister of the interior and current president of France, Nicolas Sarkozy, proposed one should establish 'on the spot fines of up to £1,000 and compulsory therapy for cannabis users' (Druglink 2004: 3). Also, how can it be considered compatible with democratic values that individuals who evidentially have been innocent have to prove their innocence in the first place to be de-listed from the UN list of terrorist suspects, as the cases quoted in the report of Dick Marty, rapporteur in charge of the Council of Europe, have demonstrated (Marty 2007)?

Eroding the possibilities for an accepted opposition to the current direction of anti-terrorism and anti-drug policies also precludes acknowledging that these policies have not proven effective. Various counter-terrorist campaigns in European countries since the 1970s have shown the impossibility of eliminating terrorism by violence alone; for instance, the German Red Army Faction dissolved in the early 1990s and not as an effect of the German anti-terrorist policies (Richardson 2006; Süddeutsche Zeitung 2008). Since the *Single Convention on Narcotic Drugs* was adopted in 1961, the corresponding anti-drug legislations of the Member States have neither led to a decrease of drug addiction and drug deaths nor to a destruction of the different drug cartels and mafias, let alone removed drugs from the planet altogether – on the contrary, since the advent of synthetic drugs, innovation in this field has been proliferating.[5]

Of course, guided by the vision of a drug- and terrorism-free world seems to be too hard a goal to achieve, but in particular with regard to terrorism 'it only eases when political compromise takes place on the issues that instigated it' (Jackson 2005: 184). While claiming that a legalization of drugs like marijuana is a better means to counter drug abuse and trafficking (as prominent figures like Milton Friedman have advocated)[6], the truth residing in this alternative suggestion targets one of the arteries of the drug problem, since the latter is also about the enormous sums of money gained by the trade and abuse. Ultimately, the room for sincere opposition is undermined.

On the possibility of different hegemonic orders

It is clear that the conceptualization of hegemony so far as a practice of imposing a decision on a non-decidable, uneven discursive terrain 'is neutral with respect to the *type* of hegemony instituted' (Norval 2000: 231). However, by reconstructing the identities of Self and Other, by affirming the relational and constructed character of Both, the analysis also highlighted the ethical quality of political life. The located productive and counter-hegemonic strategies have shown how much their movements tried to protect or disturb the establishment of a hegemonic order by defining and denying as 'independent sites of evil [. . .] those differences that pose the greatest threat to the integrity and certainty' of the respective order (Connolly 1991: ix).

Moreover, defining these sites of evil in the discourses on terrorism and drugs produces a number of consequences: first, the 'war on terror and drugs' always implies that the wars could be won, that 'the land of idle happiness' can be reached only, if the enemy is annihilated. Second, this illusion falsely promises the Self that a victory in these wars preserves its moral integrity and prevents it from becoming like the antagonistic Other. With their zero-sum logic – conversion or annihilation for enemies, commitment or association with the enemy for cooperation partners – the discourses normalize the dynamics of inclusion and exclusion; yet, most importantly, it is not the Self who has to change in order to make peace happen: 'it is the Other who must comply or die' (Agathangelou and Ling 2005: 853).

Finally, such wars do not refer to peace as their ultimate goal, even if it might seem they do. The analysis has shown how much they are about the ultimate victory over terrorism and drugs: the vision that guides is the drug-free world, the world free from terrorism while peace is banned to the second balcony. Moreover, hegemonic regimes mask and deny the responsibility of a Self towards its Other(s). Regimes allow subjects to hide behind the truths and values established by them and seem to liberate them from taking responsibility for their actions (Nuzzo 2004: 339). Yet, if a Self's identity is dependent on its antagonistic and non-antagonistic Other(s), since in the midst of a collective identity subjects construct a 'we' as the foundation of the constitution of the Other, then it is this 'we' that has crucial political consequences for the Other. It is this moment of responsibility a Self needs to assume in its confrontation with the Other, be it a terrorist or a poor individual, a drug dealer, cultivator or an addict. To assume its responsibility and entanglement of its own actions with the Other means to acknowledge being a consuming or producing country of drugs and the kinds of responsibilities it implies for the Other, be it a drug dealer or a drug addict. It equally involves recognizing that disposing of a colonial past or considering oneself as an Islamic state makes one responsible for countering terrorist violence as an effect of one's identity.

While being susceptible for the ethical quality of political life and the tensions this awareness produces for a hegemonic approach to international politics, it is important to note that the 'irreducible antagonistic element present in social relations' (Mouffe 1993b: 140) is not denied. Instead, following Chantal Mouffe who – inspired by Carl Schmitt – makes us 'aware of the dimension of the political that is linked to the existence of an element of hostility among human beings' (Mouffe 1993a: 2), disagreement and conflict form the core of the political, since they arise and are reflective of a deeper ontological condition. Indeed, fundamental antagonism cannot always be avoided and it is difficult to think about political orders without limits.

Yet, being constitutive in no way implies that disagreement, dissent and conflict are simply given; in contrast, they are subject to negotiation (Norval 2004: 154). In light of this, one needs to address whether different types of hegemonies are conceivable in order to distinguish, for instance, democratic and authoritarian hegemonic practices. However, reflections on different types of hegemonic orders are still in their infancy and mostly addressed in the context of democratic politics, as the ontological condition referred to is 'of crucial importance in the formation of democratic regimes' (Norval 2000: 153). Of course, arguing that 'the specific political distinction to which political actions and motives can be reduced are that between friend and enemy' considers the enemy as someone who must not only be defeated but also destroyed (Schmitt 1976: 26, 36) is highly problematic for democratic politics. It is imperative to allow for a nuancing of the picture of the antagonistic Other by making a case for antagonists that need not necessarily be enemies in the Schmittian sense of the term, since considering conflicts as constitutive but also as subject to negotiation alters the parameters of disagreement. For example, as Mouffe has proposed, *agonism* could be conceived as a democratic alternative to antagonism: conceptualizing the Other as adversary perceives the relationship between Self and Other as struggles between adversaries and not as a conflict between enemies (Mouffe 1993a; 1993b). Accordingly, the aim of agonism is

> to construct the 'them' in such a way that is no longer perceived as an enemy to be destroyed, but an 'adversary', i.e. somebody whose ideas we combat but whose right to defend those ideas we do not put into question.
>
> (Mouffe 2000: 15)

Having said this, we venture into unknown terrain, as further theorization and empirical investigation of the movement from enemy to adversary and of the transformation of antagonism into agonism is needed (Norval 2000: 231). The same counts for the question of whether these reflections on politics within democratic societies could be transferred to the international level. Although Mouffe argues that, in principle, agonism is possible at the global level, it would require a multipolar world which allows for the articulation of legitimate alternatives – however, in the current world these alternatives are barely visible (Mouffe 2005).

While not feeling in the position to point out practical ways for such an approach, wouldn't it be a start to more openly consider the alternative voices in the discourses on drugs and terrorism as potentially legitimate? And, most importantly, to find out more comprehensively how the Other seeks to define the Self and to acknowledge that 'as humans in society [. . .] we are all Others somewhere to someone' (George 1995: 210)? Would it not be possible to establish a type of international hegemonic regime that does not fall for the seductive sirens of the language of war, clears away the old patterns of denigration, vengeance and violence and ceasès to play the ever same games of calling someone a terrorist to legitimize one's actions or to consider drug abuse as immoral? This would ultimately allow rethinking carefully how one entered into this pattern of accusations.

This would also permit a Self to acknowledge that it cannot achieve a 'full-fledged' identity in a 'land of idle happiness' by eliminating terrorism and drugs altogether. This is an illusion. An identity will always be marked by a lack, by its constitutive split and 'land' cannot be achieved by thinking only in enemy images. Such 'a critical ontology of ourselves' (Jabri 1998: 605) would not construct the Self as the same reference point, as the single and universal standard against which all others have to be judged. This would of course imply to 'put ourselves on the line more often' (Connolly 1997: §38), stop hiding behind the hegemonic vision of a drug- and terrorism-free world and renounce holding universal moral high grounds. Such enterprise is even more necessary, if – as in the fields of international drug prohibition and terrorism – the hegemonic constructions of Self and Other ultimately decide upon peace and war.

Appendix – Overview of codes belonging to productive hegemonic and counter-hegemonic strategies

A. Productive hegemonic strategies

Basic dimension and its strategies

Universalization

STRATEGY CODES:

International cooperation only means to fight drugs/terrorism
Interest of mankind above all other interest
Praise other countries
Call for cooperation
Consensus needed/Majority, consensus needed to fight
Convention is interest of mankind
Collective responsibility

SELF CODES:

Description of Self of International Community
Not concerned but interested in control
Country engaged in the fight

OTHER CODES:

(Aware of) growing drug problem

SUBSTANTIAL CODES:

Fight via international cooperation/How to fight- via international
cooperation

Establishing an antagonistic frontier

STRATEGY CODES:

>   Fight is war on terror
>   Condemn terrorism
>   Terrorism has to be fought

OTHER CODES:

>   Drug dealers and their description
>   Addicts and their description
>   Drug traffic & its description
>   International dimension of drug traffic;
>   Drugs & their description (Drugs are dangerous)
>   Endanger individuals & society & world as a whole
>   Indiscriminate violence
>   No cause can justify

Representation

STRATEGY CODES:

>   Convention is interest of mankind (drugs only)

SELF CODES:

>   International Community as nodal point (drugs only)

CONCEPTUAL CODES:

>   Lack of International Community/world

Supplementary dimension and its strategies

Extending the antagonizing chain of equivalence

STRATEGY CODES:

>   Praise efforts already made
>   Refer to experts
>   Power to experts

SELF CODES:

Résistance is not terrorism!

Referring to a subject's agreement with the general equivalent

STRATEGY CODES:

Call for cooperation
Consensus needed/Majority, consensus needed to fight
Praise other countries
Reject doubts of engagement
Interest of mankind above all other interest
Convention is interest of mankind
Praise own efforts

STRATEGY CODES:

Willingness to cooperate

CONCEPTUAL CODES:

Disposition to cooperate
Link to identity with reference to & pro general equivalent

SUBSTANTIAL CODES:

Fight drug traffic
Fight via international cooperation
Engagement/support of every country needed

Simultaneously emphasizing and downgrading the particularity of a subject of chain A

STRATEGY CODES:

Strengthen argument via reference to own experience

SELF CODES:

Own country at the forefront
Picture of country's society (drugs only)

SUBSTANTIAL CODES:

Exemption indigenous medicine
Fight drug problem via rule of law

Crossing the antagonistic frontier in order to strengthen chain A

STRATEGY CODES:

Accuse other countries of being source of drugs
Double standard of UN
Accuse of complicity with terrorists

OTHER CODES:

Link between addicts and dealers

Enlarging the antagonized chain of equivalence

OTHER CODES:

Financial aspect of drug traffic
New danger synthetic drugs
Changing character of drugs

SUBSTANTIAL CODES:

Fight money laundering

OTHER CODES:

Link between criminals and addicts
Link drug traffic and criminal activities
Link between migrants and addicts
Link migration and terrorism

B. Counter-hegemonic strategies

Basic dimension and its strategies

Particularization

STRATEGY CODES:

Western countries responsible for terrorism
Difference between developed and underdeveloped world

Geographical representation necessary
Doubt engagement
Accuse of hypocrisy

SELF CODES:

International community has more pressing problems
Being not concerned (and not interested) in control
Description of Self of particular country
Picture of particular society

Breaking off the chain of equivalence

No codes/segments assigned

Weakening of the antagonistic frontier

OTHER CODES:

Addicts and their description

CONCEPTUAL CODES:

Responsibility towards the Other
Responsibility of producing countries

Supplementary dimension and its strategies

Autonomization of subject of chain A

STRATEGY CODES:

Do not hamper countries to go further
Special role of/for particular country

Stressing the particularity of a subject of chain A explicitly at the expense of the general equivalent

SELF CODES:

Protect national identity

CONCEPTUAL CODES:

Link to identity with reference to & contra general equivalent

SUBSTANTIAL CODES:

> Sovereignty of members
> Respect national principles

Crossing the antagonistic frontier in order to weaken it
a) Protect particularity of a subject by articulating its particularity as part
of chain Z

STRATEGY CODES:

> Accuse other countries of being terrorist

OTHER CODES:

> Résistance is not terrorism

SUBSTANTIAL CODES:

> Exclude national liberation movements
> Respect right of self determination
> State terrorism (States should not support terrorists)

b) Underscore particularity of a subject/element of chain Z

OTHER CODES:

> What are NOT drugs
> Paradoxical/changing nature of drugs

SUBSTANTIAL CODES:

> Take underlying causes into account
> (Describe) underlying causes of drug problem/terrorism

Attempts to disarticulate floating elements of chain Z

OTHER CODES:

> No link between Migration and Terrorism/drugs
> No link between Terrorism and specific cultures, religions (link between Islam,
>   Arabs and terrorism)

Notes

Introduction

1 Throughout the text, International Relations are capitalized when referring to the disciplinary domain. When referring to social practice and events that make up the world stage of international relations, it will be written in minuscule.

2 Although with some reservations, I share the position of Ole Wæver (1998b) who claims that the application of labels to schools of thoughts and theoretical approaches structure the conduct of disciplinary debates and that it is therefore useful to attach a specific label to one's own study. Still, in the present context, 'poststructuralism' is understood 'as a broad church, as a label covering a variety of intellectual trends, ranging from Foucault's analysis of discursive formations, to Lacanian psychoanalysis, Derrida's deconstruction and Barthe's semiology' (Laclau 2000: x).

3 For an explanation of what is meant by conventional constructivism, see chapter one.

4 For an exception see Bewley-Taylor 2003; Jelsma 2003.

1 On hegemony and identity in international security discourses

1 'A table is a table'. All translations from German are my own.

2 In IR terms this implies that a discourse encompasses ideational factors (ideas, norms, identity or culture) as well as material factors. If I refer in the following to 'reality' without quotation marks, reality is comprehended as a construct that can only be understood through language.

3 For recent writings on hegemony see Chomsky 2003; Agnew 2005; Friedman and Chase-Dunn 2005; David and Grondin 2006.

4 Of course, thinking on hegemony in IR cannot be reduced to the Neo-Gramscians. For instance, other critical theorists like Andrew Linklater departing equally from a Marxist tradition have reflected upon the social construction of order via the constitution of order via the constitution of political communities through processes of exclusion and inclusion and researched 'the significance of [. . .] differences between insiders and outsiders for the conduct of international relations' (Linklater 1990: 146). See also Linklater 1992; 1998.

5 The depiction of Cox' understanding of hegemony is based above all on the following works: Cox 1981; 1983; 1987; 1996. Scholars like Andreas Bieler, Stephen Gill, Adam D. Morton or Mark Rupert to name only a few have followed in Cox' vein. See Gill 1993; 2003; Rupert 1995; Bieler and Morton 2001.

6 This is what Gramsci calls a 'war of position' while the 'war of movement' (understood as a frontal attack) denotes the successful strategy in Russia. See Ives 2004: 107.

7 This distinction is crucial as it is not restricted to political discourses but is an essential feature of language in general. Consider for instance syntagmatic and paradigmatic relations (linguistics) or metonymy and metaphor (rhetoric). See Laclau 2005: 221.

8 As representatives for 'conventional' constructivism, one may consider, among others, Wendt 1994; 1999; Katzenstein 1996; Adler 1997; Marcussen *et al.* 1999.
9 Wendt has recently adopted a stronger relational understanding of identity, as he now links it with individual and collective recognition. '[I]t is through the recognition by the Other that one is constituted as a Self in the first place' (Wendt 2003: 511). However, it would be misleading to conceive of this move as one towards a relational understanding of identity because, for Wendt, actors enter the process of recognition with already fully established identities that are not constructed through this process.
10 In a similar vein Weller 1999: 254–5. Recently, constructivist approaches have been envisaged the '[n]ext step in Constructivist IR Theory', i.e. to endogenize social identities of actors and to 'break off' the agreement with rationalists in treating corporate identities as fixed and pre-social entities. However, this step consists above all in a different conceptualization of actors bearing identities: by applying a sociational perspective, scholars attempt to account for 'processes involving the appearance and disappearance of political actors' and 'the emergence and survival of democratic security communities' (Cederman and Daase 2003: 6).
11 In referring to the thinking of the Christian philosopher Augustine, Connolly identifies this drive of identity towards the antagonistic Other in the two problems of evil. First, since human beings suffer from life and the inescapable death, they search for 'sites at which responsibility can be located'. Second, this search finds its suitable object in the Other by denouncing it as that 'that exposes sore spots in one's identity as evil or irrational'. In consequence, Hansen rightly states that while leaving the Christian context 'the need for locating the responsibility in the other has been institutionalized at the individual as the collective or state level'. See Connolly 1991: 8; Hansen 2006: 39.
12 The same argument is made by Bahar Rumelili (2004: 36) who concludes that poststructuralists 'still struggle to understand how the relationship between a self and its constitutive other is in some cases characterised by discourses of fear and identity threat and in other cases by less negative representations'.
13 Like Connolly, Campbell speaks of a *temptation* and not of a necessity.
14 For noteworthy exceptions see Klein 1988; Doty 1996; Neumann 1996; 1999; Shapiro 2004; Inayatullah and Blaney 2004; Hansen 2006. For a classic example in this respect consider Said 2003.

2 Opening the 'black box': the construction of international hegemonies

1 I borrow the conceptual idea of splitting the logics of equivalence and difference in various strategies of hegemonic operations and distinguishing between *basic* and *supplementary dimensions* from Nonhoff 2006.
2 However, as hegemonic articulations articulate subjects from one single place in the discourse and consider them as equivalential with respect to a common reference point, *chain Z* is equally constructed from one specific point in the discourse – the one of the antagonizing *chain A*. This implies that the articulation of antagonistic frontiers is dependent on a subject articulated in this discourse as the frontiers are not objective phenomena that can be described in always the same manner (Diaz-Bone 2002: 222).
3 Adapted from Thomassen 2005: 5.
4 In the original example of Laclau, different letters have been used, since the example of a repressive Tsarist regime oppressing the demands of workers for higher wages was taken. Therefore, the particular signifiers A1 to A4 of *chain A* were originally designated with the letter *D* to signify the *d*emands of the oppressed workers. In contrast, the antagonistic force has been signified with the letter *T* like *T*sarism as the oppressor and enemy of the workers (Laclau 2000a: 303). In the present context, a change of letters was necessary to avoid potential confusion of *T* with terrorism and *D* with drugs.

5   The relationship has surfaced under various guises; for instance, under the heading 'explaining vs. understanding' or 'causality vs. constitution' etc. See for example Wendt 1987; Dessler 1989; Carlsnaes 1992; Wight 1999.
6   According to Laclau (2005: 222), the possibility to derive further strategies from the two logics always exists.
7   Please see the appendix for the various hegemonic strategies.
8   The debates leading to the adoption of the three conventions and to the amendment of the *Single Convention* in 1972 are available as 'Official Records' including plenary meetings or general debates and summary records of diverse technical committees. See United Nations 1964a, 1973a, b, c, d, 1991.
9   Nominal end of the debates in the 1970s was the decision of the Ad Hoc Committee on Terrorism to refuse a renewal of its mandate in 1979.
10 One may object to this decision with reference to the debates at the Council of Europe, which met in the *European Convention on the Suppression of Terrorism* (1977). However, these discussions never tried to define terrorism but intended to de-politicize the issue.
11 One may object this decision by pointing to the Counter-Terrorism Committee of the UN Security Council, founded shortly after 11 September 2001 (UN Security Council 2001). Despite the Counter-Terrorism Committee not dealing with the comprehensive convention, its debates are represented and reflected upon in the above-mentioned committees selected for analysis.
12 Besides, the analysis of elite discourse is not '*per se* less important than an extensive reflection on Pop-Art' (Diez 1999: 87, original emphasis).
13 The analysis of the international measures institutionalizing hegemonic practices relies to a great extent on the material gathered in the framework of a research project on the internationalization of the state monopoly of force within the Bremen *Collaborative Research Centre 597 'Transformations of the State'*. The project investigated the evolution of international police cooperation since the 1960s in the fields of international terrorism and drug trafficking. See for the project proposal http://www.sfb597.uni-bremen.de/pages/forProjektBeschreibung.php?SPRACHE=en&ID=17 (accessed 26 April 2010).
14 The documents in the drugs discourse are evenly distributed over the entire period (1961–1988) with 252 UN documents. In the discourse on terrorism, two-thirds of the documents stem from the recent period (1997–2010) with 197 UN documents. Of 486 documents, 37 referred to international measures..
15 While being developed in the context of the grounded theory approach, the requirement of recursivity of the latter remains crucial to the present context: by constant reference to the data, one's findings are refined, corrected and validated. For the approach, see among others Strauss and Corbin 1996.
16 Please see the appendix for the codes assigned to each hegemonic strategy.

3   International drug prohibition: constructing the 'drug-free world'

1   For further information on the 'opium wars' and their role in the establishment of drug prohibition see Bruun *et al.* 1975 and Boekhaut van Solinge 2002: 33–8.
2   For an overview of the international legal framework of the UN (including EU and the Council of Europe) see De Ruyver *et al.* 2002.
3   Only the 1936 Illicit Trafficking Convention remained into force because delegations have been unable to agree which of its provisions to incorporate into the *Single Convention*. See McAllister 2000: 208.
4   See http://www.unodc.org/unodc/en/treaties/index.html (accessed 12 April 2010).
5   The distinction between addict in general and sufferers or patients receives unanimous support. The latter are people who suffer from an (incurable) disease and 'who really need' narcotics to bear their pain but were not previously consumers, thus, who are not addicted to drugs. See United Nations 1964a: 2.

6   This movement allows reconstructing sub-strategy *Underscore particularity of a subject of chain Z* of supplementary counter-hegemonic strategy *Crossing the antagonistic frontier in order to weaken it.*

7   Formulations linked to the goal of a universally acceptable convention are: comprehensive multilateral convention, new convention, new instrument, strong convention, universally acceptable convention.

8   This finding is sustained by a recurrent use of the pronouns 'we', 'us' or 'our' in conjunction with the international drug control.

9   Formulations connected with the international drug control are: illicit traffic, control, drug abuse, fight and combat.

10   Point de capiton means 'quilting point' literally. See Lacan 1973: 805.

11   Formulations connected with the potential points are: international community – mankind, world, community, globe, humanity, societies, society, United Nations and public; international drug control – illicit traffic, control, drug abuse, fight and combat; drugs – drug, evil, plague, menace, scourge, narcotics, illicit substances, enemy, threat, abuse, traffickers and traffic. The terms themselves were the result of the coding process and the frequency of their codes signalled their relevance.

12   This is supported by the already invoked number of co-occurrences of the international community with the control (957 hits).

13   See http://www.incb.org/incb/en/mandate.html (accessed 12 April 2010).

14   See Klein 2000; Daily Mirror 2002; Financial Times 2002; The Observer 2002; United Kingdom Home Office 2002b; Foreign and Commonwealth Office 2004; Scotland on Sunday 2004; The Daily Telegraph 2004.

15   Keep in mind the *French Connection*, when the United States pressured the French police to cooperate with US police forces cracking down on cross-border drug traffic (Cusack 1974: 242–4). This cooperation led to a Franco-US Protocol in 1971 (Ministère de l'Intérieur 1971) and a German-US Protocol in 1978 (Rebscher 1981: 168).

16   For an overview on the European increase of drug death rates from the mid 1980s and on, see http://stats05.emcdda.europa.eu/en/elements/drdfig08-en.html (accessed 12 April 2010).

17   See Article 3(4) of the 1988 UN Convention available at http://www.unodc.org/pdf/convention_1988_en.pdf (accessed 12 April 2010).

18   European Monitoring Centre for Drugs and Drug Addiction, http://www.emcdda.europa.eu/stats07/DRD (accessed 12 April 2010). Still, the difficulties with such numbers are manifold. Most importantly, definitions of crime are socially constructed. Hence, they are subject to changes and can be easily criticized. Moreover, once a social phenomenon has been defined as a crime and moved into the focus of the prosecuting agencies, official numbers might rise: if more effort is put into crime detection, more crimes will be detected.

19   Since only one sub-strategy of counter-hegemonic strategy *Crossing the antagonistic frontier in order to weaken it* has been located, this explains the result of three and a half strategies.

20   The necessity to revitalize from time to time the consensus on drugs can also be reconstructed from the quest for a consolidation of the regime with three consecutive agreements and (after the apparent 'completion' of the regime) the organization of further conferences (for instance, the 2000 UN *Convention against transnational organized crime*). Hence, without denying the 'existence' of events such as an increase in drug traffic and overall drug criminality, it is the interpretation that these events threaten the established consensus that matters.

4 Writing the 'war on terror': the struggle of hegemonic projects

1   The second convention set up an International Criminal Court with jurisdiction over terrorist crimes (Wilkinson 1997: 666–7). On the anti-terrorism conventions of the League of Nations see Dubin 1991.

2 See http://untreaty.un.org/English/Terrorism.asp (accessed 14 April 2010).

3 Of course, the literature on terrorism in general is huge; however, I concentrate on the few works dealing explicitly with the UN attempts to define terrorism.

4 See Connolly 1997; Booth and Dunne 2002; Silke 2004; Bigo 2005; Booth 2005; Jackson 2005; MacCoun and Reuter 2005; European Political Science 2007; Ranstorp 2007; Neal 2010.

5 The high frequencies of these requests show their relevance: 'exclude national liberation movements' (including the assertion that 'freedom fighters have legitimate motives') – 108 hits; 'take underlying causes into account' – 621 hits; 'state terrorism' – 184 hits in 197 documents.

6 The requests are supported by a recurrent reference that the legitimacy of the liberation struggles has been proclaimed by the United Nations.

7 It should be noted that the 'accusation of being terrorist' is considered as a counter-hegemonic strategy, whereas the 'accusation of being a source of drugs' has been subsumed under productive hegemonic strategies. The main difference lies in the rearticulation and strengthening of an *already established* antagonistic frontier (drugs) in contrast to the attempts to establish a frontier in the first place (terrorism).

8 These are the already-mentioned *Convention on Offences and Certain Other Acts Committed on Board Aircraft* (1963), *Convention for the Suppression of Unlawful Seizure of Aircraft* (1970) and *Convention for the Suppression of Unlawful Acts Against the Safety of Civil Aviation* (1971).

9 It is worth re-emphasizing a fundamental insight in order not to be misunderstood: referring to an event dislocating a discourse by no means implies that I am speaking of an extra-discursive reality. The materiality of the Munich attacks exists outside of the discourse but they cannot constitute themselves as objects outside of a discourse, i.e. to acquire meaning they must be part of a language-meaning framework.

10 The importance of these common goals is underlined by their high frequency: universally acceptable definition is necessary – 715 hits; need for a comprehensive convention on terrorism – 844 hits in 197 documents.

11 Formulations connected with the fight against international terrorism are 'fight', 'combat', 'war', 'struggle'.

12 For rare references in the second round see UN Sixth Committee 2000a: 4 and UN Sixth Committee 2005a: 14.

13 Formulations connected with the potential points are (next to the term itself): for international community – mankind, world, humanity, civilization, societies, society; for international terrorism – evil, plague, menace, scourge, enemy, adversary, threat, barbar* (barbarism, barbarous, barbarian, barbarians), heinous, violen* (violence, violent). The nodal points have been identified at the end of the coding process. The terms themselves have been a result of the coding process and the frequency of their codes signalled their relevance.

14 See http://www.unodc.org/unodc/en/terrorism/conventions.html (accessed 14 April 2010).

15 See http://www.unodc.org/unodc/en/terrorism/global-action-against-terrorism.html (accessed 14 April 2010).

16 See http://www.un.org/sc/ctc/action.html (accessed 14 April 2010).

17 See http://untreaty.un.org/English/Terrorism.asp (accessed 14 April 2010).

18 In the aftermath of 11 September 2001, the European Union established a similar list. The criteria for inclusion on a list were also very vague (Tappeiner 2005). It was left to the Member States to decide according to their national rules what names they would put forward for the list. The EU considered itself bound to carry out the SC resolution and said so in the Common Position. But the EU list includes not only the Sanctions UN-Committee list but also adds other persons whom the Member States have proposed from their national perspectives (Guild 2008: 182).

19 Or take the example introduced by Dick Marty, rapporteur in charge of the Council of Europe, who reported the case of Mr Y: 'Mr. Y. has lived for more than 30 years in a small Italian enclave in Switzerland. He is a successful businessman. At the end of 2001, his name is included on the "black list" of the UN Security Council because he is suspected of having funded the attacks of 11 September. This means that all his assets are frozen and that he is barred from leaving the country: he is thus forbidden from leaving the tiny enclave in which he and his family have been living for decades, without ever having been informed of this fact, without having been heard and without possibility of appeal. The prosecutor's office of the Swiss Confederation opens an investigation. After almost four years, the investigation must be closed because no elements exist to charge him, the Swiss state is obliged to pay his lawyer and that of one of his co-workers the equivalent of € 80,000. Despite the closed investigation, Mr. Y. remains on the "black list". He has begun civil proceedings against Switzerland to claim damages; but any award would be immediately frozen on the basis of the decision of the Security Council. The latter are clearly embarrassed, as they are not even sure about what would be the last instance competent to decide in order to enable Mr. Y. to finally apply to the European Court of Human Rights. All this is taking place in a climate of indifference: Mr. Y. is an Italian national, of Egyptian origin, and was professionally active in Switzerland, where his assets have been frozen for five years, without the least proof of guilt. Mr. Y. is a Muslim and has been a member of the Muslim Brothers for a very long time (which he has never kept a secret): is this a sufficient blemish to justify that this person, who is 75 years old and has serious health problems, sees the fruit of a working life destroyed and cannot visit his children and grandchildren? The story of Mr. Y. is only one among others' (Marty 2007: 1).
20 See UN Security Council Committee established pursuant to Resolution 1267 (1999) concerning Al-Qaida and the Taliban and associated individuals and entities (2008).
21 See http://www.un.org/News/Press/docs//2009/sc9825.doc.htm (accessed 15 April 2010).
22 In the US arena, the approach to focus on sanctioning and punishing individuals has reached a climax when shortly after the attacks of 11 September 2001, US government officials considered Usama bin Laden as prime suspect and offered a reward of 25 Million US-dollars for information leading to his capture or death. In July 2007, the US Senate nearly unanimously (only one dissenting vote) doubled this figure to 50 Million US-dollars. See Federal Bureau of Investigation 2003; BBC News 2007; Spiegel online 2007.
23 The Framework Decision on the European Arrest Warrant (Council of the European Union 2002c) and the Framework Decision on combating terrorism (Council of the European Union 2002b) were adopted in June 2002, a second pillar Common Position establishing lists of terrorist groups was agreed upon in June 2003 (Council of the European Union 2006).
24 The agreement of 6 December 2002 is available at http://www.europol.europa.eu/legal/agreements/Agreements/16268–2.pdf (accessed 16 April 2010); the supplementary agreement is available at http://www.europol.europa.eu/legal/agreements/Agreements/16268–1.pdf (accessed 16 April 2010). A further important agreement on information exchange between the US and the EU is the transfer of passenger data to the US (Council of the European Union 2007).
25 One may object to this conclusion by arguing that in the case of data transmission a Member State has to consent before Europol is allowed to transfer the information to the US authorities. Thierry Balzacq rightly considers the prior consent clause as 'little more than a smokescreen. On the one hand, Europol requires no consent when it transmits information acquired through channels other than Member States. On the other hand, the binding character of this "prior consent clause" could be questioned as it does not appear in any of the agreements, but rather in the letter of exchange, which accompanied the agreements' (Balzacq 2008: 91).

26 See the exchange of arguments at the British House of Lords European Union Committee available at http://www.publications.parliament.uk/pa/ld200203/ldselect/ldeucom/196/196121.htm (accessed 16 April 2010).

5 Comparing the 'war on drugs' and the 'war on terror'

1 The minor frequency of productive hegemonic strategies can be explained by their low occurrence in the discourse on terrorism.
2 One may object this differentiation by pointing out that especially synthetic drugs overthrow this distinction. Whether it is 'true' or 'false', the distinction is drawn in the discourse.
3 See on the reclassification of cannabis http://www.homeoffice.gov.uk/drugs/drugs-law/cannabis-reclassification/?view=Standard (accessed 26 April 2010).
4 Their interrelation is nicely illustrated by Jerome Kirk and Mark L. Miller's example of using a thermometer: 'A thermometer that shows the same reading of 82 degrees each time it is plunged into boiling water gives a reliable measurement. A second thermometer might give a series of measurement that vary from around 100 degrees. The second thermometer would be unreliable but relatively valid, whereas the first would be invalid but perfectly reliable'. Quoted in Silverman 2001: 225.

Conclusion: Rethinking hegemonic orders

1 The supplementary productive hegemonic strategies *Extending the antagonizing chain of equivalence* and *Enlarging the antagonized chain of equivalence* have been identified during the analysis.
2 Most essentially, these associations have been circumscribed by the two variants of the supplementary counter-hegemonic strategy *Crossing the antagonistic frontier in order to weaken it*.
3 Moreover, the 'war on terror and drugs' has given both, terrorists and drug abuser, the 'recognition and attention they so desperately sought' (Jackson 2005: 185).
4 In this respect, the analysis has identified basis counter-hegemonic strategy *Particularization* and supplementary productive hegemonic strategy *Autonomization of subjects of chain A*.
5 On a latest 'drug trend' – synthetic cannabis – see Jack 2009.
6 See among others Friedman 1991; Hardy 2005.

Bibliography

Adler, E. (1997) 'Seizing the Middle Ground: Constructivism in World Politics', *European Journal of International Relations*, 3 (3): 319–63.

Agathangelou, A.M. and Ling, L.H.M. (2005) 'Power and Play through Poisies: Reconstructing Self and Other in the 9/11 Commission Report', *Millennium: Journal of International Studies*, 33 (3): 827–53.

Agnew, J. (2005) *Hegemony: The New Shape of Global Power*, Philadelphia: Temple University Press.

—— (2007) 'Know-Where: Geographies of Knowledge of World Politics', *International Political Sociology*, 1 (2): 138–48.

Albrecht, H.-J. and van Kalmthout, A. (eds) (1989) *Drug policies in Western Europe*, Freiburg im Breisgau: Max Planck Institut für ausländisches und internationales Strafrecht.

Alegre, S., Bigo, D. and Jeandesboz, J. (2009) *External Dimension of the Area of Freedom, Security and Justice*, Study for the European Parliament, PE 410.688. Available online at: <http:\\www.europarl.europa.eu/activities/committees/studies/download.do?language=en&file=25031 (accessed 17 April 2009)>.

Angermüller, J. (2005) '"Qualitative" Methods of Social Research in France: Reconstructing the Actor, Deconstructing the Subject', *Forum: Qualitative Social Research/Forum Qualitative Sozialforschung*, 6 (3). Available online at: <http://www.qualitative-research.net/index.php/fqs/article/view/8 (accessed 31 July 2010)>.

Arar Commission (2006) *Commission of Inquiry into the Actions of Officials in Relation to Maher Arar*. Available online at: <http:\\epe.lac-bac.gc.ca/100/206/301/pco-bcp/commissions/maher_arar/07–09–13/www.ararcommission.ca/default.htm (accessed 17 April 2010)>.

Archick, K. and Gallis, P. (2003) *Europe and Counterterrorism*, New York: Nova Science Publishers.

Ashley, R. (1987) 'The Geopolitics of Geopolitical Space: Toward a Critical Social Theory of International Politics', *Alternatives*, 12 (4): 403–34.

Austin, J.L. (1976) *How to Do Things with Words. The William James Lectures Delivered at Harvard University in 1955*, 2 edn, Oxford: Oxford University Press.

Balzacq, T. (2008) 'The Policy Tools of Securitization: Information Exchange, EU Foreign and Interior Policies', *Journal of Common Market Studies*, 46 (1): 75–100.

BBC News (2007) 'Senate doubles Bin Laden reward. The US Senate has voted 87–1 to double the reward for the death or capture of al-Qaeda chief Osama bin Laden to $50m', *BBC News*. Available online at: <http://news.bbc.co.uk/go/pr/fr/-/2/hi/americas/6898075.stm (accessed 17 April 2010)>.

Berridge, V. and Edwards, G. (1981) *Opium and the People: Opiate Use in Nineteenth-Century England*, London, New York: Allen Lane/St. Martin's Press.

Bewley-Taylor, D.R. (1999) *The United States and International Drug Control, 1909–1997*, London, New York: Pinter.

—— (2003) 'Challenging the UN drug control conventions: problems and possibilities', *The International Journal of Drug Policy*, 14: 171–9.

Bichsel, P. (1969) *Kindergeschichten*, Zürich: Buchclub Ex Libris.

Bieler, A. and Morton, A.D. (2001) *Social Forces in the Making of the New Europe: The Restructuring of European Social Relations in the Global Political Economy*, New York: Palgrave.

Bigo, D. (2005) 'From Foreigners to "Abnormal Aliens". How the Faces of the Enemy Have Changed Following September the 11th', in E. Guild and J. van Selm (eds), *International Migration and Security. Opportunities and Challenges*, London, New York: Routledge, pp. 64–81.

Bittner, R. (2005) 'Morals in Terrorist Times', in G. Meggle (ed.), *Ethics of Terrorism and Counter-Terrorism*, Frankfurt: Ontos Verlag, pp. 207–13.

Boekhaut van Solinge, T. (2002) *Drugs and Decision Making in the European Union*, Amsterdam: CEDRO.

—— (2004) *Dealing with Drugs in Europe. An Investigation of European Drug Control Experiences: France, the Netherlands and Sweden*, The Hague: BJu Legal Publishers.

Booth, K. (ed.) (2005) *Critical Security Studies and World Politics*, Boulder: Lynne Rienner.

Booth, K. and Dunne, T. (2002) *Worlds in Collision. Terror and the Future of Global Order*, Basingstoke: Palgrave Macmillan.

Boulden, J. and Weiss, T.G. (2004) *Terrorism and the UN: Before and After September 11*, Bloomington: Indiana University Press.

Briesen, D. (2005) *Drogenkonsum und Drogenpolitik in Deutschland und den USA. Ein historischer Vergleich.*, Frankfurt, New York: Campus Verlag.

Bruun, K., Lynn, P. and Rexed, I. (1975) *The Gentlemen's Club: International Control of Drugs and Alcohol*, Chicago, London: The University of Chicago Press.

Bundesministerium für wirtschaftliche Zusammenarbeit und Entwicklung and Gesellschaft für Technische Zusammenarbeit (2004) *Entwicklungsorientierte Drogenkontrolle: Politik, Strategien, Erfahrungen und Intersektorale Lösungsansätze*, Bonn, Eschborn: Bundesministerium für wirtschaftliche Zusammenarbeit und Entwicklung.

Busch, H. (2001) *Polizeiliche Drogenbekämpfung, eine internationale Verstrickung*, Münster: Westfälisches Dampfboot.

Butler, J. (1993) *Bodies That Matter: On the Discursive Limits of 'Sex'*, London, New York: Routledge.

Buzan, B., Wæver, O. and de Wilde, J. (1998) *Security. A New Framework for Analysis*, Boulder: Lynne Rienner.

Campbell, D. (1993) *Politics without Principle: Sovereignty, Ethics, and the Narratives of the Gulf War*, Boulder: Lynne Rienner.

—— (1998a) *National Deconstruction. Violence, Identity, and Justice in Bosnia*, London, Minneapolis: University of Minnesota Press.

—— (1998b) *Writing Security. United States Foreign Policy and the Politics of Identity*, revised edn, Minneapolis: University of Minnesota Press.

Carlsnaes, W. (1992) 'The Agency-Structure Problem in Foreign Policy Analysis', *International Studies Quarterly*, 36 (3): 245–70.

Cederman, L.-E. and Daase, C. (2003) 'Endogenizing Corporate Identities: The Next Step in Constructivist IR Theory', *European Journal of International Relations*, 9 (1): 5–35.

Chalk, P. (1996) *West European Terrorism and Counter-Terrorism. The Evolving Dynamic*, London: Macmillan Press.

Charbonneau, B. and Cox, W.S. (2008) 'Global Order, US Hegemony and Military Integration: The Canadian-American Defense Relationship', *International Political Sociology*, 2 (4): 305–21.

Chilton, P.A. (1996) *Security Metaphors. Cold War Discourse From Containment to Common House*, New York: Peter Lang Publishing.

Chirac, J. (2003) *Discours lors de la cérémonie d'ouverture de la conférence internationale sur les routes de la drogue*, 22 May 2003. Available online at: <http://www.elysee.fr/elysee/elysee.fr/francais_archives/actualites/a_1_elysee/2007/mai/declaration_televisee_de_m_jacques_chirac.76615.html (accessed 26 April 2010)>.

Chomsky, N. (2003) *Hegemony or Survival: America's Quest for Global Dominance*, London: H. Hamilton.

Clark, I. (2009) 'Towards an English School Theory of Hegemony', *European Journal of International Relations*, 15 (2): 203–28.

Coffey, A. and Atkinson, P. (1996) *Making sense of qualitative data*, Thousand Oaks: Sage.

Connolly, W.E. (1991) *Identity/ Difference. Democratic Negotiations of Political Paradox*, Ithaca, London: Cornell University Press.

—— (1997) 'Drugs, the Nation and Free Lancing: Decoding the Moral Universe of William Bennett', *Theory and Event*, 1 (1). Available online at: <http://muse.jhu.edu/journals/theory_and_event/ (accessed 2 October 2010)>.

Council of Europe (1990) 'Convention on Laundering, Search, Seizure and Confiscation of the Proceeds from Crime', *European Treaty Series*, No. 141, 8 November 1990.

Council of the European Union (2002a) *2423rd Council meeting – Justice, Home Affairs and Civil Protection – 25–26 April 2002*, Luxembourg. Available online at: <http://www.rklambda.at/dokumente/euplan/Rat-E-020425.pdf (accessed 17 April 2010)>.

—— (2002b) 'Council Framework Decision of 13 June 2002 on Combating Terrorism (2002/475/JHA)', *Official Journal*, L 164: 3–7.

—— (2002c) 'Council Framework Decision of 13 June 2002 on the European Arrest Warrant and the Surrender Procedures Between Member States (2002/584/JHA)', *Official Journal*, L 190: 1–18.

—— (2003a) 'Agreement on extradition between the European Union and the United States of America', *Official Journal of the European Union*, L 181: 27–33.

—— (2003b) 'Agreement on mutual legal assistance between the European Union and the United States of America', *Official Journal of the European Union*, L 181: 34–42.

—— (2006) 'Council Common Position 2006/231/CFSP of 20 March 2006 updating Common Position 2001/931/CFSP on the application of specific measures to combat terrorism and repealing Common Position 2005/936/CFSP', *Official Journal of the European Union*, L 82: 20.

—— (2007) 'On the Conclusion of an Agreement between the European Community and the United States of America on the Processing and Transfer of PNR Data by Air Carriers to the United States Department of Homeland Security (DHS) (2007 PNR Agreement) (2007/551/CFSP/JHA)', *Official Journal of the European Union*, L 204: 16–7.

Cox, R.W. (1981) 'Social Forces, States and World Orders: Beyond International Relations Theory', *Millennium: Journal of International Studies*, 10 (2): 126–55.

—— (1983) 'Gramsci, Hegemony and International Relations: An Essay in Method', *Millennium: Journal of International Studies*, 12 (2): 162–75.

—— (1987) *Production, Power, and World Order*, New York: Columbia University Press.

—— (1996) *Approaches to world order*, Cambridge: Cambridge University Press.

Cox, R.W. and Schecter, M.G. (2002) *The Political Economy of a Plural World: Critical Reflections on Power, Morals, and Civilisation*, London: Routledge.

Crenshaw, M. and Pimlott, J. (1997) *Encyclopedia of World Terrorism, vol. 1*, Armonk: M.E. Sharpe.

Cusack, J. (1974) 'Response of the Government of France to the International Heroin Problem', in L.R.S. Simmons and A.A. Said (eds), *Drugs Politics and Diplomacy: the International Connection*, London: Sage, pp. 229–56.

Daily Mirror (2002) 'Lethal crop that leads to deaths like Rachel's', *Daily Mirror*, 6 March 2002.

David, C.-P. and Grondin, D. (2006) *Hegemony or Empire? The Redefinition of US Power under George W. Bush*, Aldershot: Ashgate.

De Ruyver, B., Vermeulen, G., Vander Beken, T., Vander Laenen, F. and Geenens, K. (2002) *Multidisciplinary Drug Treaties and the UN Drug Treaties*, Antwerpen-Apeldoorn: Maklu.

Derrida, J. (1972) 'La différance', in J. Derrida (ed.), *Marges de la philosophie*, Paris: Minuit, pp. 1–30.

—— (1980) *Writing and Difference*, Chicago: The University of Chicago Press.

Dessler, D. (1989) 'What's at stake in the agent-structure debate?' *International Organization*, 43 (3): 441–73.

Deutsche Welle World (2005) 'Drogen schaden dem Aufbau Afghanistans', *Deutsche Welle World*. Available online at: <http://www.dw-world.de/dw/article/0,,1597605,00.html (accessed 26 April 2010)>.

Diaz-Bone, R. (2002) *Kulturwelt, Diskurs und Lebensstil. Eine Diskurstheoretische Erweiterung der Bourdieuschen Distinktionstheorie*, Opladen: Leske + Budrich.

Diaz-Bone, R. and Schneider, W. (2003) 'Qualitative Datenanalysessoftware in der Sozialwissenschaftlichen Diskursanalyse – Zwei Praxisbeispiele', in R. Keller, A. Hirseland, W. Schneider and W. Viehöver (eds), *Handbuch Sozialwissenschaftliche Diskursanalyse, vol. 2*, Opladen: Leske + Budrich, pp. 457–95.

Diez, T. (1999) *Die EU Lesen. Diskursive Knotenpunkte in der Britischen Europadebatte*, Opladen: Leske + Budrich.

—— (2001) 'Europe as a Discursive Battleground. Discourse Analysis and European Integration Studies', *Cooperation and Conflict*, 36 (1): 5–38.

—— (2004) 'Europe's Others and the Return of Geopolitics', *Cambridge Review of International Affairs*, 17 (2): 319–35.

—— (2006) 'Postmoderne Ansätze', in S. Schieder and M. Spindler (eds), *Theorien der Internationalen Beziehungen*, 2. Auflage, Opladen: Leske + Budrich, pp. 449–76.

Dombrowski, P. (1998) 'Haute Finance and High Theory: recent scholarship on global financial relations', *Mershon International Studies Review*, 42 (1): 1–28.

Dorn, N., Murji, K. and South, N. (1992) *Traffickers. Drugs Market and Law Enforcement*, London: Routledge.

Doty, R.L. (1996) 'Sovereignty and the Nation: Constructing the Boundaries of National Identity', in T.J. Biersteker and C. Weber (eds), *State Sovereignty as Social Construct*, Cambridge: Cambridge University Press, pp. 121–47.

—— (1997) 'Aporia: A Critical Exploration of the Agent-Structure Problematique in International Relations Theory', *European Journal of International Relations*, 3 (3): 365–92.

—— (2003) *Anti-immigratianism in western democracies: statecraft, desire, and the politics of exclusion*, London: Routledge.

Dreyfus, H.L. and Rabinow, P. (1994) *Michel Foucault: Jenseits von Strukturalismus und Hermeneutik*, Frankfurt am Main: Beltz Athenaeum Verlag.

Driscoll, L. (2000) *Reconsidering Drugs. Mapping Victorian and Modern Drug Discourses*, New York, Basingstoke: Palgrave.

Drogenbeauftragte der Bundesregierung (2003) *Aktionsplan Drogen und Sucht*, November 2003. Available online at: <http://infomed.mds-ev.de/sindbad.nsf/51293108f720804cc1 2571e700442bde/b8e38fd8e7f0d57300256e7f00368971?OpenDocument (accessed 26 April 2010)>.

Druglink (2004) 'Europe's new hard line on drugs', *Druglink*, 18 (1): 3.

Dubin, M.D. (1991) *International Terrorism: Two League of Nations Conventions, 1934–1937*, Millwood: Kraus International Publiations.

Dubois, D. (2002) 'The Attacks of 11 September: EU–US Cooperation Against Terrorism in the Field of Justice and Home Affairs', *European Foreign Affairs Review*, 7: 317–35.

Dyrberg, T.B. (1998) 'Diskursanalyse als Postmoderne Politische Theorie', in O. Marchart (ed.), *Das Undarstellbare der Politik: zur Hegemonietheorie Ernesto Laclaus*, Wien: Turia + Kant, pp. 23–51.

—— (2004) 'The Political and Politics in Discourse Analysis', in S. Critchley and O. Marchart (eds), *Laclau. A critical reader*, London, New York: Routledge, pp. 241–55.

Elvins, M. (2003) *Anti-Drug Policies of the European Union. Transnational Decision-Making and the Politics of Expertise*, Basingstoke: Palgrave Macmillan.

Emcke, C. (2005) 'War on Terrorism and the Crises of the Political', in G. Meggle (ed.), *Ethics of Terrorism & Counter-Terrorism*, Frankfurt: Ontos verlag, pp. 227–43.

Estievenart, G. (ed.) (1995) *Policies and strategies to combat drugs in Europe: The Treaty on European Union – Framework for a New European Strategy to Combat Drugs?*, Dordrecht: Marinus Njihoff Publishers.

European Parliament and European Council (2005) 'Directive 2005/60/EC of 26 October 2005 on the prevention of the use of the financial system for the purpose of money laundering and terrorist financing', *Official Journal of the European Union*, L 309: 15.

European Political Science (2007) 'Symposium: The case for critical terrorism studies', *European Political Science*, 6 (4): 225–68.

Europol (2002) *Supplemental Agreement between the Europol Office and the United States of America on the Exchange of Personal Data and Related Information*. Available online at: <http://www.europol.europa.eu/legal/agreements/Agreements/16268-1.pdf (accessed 16 April 2010)>.

Fairclough, N. (2000) *New Labour, New Language?*, London: Routledge.

—— (2003) *Analysing Discourse*, London: Routledge.

Federal Bureau of Investigation (2003) *Five years ago today. Usama bin Laden: Wanted for Murder*. Available online at: <http://www.fbi.gov/page2/nov03/laden110503.htm (accessed 17 April 2010)>.

Fierke, K.M. (1998) *Changing Games, Changing Strategies. Critical Investigations in Security*, Manchester, New York: Manchester University Press.

Financial Times (2002) 'Afghanistan opium crop threatens Europe', *Financial Times*, 18 February 2002.

Finger, S.M. (1976) 'International Terrorism and the United Nations', in Y. Alexander (ed.), *International Terrorism: National, Regional, and Global Perspectives*, New York: Praeger, pp. 323–48.

Foreign and Commonwealth Office (2004) *Speech by the Foreign Secretary Jack Straw at the International Institute for Strategic Studies, press release (28 October 2004)*. Available online at: <http:\\www.fco.gov.uk (accessed 22 April 2010)>.

Foucault, M. (1982) 'Afterword. The Subject and Power', in H.L. Dreyfus and P. Rabinow (eds), *Michel Foucault. Beyond Structuralism and Hermeneutics*, Chicago: The University of Chicago Press, pp. 208–26.

—— (1990) *The History of Sexuality, vol. I*, Harmondsworth: Pelican.

—— (2006) 'Polemics, Politics and Problematization', in P. Rabinow (ed.), *Ethics, Subjectivity and Truth. Essential Works of Foucault 1954–1984, vol. 1*, New York: New Press, pp. 111–20.

France (2003) *Situation en France sur la consommation et le trafic d'héroïne*. Available online at: <http:\\www.archives.diplomatie.gouv.fr (accessed 21 April 2010)>.

Franck, T.M. and Lockwood, B.B. (1974) 'Preliminary Thoughts Towards an International Convention on Terrorism', *The American Journal of International Law*, 68 (1): 69–90.

Frankfurter Allgemeine Zeitung (2000) 'Verstärkter Kampf gegen Steuerhinterziehung', *Frankfurter Allgemeine Zeitung*, 1 July 2000.

Friedman, J. and Chase-Dunn, C. (eds) (2005) *Hegemonic Definitions: Present and Past*, Cambridge: Cambridge University Press.

Friedman, M. (1991) 'The War We are Loosing', in M.B. Krauss and E.P. Lazear (eds), *Searching for Alternatives: Drug-Control Policy in the United States*, Stanford: Hoover Institution Press, pp. 53–67.

Friedrichs, J. (2006) 'Defining the International Public Enemy: The Political Struggle behind the Legal Debate on International Terrorism', *Leiden Journal of International Law*, 19: 69–91.

—— (2007) *Fighting Terrorism and Drugs. Europe and International Police Cooperation*, London, New York: Routledge.

Friesendorf, C. (2007) *US Foreign Policy and the War on Drugs: Displacing the Cocaine and Heroin Industry*, London, New York: Routledge.

Friman, R. (1996) *NarcoDiplomacy: Exporting the US War on Drugs*, Ithaca, London: Cornell University Press.

Frowein, J. (2006) 'The UN-antiterror administration and the rule of law', in P.-M. Dupuy (ed.), *Völkerrecht als Weltordnung. Festschrift für Christian Tomuschat*, Kehl: Engel, pp. 785–95.

Gal-Or, N. (1985) *International Cooperation to Suppress Terrorism*, London, Sydney: Croom Helm.

George, J. (1995) 'Realist "Ethics", International Relations, and Postmodernism: Thinking beyond the Egoism-Anarchy Thematic', *Millennium: Journal of International Studies*, 24 (2): 195–223.

Gerber, J. and Jensen, E.L. (eds) (2001) *Drug War, American Style: The Internationalization of Failed Policy and its Alternatives*, New York: Garland.

Germany (1992) 'Gesetz zur Bekämpfung des illegalen Rauschgifthandels und anderer Erscheinungsformen der Organisierten Kriminalität (OrgKG)', *Bundesgesetzblätter I*: 1302.

—— (2000) 'Drittes Betäubungsmittelgesetz – Änderungsgesetz', *Bundesgesetzblätter I*: 302.

—— (2002) 'Gesetz zur Verbesserung der Bekämpfung der Geldwäsche und der Bekämpfung der Finanzierung des Terrorismus', *Bundesgesetzblätter I*: 3105.

Giddens, A. (1984) *The Constitution of Society*, Berkely: University of California Press.

Gill, S. (1993) *Gramsci, Historical materialism and International Relations*, Cambridge: Cambridge University Press.

—— (2003) *Power and Resistance in the New World Order*, Basingstoke: Palgrave Macmillan.

Gilmore, W.C. (2004) *Dirty Money. The Evolution of International Measures to Counter Money Laundering and the Financing of Terrorism*, 3 edn, Strasbourg: Council of Europe Publishing.

Gilpin, R. (1975) *US Power and the Multinational Cooperation*, New York: Basic Books.

Gioia, A. (2006) 'The UN Conventions on the Prevention and Suppression of International Terrorism', in G. Nesi (ed.), *International Cooperation in Counter-Terrorism: the United Nations and Regional Organizations in the Fight Against Terrorism*, Aldershot, Bourlington: Ashgate, pp. 3–23.

Glynos, J. and Howarth, D. (2007) *Logics of Critical Explanation in Social and Political Theory*, London, New York: Routledge.

Gramsci, A. (1971) *Selections from the Prison Notebooks of Antonio Gramsci*, London: Laurence and Wishart.

Guelke, A. (2006) *Terrorism and Global Disorder: Political Violence in the Contemporary World*, London: Tauris.

Guild, E. (2008) 'The Uses and Abuses of Counter-Terrorism Policies in Europe: The Case of the "Terrorist Lists"', *Journal of Common Market Studies*, 46 (1): 173–93.

Gusfield, J.R. (1981) *The Culture of Public Problems. Drinking, Driving and the Symbolic Order*, Chicago: The University of Chicago Press.

Hall, S. (1996) 'Introduction: Who Needs Identity?' in S. Hall and P. du Gay (eds), *Questions of Cultural Identity*, London, Thousand Oaks, New Delhi: Sage, pp. 1–17.

Halliday, F. (2002) 'The pertinence of imperialism', in M. Rupert and H. Smith (eds), *Historical Materialism and Globalization*, London, New York: Routledge, pp. 75–89.

Hansen, L. (1997) 'A Case for Seduction? Evaluating Poststructuralist Conceptualization of Security', *Cooperation and Conflict*, 32 (4): 369–97.

—— (2006) *Security as Practice. Discourse Analysis and the Bosnian War*, London, New York: Routledge.

Forbes.com (2005) 'Milton Friedman: Legalize it!' *Forbes.com*, 6 February 2005. Available online at: <http://www.forbes.com/2005/06/02/cz_qh_0602pot.html (accessed 17 April 2010).>.

Herschinger, E., Jachtenfuchs, M. and Kraft-Kasack, C. (2010) 'International Policing: Embedding the State Monopoly of Force', in H. Enderlein, S. Wälti and M. Zürn (eds), *Handbook on Multi-level Governance*, Edward Elgar Publishers, forthcoming.

—— (forthcoming) 'Transgouvernementalisierung und die ausbleibende gesellschaftliche Politisierung der inneren Sicherheit', in M. Zürn and M. Ecker-Ehrhardt (eds), *Gesellschaftliche Politisierung und internationale Institutionen*, Frankfurt am Main: Suhrkamp.

Herschinger, E. and Nonhoff, M. (2008) 'Who's afraid of . . . strategy? Exploring the potential of an unloved concept', paper presented at the Inaugural World Conference: Ideology and Discourse Analysis, University of Roskilde, Denmark, September 8–10.

Hoffmann, B. (1998) *Inside Terrorism*, New York: Columbia University Press.

Höhne, T. (2001) 'Alles konstruiert, oder was? Über den Zusammenhang von Konstruktivismus und empirischer Forschung', in J. Angermüller, K. Bunzmann and M. Nonhoff (eds), *Diskursanalyse: Theorien, Methoden, Anwendungen*, Hamburg: Argument, pp. 23–35.

Howarth, D. (1997) 'Complexities of identity/difference: Black Consciousness ideology in South Africa', *Journal of Political Ideologies*, 2 (1): 51–78.

—— (2000) *Discourse*, Buckingham, Philadelphia: Open University Press.

—— (2004) 'Hegemony, Political Subjectivity, and Radical Democracy', in S. Critchley and O. Marchart (eds), *Laclau. A Critical Reader*, London: Routledge, pp. 256–76.

Howarth, D. and Stavrakakis, Y. (2000) 'Introducing discourse theory and political analysis', in D. Howarth, A.J. Norval and Y. Stavrakakis (eds), *Discourse Theory and Political Analysis: Identities, Hegemonies and Social Change*, Manchester, New York: Manchester University Press, pp. 1–23.

Inayatullah, N. and Blaney, D.L. (2004) *International Relations and the Problem of Difference*, London, New York: Routledge.

International Drug Policy Consortium (2008) *The International Narcotics Control Board: Current Tensions and Options for Reform*, IDCP Briefing Paper 7. Available online at: <www.idpc.net/sites/default/files/library/IDPC_BP_07_INCB_TensionsAndOptions_EN.pdf (accessed 26 April 2010)>.

International Narcotics Control Board (2009) *Report of the International Narcotics Control Board for 2008*, Nr. E/INCB/2008/1, United Nations, New York. Available online at: <http://www.incb.org/pdf/annual-report/2008/en/AR_08_English.pdf (accessed 25 April 2010)>.

Ives, P. (2004) *Language and Hegemony in Gramsci*, London, Ann Arbor: Pluto Press.

Jabri, V. (1998) 'Restyling the Subject of Responsibility in International Relations', *Millennium: Journal of International Relations*, 27 (3): 591–611.

Jachtenfuchs, M., Friedrichs, J., Herschinger, E. and Kraft-Kasack, C. (2008) *Policing Among Nations. Embedding the Monopoly of Force*, Hertie School of Governance – working paper series, Nr. 28. Available online at: <http://www.hertie-school.org/binaries/addon/526_hsog_wp_no._28.pdf (accessed 26 April 2010)>.

Jack, A. (2009) 'A new leaf. The first synthetic cannabis-type drug has reached the streets and, for the moment, it's perfectly legal', *Financial Times*, February 14–15, p. 19 (Life&Arts).

Jackson, R. (2005) *Writing the War on Terrorism: Language, Politics and Counter-terrorism*, Manchester: Manchester University Press.

Jelsma, M. (2003) 'Drugs in the UN system: the unwritten history of the 1998 United Nations General Assembly Special Session on drugs', *International Journal of Drug Policy*, 14 (2): 181–95.

Jenkins, B.M. (1986) 'Defense Against Terrorism', *Political Science Quarterly*, 101 (5, special issue: Reflections on Providing for 'The Common Defense'): 773–86.

Jepperson, R.L., Wendt, A. and Katzenstein, P.J. (1996) 'Norms, Identity and Culture in National Security', in P.J. Katzenstein (ed.), *The Culture of National Security. Norms and Identity in World Politics*, New York: Columbia University Press, pp. 33–75.

Katzenstein, P.J. (1996) 'Introduction: Alternative Perspectives on National Security', in P.J. Katzenstein (ed.), *The Culture of National Security: Norms and Identity in World Politics*, New York: Columbia University Press, pp. 1–32.

Katzenstein, P.J., Keohane, R.O. and Krasner, S.D. (1999) *Exploration and Contestation in the Study of World Politics*, Cambridge: MIT Press.

Keeley, J.F. (1990) 'Toward a Foucauldian Analysis of International Regimes', *International Organization*, 44 (1): 83–105.

Keohane, R.O. (1980) 'The Theory of Hegemonic Stability and Changes in International Economics Regimes, 1967–1977', in O.R. Holsti, M.S. Randolph and A.L. George (eds), *Change in the International System*, Boulder: Westview, pp. 131–62.

—— (1984) *After Hegemony: Cooperation and Discord in the World Political Economy*, Princeton: Princeton University Press.

188   Bibliography

—— (1989) 'International Relations Theory: Contributions of a Feminist Standpoint', *Millennium: Journal of International Studies*, 18 (2): 245–53.

Kindleberger, C.P. (1973) *The World in Depression, 1929–1939*, Berkley, Los Angeles: University of California Press.

Klein, A. (2000) 'Misguided Missiles: Drugs War in Colombia', *Druglink*, 15 (3): 16–7.

Klein, B.S. (1988) 'Beyond the Western Alliance. The Politics of Post-Atlanticism', in S. Gill (ed.), *Atlantic Relations: beyond the Reagan era*, Hemel Hempstead, Hertfordshire, New York: Harvester Wheatsheaf, pp. 196–211.

—— (1989) 'The Textual Strategies of the Military: Or Have You Read Any Good Defense Manuals Lately?' in J. Der Derian and M.J. Shapiro (eds), *International/Intertextual Relations. Postmodern Readings of World Politics*, New York, Toronto, Oxford, Singapore, Sydney: Lexington Books, pp. 97–112.

—— (1990) 'How the West was One: Representational Politics of NATO', *International Studies Quarterly*, 34 (3): 311–25.

—— (1994) *Strategic Studies and World Order*, Cambridge: Cambridge University Press.

Lacan, J. (1973) 'Subversion des Subjekts und Dialektik des Begehrens im Freudschen Unbewußten', in J. Lacan (ed.), *Schriften II*, Olten, Freiburg im Breisgau: Walter – Verlag, pp. 165–204.

—— (2006) *Écrits*, New York: W. W. Norton.

Laclau, E. (1990) 'New Reflections on the Revolution of Our Time', in E. Laclau (ed.), *New Reflections on the Revolution of Our Time*, London, New York: Verso, pp. 3–87.

—— (1994a) 'Introduction', in E. Laclau (ed.), *The Making of Political Identities*, London, New York: Verso, pp. 1–8.

—— (1994b) 'Why do Empty Signifiers Matter to Politics?' in J. Weeks (ed.), *The Lesser Evil and the Greater God*, London: Rivers Oran Press, pp. 167–78.

—— (1995) 'Subject of Politics, Politics of the Subject', *A Journal of Feminist Cultural Studies*, 7 (1): 146–64.

—— (1996) 'Deconstruction, Pragmatism, Hegemony', in C. Mouffe (ed.), *Deconstruction and Pragmatism. Simon Critchley, Jacques Derrida, Ernesto Laclau and Richard Rorty*, London, New York: Routlegde, pp. 47–67.

—— (1997a) 'Inklusion, Exklusion und die Logik der Äquivalenz', in P. Weibel and S. Žižek (eds), *Inklusion-Exklusion: Probleme des Postkolonialismus und der globalen Migration*, Wien: Passagen, pp. 45–74.

—— (1997b) 'On the names of God', in S. Golding (ed.), *The Eight Technologies of Otherness*, London: Routledge, pp. 253–64.

—— (2000a) 'Constructing Universality', in J. Butler, E. Laclau and S. Žižek (eds), *Contingency, Hegemony, Universality. Contemporary Dialogues on the Left*, London, New York: Verso, pp. 281–307.

—— (2000b) 'Foreword', in D. Howarth, A.J. Norval and Y. Stavrakakis (eds), *Discourse Theory and Political Analysis: Identities, Hegemonies and Social Change*, Manchester, New York: Manchester University Press, pp. x-xi.

—— (2000c) 'Structure, History and the Political', in J. Butler, E. Laclau and S. Žižek (eds), *Contingency, Hegemony, Universality. Contemporary Dialogues on the Left*, London, New York: Verso, pp. 182–212.

—— (2004) 'Glimpsing the Future', in S. Critchley and O. Marchart (eds), *Laclau. A Critical Reader*, London, New York: Routledge, pp. 279–328.

—— (2005) *On Populist Reason*, London, New York: Verso.

Laclau, E. and Mouffe, C. (2001) *Hegemony and Socialist Strategy. Towards a Radical Democratic Politics*, London: Verso.

Laclau, E. and Zac, L. (1994) 'Minding the Gap: The Subject of Politics', in E. Laclau (ed.), *The Making of Political Identities*, London: Verso, pp. 11–39.

Lake, D.A. (1993) 'Leadership, Hegemony and the International Economy: Naked Emperor or Tattered Monarch with Potential?' *International Studies Quarterly*, 37 (4): 459–89.

Laqueur, W. (1987) *The Age of Terrorism*, Boston: Little Brown and Company.

——. (1999) *The New Terrorism. Fanaticism and the Arms of Mass Destruction*, London: Phoenix Press.

—— (2003) *No End to War: Terrorism in the Twenty-first Century*, New York: Continuum.

Lash, S. (2007) 'Power after Hegemony', *Theory, Culture & Society* 24 (3): 55–78.

Lavranos, N. (2003) 'Europol and the Fight Against Terrorism', *European Foreign Affairs Review*, 8 (2): 259–75.

Lentner, H.H. (2006) 'Hegemony and Power in International Politics', in H. Haugaard and H.H. Lentner (eds), *Hegemony and Power: Consensus and Coercion in Contemporary Politics*, Lanham: Lexington Books, pp. 89–108.

Levine, H.G. (2003) 'Global drug prohibition: its uses and crises', *International Journal of Drug Policy*, 14 (2): 145–53.

Linklater, A. (1990) 'The Problem of Community in International Relations', *Alternatives*, 15 (2): 135–53.

—— (1992) 'The Question of the Next State in International Relations Theory: A Critical Theoretical Point of View', *Millennium: Journal of International Relations*, 21 (1): 77–98.

—— (1998) 'The Idea of Citizenship and the Development of the Modern State', in U.K. Preuss and F. Requejo (eds), *European Citizenship, Multiculturalism and the State*, Baden-Baden: Nomos, pp. 51–66.

MacCoun, R.J. and Reuter, P. (2005) 'Philosophical Underpinnings', in L.E. Huggins (ed.), *Drug War Deadlock: the Policy Battle Continues*, Stanford: Hoover Institution Press, pp. 33–50.

Manzo, K. (1992) *Domination, Resistance and Social Change in South Africa: The Local Effects of Global Power*, New York: Praeger.

Marcussen, M., Risse, T., Engelmann-Martin, D., Knopf, H.J. and Roscher, K. (1999) 'Constructing Europe? The Evolution of French, British and German Nation State Identities', *Journal of European Public Policy*, 6 (4): 614–33.

Marty, D. (2007) *UN Security Council Blacklists*, (as/jur(2007)14), 19 March 2007, Strasbourg: Parliamentary Assembly, Council of Europe.

Mascianduro, D. (ed.) (2004) *Global Financial Crime: Terrorism, Money Laundering and Offshore Centres*, Aldershot: Ashgate.

McAllister, W.B. (2000) *Drug Diplomacy in the Twentieth Century: An International History*, London, New York: Routledge.

McLean, I. and McMillan, A. (2003) *Oxford Concise Dictionary of Politics*, Oxford: Oxford University Press.

Mercer, J. (1995) 'Anarchy and Identity', *International Organization*, 49 (2): 229–52.

Miles, M.B. and Huberman, A.M. (1994) *Qualitative Data Analysis. An Expanded Sourcebook*, Thousand Oaks, London, New Delhi: Sage.

Milliken, J. (1999) 'The Study of Discourse in International Relations: A Critique of Research and Methods', *European Journal of International Relations*, 5 (2): 225–54.

—— (2001) *The Social Construction of the Korean War: Conflict and its Possibilities*, Manchester: Manchester United Press.

Ministère de l'Intérieur (1971) *Accord entre la Direction Générale de la Police Nationale française (Direction Centrale de la Police Judiciaire) et the United States Bureau of Narcotics and Dangerous Drugs signé par le Ministre de l'intérieur du Gouvernement de la République Française, Raymond Marcellin, Et the Attorney General of the United States of America, John Mitchell*, Versement No 19920026 – Article 1–6, Fontainebleau: Centre des Archives Contemporaines.

Ministère des Affaires étrangères (undated document-a) *Fonds de solidarité prioritaire: Burkina Faso – Appui à la police*. Available online at: <www.archives.diplomatie.gouv. fr (accessed 21 April 2010)>.

——(undated document-b) *Fonds de solidarité prioritaire: Niger – Appui au centre national de répression du trafic illicite des drogues*. Available online at: <www.archives.diplomatie. gouv.fr (accessed 21 April 2010)>.

Mission interministérielle de la lutte contre la drogue et la toxicomanie (1999) *Plan triennal de lutte contre la drogue et de prévention des dépendances, 1999–2001: rapport officiel*, Paris: La Documentation Française.

Mitsilegas, V. (2003a) *Money Laundering Counter-Measures in the European Union. A New Paradigm of Security Governance versus Fundamental Legal Principles*, Den Haag: Kluwer.

——(2003b) 'The New EU–USA Cooperation on Extradition, Mutual Legal Assistance and the Exchange of Police Data', *European Foreign Affairs Review*, 8: 515–36.

——(2007) 'The External Dimension of EU Action in Criminal Matters', *European Foreign Affairs Review*, 12: 457–97.

Montebourg, A. (2000) *La lutte contre le blanchiment des capitaux en France: un combat à poursuivre. Rapport d'information n° 2311, Tome II, Vol. 1 – Rapport et annexes, 30 mars 2000*, Paris: Assembleé Nationale.

Mouffe, C. (1979) 'Hegemony and Ideology in Gramsci', in C. Mouffe (ed.), *Gramsci and Marxist Theory*, London, Boston, Henley: Routledge & Kegan Paul, pp. 168–204.

——(1993a) 'Introduction: For an Agonistic Pluralism', in C. Mouffe (ed.), *The Return of the Political*, London, New York: Verso, pp. 1–8.

——(1993b) 'Pluralism and Modern Democracy', in C. Mouffe (ed.), *The Return of the Political*, London, New York: Verso, pp. 117–34.

——(2000) *Deliberative Democracy or Agonistic Pluralism*, Political Science Series Nr. 72, Institute for Advanced Studies, Vienna. Available online at: <http://www.ihs.ac.at/ publications/pol/pw_72.pdf (accessed 25 April 2010)>.

——(2005) *Speech of Chantal Mouffe at the Workshop 'Discourse, Democracy, Hegemony. Résumé and Future Prospect of the Political Theory of Ernesto Laclau and Chantal Mouffe'*, Bremen, December 9–10, 2005.

Müller, H. (2002) 'Security Cooperation', in W. Carlsnaes, T. Risse and B.A. Simmons (eds), *Handbook of International Relations*, London, Thousand Oaks, New Delhi: Sage Publications, pp. 369–91.

Musto, D. (1999) *The American Disease. Origins of Narcotics Control*, New York, Oxford: Oxford University Press.

Nadelmann, E.A. (1990) 'Global prohibition regimes: the evolution of norms in international society', *International Organization*, 44 (4): 479–526.

——(1993) *Cops Across Borders. The Internationalization of US Criminal Law Enforcement*, University Park, PA: Pensylvannia University Press.

Neal, A. (2010) *Exceptionalism and the Politics of Counter-terrorism: Liberty, Security and the War on Terror*, London: Routledge.

Neumann, I.B. (1996) 'Self and Other in International Relations', *European Journal of International Relations*, 2 (2): 139–74.

—— (1999) *Uses of the Other. 'The East' in European Identity Formation*, Manchester: Manchester University Press.

Nonhoff, M. (2001) 'Soziale Marktwirtschaft – ein leerer Signifikant? Überlegungen im Anschluss an die Diskurstheorie Ernesto Laclaus', in J. Angermüller, K. Bunzmann and M. Nonhoff (eds), *Diskursanalyse: Theorien, Methoden, Anwendungen*, Hamburg: Argument, pp. 193–208.

—— (2006) *Politischer Diskurs und Hegemonie. Das Projekt 'Soziale Marktwirtschaft'*, Bielefeld: Transcript.

Norval, A.J. (2000) 'Trajectories of future research in discourse theory', in D. Howarth, A.J. Norval and Y. Stavrakakis (eds), *Discourse Theory and Political Analysis: Identities, Hegemonies and Social Change*, Manchester, New York: Manchester University Press, pp. 219–36.

—— (2004) 'Democratic decisions and the question of universality: rethinking recent approaches', in S. Critchley and O. Marchart (eds), *Laclau. A Critical Reader*, London, New York: Routledge, pp. 140–66.

Nutt, D., King, L.A., Saulsbury, W. and Blakemore, C. (2007) 'Development of a rational scale to assess the harm of drugs of potential misuse', *The Lancet*, 369 (9566): 1047–53.

Nuzzo, A. (2004) 'Reasons for Conflict. Political Implications of a Definition of Terrorism', *Metaphilosophy* 35 (3): 332–44.

Osman, M.A. (2003) *The United Nations and Peace Enforcement: Wars, Terrorism and Democracy*, Aldershot: Ashgate.

Pêcheux, M. (1969) *Analyse automatique du discours*, Paris: Dunod.

Ranstorp, M. (ed.) (2007) *Mapping Terrorism Research: State of the Art, Gaps and Future Direction*, London: Routledge.

Rebscher, E. (1981) 'Rechtliche und organisatorische Grundlagen der internationalen Zusammenarbeit bei der Drogenbekämpfung', in Bundeskriminalamt (ed.), *Polizeiliche Drogenbekämpfung*, Wiesbaden: Bundeskriminalamt, pp. 155–76.

Reyes, O. (2005) 'New Labour's Politics of the Hard-working Family', in D. Howarth and J. Torfing (eds), *Discourse Theory in European Politics:Identity, Policy and Governance*, Basingstoke: Palgrave Macmillan, pp. 231–54.

Richardson, L. (2006) *What Terrorists Want: Understanding the Terrorist Threat*, Manchester: John Murray.

Rumelili, B. (2004) 'Constructing Identity and Relating to Difference: Understanding the EU's Mode of Differentiation', *Review of International Studies*, 30: 27–47.

Rupert, M. (1995) *Producing Hegemony: The Politics of Mass Production and American Global Power*, Cambridge: Cambridge University Press.

Saco, D. (1999) 'Colonizing Cyberspace: "National Security" and the Internet', in J. Weldes, M. Laffey, R. Duvall and H. Gusterson (eds), *Cultures of Insecurity*, Minneapolis: University of Minnesota Press, pp. 261–92.

Said, E. (2003) *Orientalism*, 3 edn, London: Penguin Books.

Savona, E.U. (1997) *Responding to Money Laundering: International Perspectives*, London: Harwood.

Schmid, A.P. (1993) *Western Responses to Terrorism*, London, Portland: Frank Cass.

—— (1997) 'The Problems of Defining Terrorism', in M. Crenshaw and J. Pimlott (eds), *Encyclopaedia of World Terrorism, Vol. 1*, Armonk, NY: M.E. Sharpe, pp. 12–22.

Schmitt, C. (1976) *The Concept of the Political*, New Brunswick: Rutgers University Press.

Schreier, M. (1997) *Das Erkennen sprachlicher Täuschung. Über Absichtlichkeitsindikatoren beim unintegren Argumentieren*, Münster: Aschendorff Verlag.

Scotland on Sunday (2004), 'Britain losing war on Afghan heroin', *Scotland on Sunday*, 7 November 2004.

Shapiro, M.J. (1989) 'Textualizing Global Politics', in J. Der Derian and M.J. Shapiro (eds), *International/Intertextual Relations. Postmodern Readings of World Politics*, New York: Lexington Books, pp. 11–22.

—— (1999) 'The Ethics of Encounter: Unreading, Unmapping the Imperium', in D. Campbell and M.J. Shapiro (eds), *Moral Spaces. Rethinking Ethics and World Politics*, Minneapolis: University of Minnesota Press, pp. 57–91.

—— (2004) *Methods and Nations. Cultural Governance and the Indigenous Subject*, London: Routledge.

Silke, A. (ed.) (2004) *Research on Terrorism: Trends, Achievements and Failures*, London: Frank Cass.

Silverman, D. (2001) *Interpreting Qualitative Data: Methods for Analysing Talk, Text and Interaction*, 2nd edn, London: Sage.

Spiegel online (2007) 'Kopfgeld verdoppelt. 50 Millionen Dollar für Bin Laden – tot oder lebendig', *Spiegel online*, 13 July 2007. Available online at: <http://www.spiegel.de/politik/ausland/0,1518,494365,00.html (accessed 17 April 2010)>.

Stäheli, U. (1999) 'Die politische Theorie der Hegemonie: Ernesto Laclau und Chantal Mouffe', in A. Brodocz and G.S. Schaal (eds), *Politische Theorien der Gegenwart*, Opladen: Leske+ Budrich, pp. 141–65.

—— (2004) 'Competing figures of the limit: dispersion, transgression, antagonism and difference', in S. Critchley and O. Marchart (eds), *Laclau. A Critical Reader*, London, New York: Routledge, pp. 226–40.

Stoll, P.-T., Mißling, S. and Juretko, B. (2004) *Doppelte Sicherheit. Über die zwischen-staatliche Zusammenarbeit im Kampf gegen den internationalen Terrorismus*, Berlin: Heinrich-Böll Stiftung.

Strauss, A.L. and Corbin, J. (1996) *Grounded Theory: Grundlagen qualitativer Sozialforschung*, Weinheim: Beltz.

Süddeutsche Zeitung (2001a) 'Oasen bekommen den Segen', *Süddeutsche Zeitung*, 19 November 2001.

Süddeutsche Zeitung (2001b) 'Papiertiger OECD', *Süddeutsche Zeitung*, 30 July 2001.

Süddeutsche Zeitung (2008) 'Zehnter Jahrestag der RAF Auflösung: "Das Ergebnis kritisiert uns"', *Süddeutsche Zeitung*, 20 April 2008. Available online at: <http://www.sueddeutsche.de/politik/113/439855/text/ (accessed 17 April 2010)>.

Sylvester, C. (1994) *Feminist Theory and International Relations in a Postmodern Era*, Cambridge: Cambridge University Press.

Tappeiner, I. (2005) 'The Fight Against Terrorism: The Lists and the Gaps', *Utrecht Law Review*, 1 (1): 97–125.

The Daily Telegraph (2004) 'Poverty and terrorism fuel booming drug trade in Afghanistan', *The Daily Telegraph*, 24 August 2004.

The Observer (2002) 'Blair sets up team to stem tide of Afghan heroin into UK', *The Observer*, 24 March 2002.

Thomas, C. (2003) 'Disciplining globalization: international law, illegal trade, and the case of narcotics', *Michigan Journal of International Law*, 24 (2): 549–75.

Thomassen, L. (2005) *From Antagonism to Heterogeneity: Discourse Analytical Strategies*, Essex Papers in Politics and Government: Sub-Series in Ideology and Discourse Analysis, Nr. 21. Available online at: <http://www.essex.ac.uk/government/resources/EssexPapers/IDA21thomassenAbstract.pdf (accessed 19 April 2010)>.

Todorov, T. (1992) *The Conquest of America. The Question of the Other*, New York: Harper and Row Publishers.

—— (2008) *La peur des barbares. Au-delà du choc des civilisations*, Paris: Laffont.

Torfing, J. (1991) 'A hegemony approach to capitalist regulation', in R.B. Bertramsen, J.P. Frolund and J. Torfing (eds), *State, Economy and Society*, London, Boston, Sydney, Wellington: Unwin Hyman, pp. 35–93.

—— (1998) *Politics, Regulation, and the Modern Welfare State*, New York: St. Martin's Press.

—— (1999) *New Theories of Discourse: Laclau, Mouffe, and Žižek*, Oxford: Blackwell Publishers.

—— (2005) 'Discourse Theory: Achievements, Arguments, and Challenges', in D. Howarth and J. Torfing (eds), *Discourse Theory in European Politics. Identity, Policy and Governance*, London: Palgrave, Macmillan, pp. 1–32.

Transnational Institute (2005) *Drug Policy Briefing N° 11*. Available online at: <http://www.tni.org/sites/www.tni.org/files/download/brief11.pdf (accessed 24 April 2010)>.

UN Ad Hoc Committee on International Terrorism (1973a) *Observations of States*, A/AC.160/1, New York: United Nations, 16 May 1973.

—— (1973b) *Observations of States (continued)*, A/AC.160/1/Add.1, New York: United Nations, 12 June 1973.

—— (1973c) *Report*, Supplement Nr. 28 (A/9028), New York: United Nations.

—— (1979a) *Consideration of the Observations of States and Formulation of Recommendations Pursuant to General Assembly Resolution 32/147*, A/AC.160/SR.13, New York: United Nations, 26 March 1979.

—— (1979b) *Consideration of the Observations of States and Formulation of Recommendations Pursuant to General Assembly Resolution 32/147 (continued)*, A/AC.160/SR.15, New York: United Nations, 28 March 1979.

—— (1979c) *Summary Record of the 11th Meeting*, A/AC.160/SR.11, New York: United Nations, 22 March 1979.

—— (1979d) *Summary Record of the 19th Meeting*, A/AC.160/SR.19, New York: United Nations, 6 April 1979.

—— (2010) *Report*, Supplement Nr. 37 (A/65/37), New York: United Nations, 12–16 April 2010.

UN General Assembly (1970) *Declaration on the Principles of International Law Concerning Friendly Relations and Co-operation Among States in Accordance with the Charter of the United Nations*, United Nations, New York. Available online at: <http://documents.un.org (accessed 17 April 2010)>.

—— (1972) *Organization of the Twenty-seventh Session of the General Assembly: Memorandum by the Secretary General*, A/BUR/SR.199, New York: United Nations, 20 September 1972.

—— (2006) *Resolution: The United Nations Global Counter-Terrorism Strategy*, A/RES/60/288. Available online at: <http://www.un.org/terrorism/strategy-counter-terrorism.shtml#resolution (accessed 17 April 2010)>.

UN Security Council (1999) *Security Council Resolution 1267 (On Measures against the Taliban)*, S/RES/1267. Available online at: <http://documents.un.org (accessed 17 April 2010)>.

—— (2000) *Security Council Resolution 1333 (On measures against the Taliban)*, S/RES/1333. Available online at: <http://documents.un.org (accessed 17 April 2010)>.

—— (2001) *Security Council Resolution 1373 (Threats to international peace and security caused by terrorist acts)*, S/RES/1373 (2001). Available online at: <http://documents.un.org (accessed 17 April 2010)>.

UN Security Council Committee established pursuant to Resolution 1267 (1999) concerning Al-Qaida and the Taliban and associated individuals and entities (2008) *Guidelines of the Committee for the Conduct of its Work*. Available online at: <http://www.un.org/sc/committees/1267/pdf/1267_guidelines.pdf (accessed 17 April 2010)>.

UN Sixth Committee (1972a) *Agenda item 92 (continued) – A/C.6/L.866*, New York: United Nations, 9 November 1972.

—— (1972b) *Agenda item 92 (continued) – A/C.6/SR.1355*, New York: United Nations, 9 November 1972.

—— (1972c) *Agenda item 92 (continued) – A/C.6/SR.1357*, New York: United Nations, 13 November 1972.

—— (1972d) *Agenda item 92 (continued) – A/C.6/SR.1358*, New York: United Nations, 14 November 1972.

—— (1972e) *Agenda item 92 (continued) – A/C.6/SR.1360*, New York: United Nations, 15 November 1972.

—— (1972f) *Agenda item 92 (continued) – A/C.6/SR.1361*, New York: United Nations, 16 November 1972.

—— (1972g) *Agenda item 92 (continued) – A/C.6/SR.1364*, New York: United Nations, 17 November 1972.

—— (1972h) *Agenda item 92 (continued) – A/C.6/SR.1365*, New York: United Nations, 20 November 1972.

—— (1972i) *Agenda item 92 (continued) – A/C.6/SR.1366*, New York: United Nations, 20 November 1972.

—— (1972j) *Agenda item 92 (continued) – A/C.6/SR.1367*, New York: United Nations, 21 November 1972.

—— (1972k) *Agenda item 92 (continued) – A/C.6/SR.1368*, New York: United Nations, 21 November 1972.

—— (1972l) *Agenda item 92 (continued) – A/C.6/SR.1370*, New York: United Nations, 22 November 1972.

—— (1972m) *Agenda item 92 (continued) – A/C.6/SR.1372*, New York: United Nations, 27 November 1972.

—— (1972n) *Agenda item 92 (continued) – A/C.6/SR.1386*, New York: United Nations, 8 December 1972.

—— (1972o) *Agenda item 92 (continued) – A/C.6/SR.1387*, New York: United Nations, 8 December 1972.

—— (1972p) *Agenda item 92 (continued) – A/C.6/SR.1389*, New York: United Nations, 11 December 1972.

—— (1972q) *Agenda item 92 (continued) – A/C.8/SR.1386*, New York: United Nations, 8 December 1972.

—— (1972r) *Agenda item 92: Measures to prevent international terrorism which endangers or takes innocent human lives or jeopardizes fundamental freedoms, and study of the underlying causes of those forms of terrorism and acts of violence which lie in misery, frustration, grievance and despair and which cause some people to sacrifice human lives, including their own, in an attempt to effect radical changes (continued) – A/C.6/418*, New York: United Nations, 2 November 1972.

—— (1972s) *Organization of work – A/C.6/SR. 1311*, New York: United Nations, 25 September 1972.

—— (1997a) *Agenda item 152: Measures to Eliminate International Terrorism – A/C.6/52/SR.27*, New York: United Nations, 13 November 1997.

—— (1997b) *Agenda item 152: Measures to Eliminate International Terrorism (continued) – A/C.6/52/SR.33*, New York: United Nations, 19 November 1997.

—— (1997c) *Agenda item 152: Measures to Eliminate International Terrorism (continued) – A/C.6/52/SR.34*, New York: United Nations, 21 November 1997.

—— (1998) *Agenda item 155: Measures to Eliminate International Terrorism (continued) – A/C.6/53/SR.26*, New York: United Nations, 11 November 1998.

UN Sixth Committee (1999) *Agenda item 160: Measures to Eliminate International Terrorism – Report of the Sixth Committee – A/54/615*, New York: United Nations, 10 December 1999.

—— (2000a) *Agenda item 164: Measures to Eliminate International Terrorism – A/C.6/55/SR.27*, 13 November 2000.

—— (2000b) *Agenda item 164: Measures to Eliminate International Terrorism (continued) – A/C.6/55/SR.28*, 14 November 2000.

—— (2000c) *Agenda item 164: Measures to Eliminate International Terrorism (continued) – A/C.6/55/SR.29*, New York: United Nations, 15 November 2000.

—— (2000d) *Agenda item 166: Measures to Eliminate International Terrorism – Draft comprehensive convention on international terrorism – Working document submitted by India – A/C.6/55/1*, New York: United Nations, 28 August 2000.

—— (2001) *Agenda item 166: Measures to Eliminate International Terrorism (continued) – A/C.6/56/SR.28*, New York: United Nations, 21 November 2001.

—— (2002a) *Agenda item 160: Measures to Eliminate International Terrorism (continued) – A/C.6/57/SR.9*, New York: United Nations, 3 October 2002.

—— (2002b) *Agenda item 160: Measures to Eliminate International Terrorism (continued) – A/C.6/57/SR.10*, New York: United Nations, 4 October 2004.

—— (2003a) *Agenda item 156: Measures to Eliminate International Terrorism – A/C.6/58/SR.6*, New York: United Nations, 15 October 2003.

—— (2003b) *Agenda item 156: Measures to Eliminate International Terrorism (continued) – A/C.6/58/SR.7*, New York: United Nations, 17 October 2003.

—— (2004) *Agenda item 148: Measures to Eliminate International Terrorism – A/C.6/59/SR.7*, New York: United Nations, 18 October 2004.

—— (2005a) *Agenda item 108: Measures to Eliminate International Terrorism – A/C.6/60/SR.3*, New York: United Nations, 6 October 2005.

—— (2005b) *Agenda item 108: Measures to Eliminate International Terrorism (continued) – A/C.6/60/SR.4*, New York: United Nations, 7 October 2005.

—— (2005c) *Agenda item 108: Measures to Eliminate International Terrorism (continued) – A/C.6/60/SR.5*, New York: United Nations, 15 October 2005.

—— (2005d) *Agenda item 108: Measures to Eliminate International Terrorism (continued) – A/C.6/60/SR.6*, New York: United Nations, 10 October 2005.

—— (2006) *Agenda item 100: Measures to Eliminate International Terrorism (continued) – A/C.6/61/SR.3*, New York: United Nations, 12 October 2006.

—— (2007) *Agenda item 108: Measures to Eliminate International Terrorism -A/C.6/62/SR.3*, New York: United Nations, 10 October 2007.

—— (2008a) *Agenda item 99: Measures to Eliminate International Terrorism (continued) – A/C.6/63/SR.2*, New York: United Nations, 8 October 2008.

—— (2008b) *Agenda item 99: Measures to Eliminate International Terrorism (continued) – A/C.6/63/SR.4*, New York: United Nations, 9 October 2008.

—— (2009) *Agenda item 106: Measures to Eliminate International Terrorism (continued) – A/C.6/64/SR.3*, New York: United Nations, 7 October 2009.

United Kingdom (2002) *Proceeds of Crime Act 2002*. Available online at: <https://www.opsi. gov.uk/acts/acts2002/pdf/ukpga_20020029_en.pdf (accessed 23 April 2010)>.

United Kingdom Home Office (2002a) *All Controlled Drugs are Harmful, all will Remain Illegal*, Press release 192/2002, London: Home Office, 10 June 2002.

—— (2002b) *The Government's Drugs Policy: Is it Working? The Government Reply to the Third Report from the Home Affairs Committee*, Nr. Cm 5573, London: Home Office.

—— (2002c) *Speech by Home Office Minister Bob Ainsworth – Home Office press release (N° 213/02)* London: Home Office, 25 July 2002.

—— (2002d) *Updated Drug Strategy 2002*, London: Home Office.

—— (2003) *New Guidance to Treat Heroin Addiction*, Press release 136/2003, London: Home Office, 16 May 2003.

United Nations (1964a) *Official Records of United Nations Conference for the Adoption of a Single Convention on Narcotic Drugs, New York, 1961 (24 January – 25 March), Vol. I*, New York: United Nations.

—— (1964b) *Official Records of United Nations Conference for the Adoption of a Single Convention on Narcotic Drugs, New York, 1961 (24 January – 25 March), Vol. II*, New York: United Nations.

—— (1972) *Draft Convention*, A/C.6/L.850, New York: United Nations, 25 September 1972.

—— (1973a) *Official Records of United Nations Conference for the Adoption of a Protocol on Psychotropic Substances (Vienna, 11 January – 19 February 1971), Vol. I*, New York: United Nations.

—— (1973b) *Official Records of United Nations Conference for the Adoption of a Protocol on Psychotropic Substances (Vienna, 11 January – 19 February 1971), Vol. II*, New York: United Nations.

—— (1973c) *Official Records of United Nations Conference to Consider Amendments to the Single Convention on Narcotic Drugs, 1961 (Geneva, 6–24 March 1972), Vol. I*, New York: United Nations.

—— (1973d) *Official Records of United Nations Conference to Consider Amendments to the Single Convention on Narcotic Drugs, 1961 (Geneva, 6–24 March 1972), Vol. II*, New York: United Nations.

—— (1991) *Official Records of United Nations Conference for the Adoption of a Convention Against Illicit Traffic in Narcotic Drugs and Psychotropic Substances (Vienna, 25 November – 20 December 1988), Vol. II*, New York: United Nations.

—— (1998) *Commentary on the United Nations Convention Against Illicit Traffic in Narcotic Drugs and Psychotropic Substances, Done at Vienna on 20 December 1988*, New York: United Nations Publications.

van der Veen, H.T. (2000) 'The International Drug Complex', in R. Schönenberg (ed.), *Internationaler Drogenhandel und gesellschaftliche Transformation*, Wiesbaden: Deutscher Universitätsverlag, pp. 143–68.

van Krieken, P.J. (ed.) (2002) *Terrorism and the International Legal Order: With Special Reference to the UN, the EU and Cross-border Aspects*, The Hague: TMC Asser Press.

Vennemann, N. (2004) 'Country Report on the European Union', in C. Walter, S. Vöneky, V. Roben and F. Schorkopf (eds), *Terrorism as a Challenge for National and International Law: Security versus Liberty?*, Berlin: Springer, pp. 217–66.

Wæver, O. (1998a) 'Insecurity, Security and Asecurity in the West European Non-war Community', in E. Adler and M. Barnett (eds), *Security Communities*, Cambridge: Cambridge University Press, pp. 69–118.

—— (1998b) 'The Sociology of a Not so International Discipline: American and European Developments in International Relations', *International Organization*, 52 (4): 687–727.

—— (2000) 'European Security Identities 2000', in P.J. Burgess and O. Tunander (eds), *European Security Identities – Contested Understandings of EU and NATO*, Oslo: International Peace Research Institute.

—— (2004) 'Discursive Approaches', in A. Wiener and T. Diez (eds), *European Integration Theory*, Oxford: Oxford University Press, pp. 197–215.

—— (2005) 'European Integration and Security: Analysing French and German Discourses on State, Nation, and Europe', in D. Howarth and J. Torfing (eds), *Discourse Theory in European Politics. Identity, Policy and Governance*, Basingstoke: Palgrave Macmillan, pp. 33–67.

Wagner, W. (2006) 'Polizei ohne wirksame Kontrolle? Schwierigkeiten parlamentarischer und gerichtlicher Kontrolle Europols', in M.H.W. Möllers and R.v. Ooyen (eds), *Europäisierung und Internationalisierung der Polizei*, Frankfurt am Main: Verlag für Polizeiwissenschaft, pp. 89–111.

Waldmann, P. (ed.) (2004) *Determinanten des Terrorismus*, Weilerswist: Velbrück Wissenschaft.

Walker, R.B.J. (1990) 'Security, Sovereignty, and the Challenge of World Politics', *Alternatives*, 15: 3–27.

—— (1993) *Inside/Outside: International Relations as Political Theory*, Cambridge: Cambridge University Press.

—— (2006) 'On the Protection of Nature and the Nature of Protection', in J. Huysmans, A. Dobson and R. Prokhovnik (eds), *The Politics of Protection: Sites of Insecurity and Political Agency*, Abingdon, New York: Routledge, pp. 189–203.

—— (2010) *After the Globe, Before the World*, London, New York: Routledge.

Walt, S.M. (1991) 'The Renaissance of Security Studies', *International Studies Quarterly*, 35 (2): 211–39.

Weber, C. (1995) *Simulating Sovereignty: Intervention, the State, and Symbolic Exchange*, Cambridge: Cambridge University Press.

—— (2006) *Imagining America at War: Morality, Politics and Film*, London: Routledge.

Weil, A. (1986) *The Natural Mind: An Investigation of Drugs and Higher Consciousness*, Boston: Houghton Mifflin.

Weitzman, E.A. (2000) 'Software and qualitative research', in N.K. Denzin and Y.S. Lincoln (eds), *Handbook of Qualitative Research*, 2nd edn, Thousand Oaks, London, New Delhi: Sage, pp. 803–20.

Weller, C. (1999) 'Kollektive Identitäten in der internationalen Politik', in W. Reese-Schäfer (ed.), *Identität und Interesse. Der Diskurs der Identitätsforschung*, Opladen: Leske + Budrich, pp. 249–78.

Wendt, A. (1987) 'The Agent-Structure Problem in International Relations', *International Organization*, 41 (2): 335–70.

—— (1994) 'Collective Identity Formation and the International State', *The American Political Science Review*, 88 (2): 384–96.

—— (1996) 'Identity and Structural Change in International Politics', in Y. Lapid and F. Kratochwil (eds), *The Return of Culture and Identity*, Boulder, CO., London: Lynne Rienner, pp. 47–64.

—— (1999) *Social Theory of International Politics*, Cambridge: Cambridge University Press.

—— (2003) 'Why a World State is Inevitable', *European Journal of International Relations*, 9 (4): 491–542.

Whitehouse, A. (2003) 'A brave new world: the impact of domestic and international regulation on money laundering prevention in the UK', *Journal of Financial Regulation and Compliance*, 11 (2): 138–45.

Wiesbrock, K. (2002) 'Wer ist Terrorist?' *Vereinte Nationen*, 50 (2): 72–3.

Wight, C. (1999) 'They Shoot Dead Horses Don't They? Locating Agency in the Agent-Structure Problematique', *European Journal of International Relations*, 5 (1): 109–42.

Wilkinson, P. (1974) *Political Terrorism*, London: Macmillan.

—— (1997) 'International Cooperation against Terrorism', in M. Crenshaw and J. Pimlott (eds), *Encyclopaedia of World Terrorism, Vol. 3*, Armonk, NY: M.E. Sharpe, pp. 666–72.

—— (2006) *Terrorism Versus Democracy: the Liberal State Response*, revised edn, London, New York: Routledge.

Wittgenstein, L. (2001) *Philosophical Investigations. The German text, with a revised English translation*, 3 edn, Malden, Oxford: Blackwell Publishing.

Wodak, R., de Cillia, R., Reisigl, M., Liebhart, K., Klaus, H. and Kargl, M. (1998) *Zur diskursiven Konstruktion nationaler Identität*, Frankfurt am Main: Suhrkamp Verlag.

The Independent (2007a) 'Heroin on the NHS and a document too hot to handle. Secret Home Office brief to Tony Blair and David Blunkett urges dramatic steps to counter rising criminality', *The Independent*, 25 February 2007. Available online at: <http://www.independent.co.uk/news/uk/politics/heroin-on-the-nhs-and-a-document-too-hot-to-handle-437762.html (accessed 17 April 2010)>.

The Independent (2007b) 'Home Office backs heroin on the NHS in effort to cut crime', *The Independent*, 25 February 2007. Available online at: <http://www.independent.co.uk/news/uk/politics/home-office-backs-heroin-on-the-nhs-in-effort-to-cut-crime-437803.html (accessed 17 April 2010)>.

Žižek, S. (1990) 'Beyond Discourse-Analysis', in E. Laclau (ed.), *New Reflections on the Revolution of our Time*, London, New York: Verso, pp. 249–60.

—— (1996) *The Indivisible Remainder*, London: Verso.

—— (2002) *The Sublime Object of Ideology*, London, New York: Verso.

—— (2006) 'Jack Bauer and the Ethics of Urgency', *The Guardian*. Available online at: <http://www.guardian.co.uk/media/2006/jan/10/usnews.comment (accessed 17 April 2010)>.

Index